Library of Congress Control Number (LCCN): 2005908684

Library of Congress Cataloguing in Publication Data
Condron, Barbara
MASTER LIVING
10 Essential Life Skills for Health, Prosperity, Success & Peace of Mind

Summary: The science of mind and intuitive development based upon 30 years of research and application, and illustrated through testimonials from dozens of people. An evolutionary development in educational understanding.

ISBN: 0-944386-36-9

PRINTED IN THE UNITED STATES OF AMERICA

Cover by Teresa Martin

If you desire to learn more about the research and teachings in this book,
write to School of Metaphysics World Headquarters,
Windyville, Missouri 65783.
Or call us at 417-345-8411.
Visit us on the Internet at www.som.org
or www.dreamschool.org

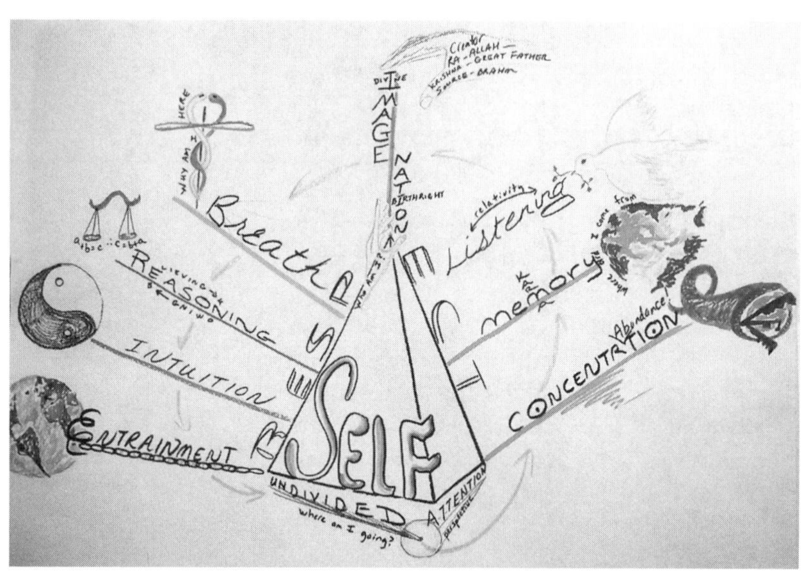

"It is only through the heart
that one sees clearly–
what is essential
is invisible to the human eye."

–Antoine de Saint-Exupéry

Contents

The Essential Life Skills to Master Living

A few beginning words

"Are you paying attention?" a parent asks in an exasperated voice. The child looks up, bright eyes shining, "I think I am," she says innocently.

"I want you to memorize this list of spelling words for Friday," the teacher says in a matter-of-fact tone to the group of eight-year-olds.

"Listen carefully," the caregiver cautions. The child looks lost. He knows something about caring and he knows something about hearing. So he tries his best.

I remember many scenarios like these through my childhood years of education in public school. I had many wonderful teachers. They were the ones who made schooling intriguing and fun. Yet, not one of them taught me how to give attention or how to improve my memory or how to listen better.

My choral teachers certainly *expected* us to listen, sometimes encouraging it with passion. They could tell us if our singing voices were flat or sharp and nudge us up or down in our intonations. That guidance came from their subconscious understandings or a "trained ear." How or where did one get a *trained* ear?– I wanted to know.

And that was the whole point, I discovered. I always wanted to KNOW! At one time, teachers almost convinced me that knowing wasn't important, but that is another area best left to a book I intend to write on the subject of Taraka Yoga, a field I am presently pioneering that applies ancient disciplines to modern *mental* technology.

Then there's that most valuable and ever-present essential life skill called breath! The only time I remember hearing about breath in school was when I had trouble "catching" mine after running around the football field three times when I was 12 years old. I learned the meaning of the word "winded" that day, from experience. I waited another 10 years to learn about the power, form, cause, and purpose of breath.

It was worth the wait.

We, as a species, are ready to move forward in our ideas of education. We are waking up to new realities within ourselves, a greater potential than book learning and high tech can offer.

Martin Luther King, Jr. described this eloquently when he accepted a Nobel Peace Prize in 1964 at the age of 35, *"Yet, in spite of these spectacular strides in science and technology, and still unlimited ones to come, something basic is missing. There is a sort of poverty of the spirit which stands in glaring contrast to our scientific and technological abundance. The richer we have become materially, the poorer we have become morally and spiritually. We have learned to fly the air like birds and swim the sea like fish, but we have not learned the simple art of living together as brothers."*

To do that we will need to learn how to live with ourselves.

Technology is an amazing testimony to humanity's creativity as a whole. It brings us a plethora of information. Yet with its virtual manmade existences, we must admit that technology cannot replace human contact in the work of nurturing the soul, the inner Being.

First and last, we need Self Respect;– the capacity to recognize ourselves as whole beings, as spiritual, mental, and emotional beings as well as physical ones. We need to develop skills to reach our full potential as homo Spiritus: the whole, functioning Self; intuitive, Spiritual Man. These skills of attention, memory, listening, and others are spoken about in our educational systems and in our societies at large, yet they are rarely taught or practiced as a discipline.

The School of Metaphysics exists to change this. The school has been teaching these life skills, essential to our daily life, since 1973. In order to know, we must do. We must have direct experience, and so this book is filled with the personal experiences with the Essential Life Skills of young and old, male and female, from varied backgrounds, cultures, and religions. These are a treasure trove of ideas that can alter the way you see and live your life. It is my hope that they will rekindle and feed your desire to know, for the best teachers show us how to use life for learning.

Just imagine when parents and teachers begin instructing the very young to, "Pay attention! Tell me what that flower looks like! What does it smell like? Feel like? Taste like? What does that flower *sound* like!"

– Barbara Condron, 2005

"Respect seems natural when you meet him (the Dalai Lama), but it is not awe. You can talk with him, and laugh with him, and discuss things with him, and although the underlying respect remains it is like being in the presence of a very old and warm friend."

– Roger Hicks and Hgakpa Chogyam in **Great Ocean**

Self Respect

Universal Language of Mind Story

Where is the Master?

One day while Bankei, a Zen Master, was working in his garden a seeker approached him asking, "Gardener, where is the Master?"

Bankei laughed and said, "By that door - inside you will find the Master."

So the man went to the door and looking inside saw Bankei, the same man who had been the gardener outside. The seeker said, "This is sacrilegious! Get down from this chair! You aren't paying respect to the Master!"

Bankei got down, sat on the ground, and said, "Now you will not find the Master in the chair - because I am the Master."

It was difficult for the man to see that a great Master could be so ordinary. He left. And he missed.

Daily Miracles

Bankei was preaching quietly to his followers one day when his talk was interrupted by a priest from another sect. This sect believed in the power of miracles.

The priest boasted that the founder of his religion could stand on one bank of the river with a brush in his hand and write a holy name on a piece of paper held by an assistant on the opposite bank of the river. Then he asked, "What miracles can you do?"

Bankei replied, "Only one. When I am hungry I eat and when I am thirsty I drink."

Sometimes we seek miracles to give meaning to our lives when all the while the miracle is in us. The miracle of consciousness is born in awareness of need. This is the birth of spiritual thinking; the revealer of Truth, the sustainer of Commitment to Self.

Spiritual Thinking is the capacity to sense with more than your physical body, to remember with more than that body's brain, to desire from more than lack. Spiritual Thinking is the activation of the mind's power in all levels of consciousness.

Reasoning replaces rationalization. Intuition replaces psychism. Enlightenment replaces divination.

Commitment to Self encourages while necessitating the transition from ego motivation to desire motivation to soul motivation. Those motivated solely by how they and things around them look to others are stimulated to move beyond the confines of their own ego. Those who lose sight of their needs in an ocean of limitless desire come to harness their ambition for a greater good. Those seeking higher guidance with respect for the Source transcend the mental confusion and emotional despair that accompany psychic infidelity.

Wherever you are on your sacred journey, commitment to Self demands: that you relinquish the old, accepting the new, that you turn from your weaknesses and build with your strengths, that you resign your mediocrity, nurturing your excellence, that you surrender physical thinking to the freedom of Spiritual Thinking.

To know who you are and where you are is self-possession. It enables you to perceive the world around you as it is. This is releasing illusion.

To know where you have come from and where you are going is power. It enables you to move in Truth toward the realization of your potential. That is embracing the miracles in daily living.

The Master Jesus addressed the reality of Self Respect when he asked the Pharisees, "Who is the greatest? He who reclines at table or he who serves?" With Self Respect we find the answer is neither, either, yet both.

INTUITIVE RESEARCH

SELF RESPECT is

"...a great capacity to place the self in another's position and to imagine the experience there and therefore form a kinship." (91397BGC8)

"Know Yourself.
To discover how conscious you are of your self-image, look at yourself as if you have just met yourself for the first time."
(SOM Lesson 1)

"Man is apart yet kindred to his fellow man and his Creator. He is free and independent while related to all."
(SOM Lesson 23)

To respect is to hold someone or something in high regard.

I was taught respect is something you earn. Love is freely and automatically given to all – people, animals, plants, but respect – respect you have to earn.

This was a good code to live by for the first 21 years of my life. It made me thoughtful of my actions. It motivated me to do good by people and do well in my endeavors. It also allowed me to become conditional in my loving.

This was one of the first lessons I learned as a 22-year-old student at the School of Metaphysics in Columbia, Missouri. I had never thought much about whether I placed conditions on my love. I loved my family and friends. I loved God as I believed He loved me. One of my first awake Self Respect exercises was examining my capacity to love.

Did I love my neighbor as I loved myself? Answering this question started me on the journey from conditional love to reverence for life. Because I was willing to continue learning after formal schooling I discovered respect is indeed something we earn for it is in the action of earning that the truth is revealed.

A great humanitarian of the 20th century Albert Schweitzer said, "Once more we dare to appeal to the whole man, to his capacity to think and feel, exhorting him to know himself and to be true to himself." Schweitzer was a scholar in both theology and philosophy. An accomplished musician, he wrote a book on Johann Sebastian Bach becoming a world-renowned interpreter of Bach's music. Even so Schweitzer was seeking, constantly asking himself "How can I help best?"

One day in 1904, when he was twenty-nine years old, he read an appeal from the French Protestant Missionary Society in Paris asking for help for the Negroes in French Equatorial Africa. "I wanted to become a doctor in order to be able to work without words. For years I had used the word. My new occupation would be not to talk about the gospel of love, but to put it into practice."

The study of medicine claimed seven years of Schweitzer's life, from 1905 to 1913. Of it he says, "The pursuit of natural sciences gave me more than just the knowledge I sought. It was for me a spiritual experience. I had always felt that the so called humanities with which I had been concerned present a psychic danger because they rarely reveal self-evident truths, but often present value judgments which masquerade as truth because of the way in which they are clothed," he said in his memoirs. "Now, suddenly, I stood in another world. I was now working with truths based on realities, and I was among men who took it for granted that every statement had to be supported by fact."

It was many years before he was enable to crystallize this philosophy into the simple formula. One day in 1915 - he was forty years old at the time - while traveling on a river in Africa, he saw the rays of the sun shimmering on the water, the tropical forest all around, and a herd of hippopotamuses basking on the banks of the river. At that moment there came to him, as if by revelation, the phrase which precisely expressed his thought: *Reverence for life*.

Schweitzer asserted that one cannot come to this reverence for life by systematic logical reasoning and knowledge, "for neither can furnish an explanation of the world and of the purpose of life." The explanation is found through what he called elemental thought which leads to a reverence for that ineffable thing which is life, an affirmation of life which is more than the will to live. "I am life that wills to live in the midst of other life that wills to live," Schweitzer said.

As the life choices of this 1954 Nobel Peace Laureate demonstrate, Self Respect is an action of seeing your Self anew, making Self in your image. Every day you and I can make this choice for the reverence of life. How, you may ask.

The following intuitive wisdom is from a Meditation Portrait of a woman in her forties. These portraits are intuitively-designed and accessed upon request by intuitive reporter/conductor partners. This response was given when the intuitive reporter was asked for suggestions for attuning the outer consciousness to superconsciousness.

> In regards to what has just been given there is a need for this one to place the Self in perspective. There is a need for this one to expand the sense of Self, the understand-

ing and the concept of Self beyond what this one has to this point. There has been a beginning of this process and there is much to do in that regard. This one's time and effort and intelligence would be best spent by investing the Self in a more complete picture of what comprises the Self. This then would afford this one a greater vantage point, a greater expanded vision of who this one is. That would foster and would help this one to more consciously be harmonized and to attune that to the greater that is in existence.

It is when this one fails to direct the thoughts in this manner that there are the doubts and fears and the other limitations that are part of the outer waking consciousness that do divorce this one from the Self and leave this one in a sense of pain or disorientation or confusion.

It is time for this one to realize that this is a choice that she makes. That it is not important what the needs of the physical Self are to this one at this time. Because they are not integrated into this one's wholeness. This will come as this one is willing to sacrifice the Self, as this one would see it, to something that is greater than herself constantly. It is through this action of disciplining the will that this one will reveal to the Self the nature of wholeness and the nature of the inner urge that exists within her.

When this one is able to set the outer Self, the limited Self to the side and to allow the strength of the whole Self to come forward this one then naturally opens a channel for which the inner urge does come forth. That does allow this one to be aligned. This is what this one needs to strive for and begin to recognize that anything less than this is a distraction. A tool for scattering and separating consciousness.

Therefore this one must resolve within the Self within the outer mind that this one will remain true to the greater cause that this one is serving. This is all. (10132001BGC1)

This Intuitive Report illustrates the enduring nature of Self Respect.

It, as Schweitzer once said, *"dare(s) to appeal to the whole man, to his capacity to think and feel, exhorting him to know himself and to be true to himself."*

Self Respect is the alpha and omega point for the full fruition of humankind's potential to be whole, to become realized as Spiritual Man. In what you will read here, watch for evidence of Self Respect as you learn and then endeavor to practice each of the Essential Life Skills presented for the purpose of developing you potential as a whole, functioning Self, a spiritual being as well as a material one.

SELF RESPECT

is looking at ourselves and others from all angles and perspectives.
Self Respect is
our foundation to add to and build onto ourselves wherever we are in our learning.

Self Respect
What is It?

At a family wedding my husband Daniel noted how most of the women present were either remembering or imaging their own wedding. I looked around and realized he was accurate. Making the moment personal was the way most of the women were sharing in the joy of the present moment.

The ability to exist out of space and time is a function of the human being's capacity for Self Respect. Such sentience, to be Self-aware, is what makes us human. The bride's Self Respect may come in striving for the ideal of being a wife. Should she cease in manifesting that ideal in her daily life, she may forget she is married, her attention wandering into an affair.

Self Respect enables us to see through different eyes. A friend is shocked because the bride is jeopardizing a perfect marriage. Her sister believes she is justified through her husband's neglect. Her husband feels betrayed and guilty. Her mother is disappointed, her father angry. Everyone around the bride has an opinion. Only the bride can say who she is – spoiler, avenger, offender, victim. The role she chooses is of her own making and to acknowledge that requires Self Respect.

Self Respect gives us the hope for change.

Self Respect makes us able to admit the changes as they occur. The greatest of these is the realization that we are thinking beings, reasoners. We are more than the bodies we inhabit. The flesh is the physical expression of who we are, but the body is no more who we are than the clothes we wear. Self Respect enables us to answer the age old question, "Who am I?"

With Self Respect we come to realize that the physical body is merely one vehicle mind uses to experience through. The voice is another. How we say our words is as revealing as the words we choose to say. It is a vehicle for the expression of Self. In Japan, Dr. Masaru Emoto has been scientifically investigating the power of sounds and words for years. You may be aware of his work with changing the structure of water through vibration.

Emoto describes how humans are slowly learning the various vibrations of the laws of nature through instinct, which is animal, and experience, which is human. The accumulated information over time has moved us from simple sounds, like vowels sounds, to more complex sounds like "love." Emoto is proving how positive words create natural crystalline structures, which are based on the hexagon. The hexagon is the basic structure of all evolution in nature. Scientifically this has to do with the chemical reaction of the benzene ring.

Researchers have found that things that do not exist naturally, those created artificially, lack this hexagonal structure.

Words convert the vibrations of nature into sound. Actions convert the vibrations of thought into the situations in our lives. Is it possible for the bride to love two men? Is it possible that her ideal of marriage may not include the assumption of monogamous fidelity? Is it possible her actions did not intend harm?

Self Respect frees us to examine our intentions. It empowers us to know ourselves through our relations with others. A bride who does not know any better can learn from the reactions of friend, father, husband.

Siddhartha, the one who would become the Buddha, was 29 when he left his father's palace and entered the streets of the city to discover the suffering in the world. He was awakened to the many problems of life. It would be years later that he would again awaken to the *cause* of such suffering.

In the same way our lives feed back to us what we know and what we do not know. Our willingness to be Self reflective, Self evaluating, Self disciplined, Self controlled, Self realized, Self determined, and so forth accelerates the learning that feeds the soul.

How much does the soul weigh? I have heard a few ounces. People have taken measurements I have read. What I know from experience is that the soul enters and leaves the physical shell. I have seen a soul depart. I have seen it not with my physical eyes, I have seen it with what the Tibetans call the *wisdom eye*, what the Theosophists and spiritualists call the *third eye*. This eye of mental perception gives us the gift of sight beyond limits of the physical world.

Dreams tell us we exist separate from the body. When in the dreamstate, the body you use can taste food, feel another's caress, and even experience pain. It is real in its level of existence. Yet where does that dream body go when you awake? What remains of the dream experience is awareness in the form of memory. We exist beyond the physical.

With all the evidence of our research into the mind for almost four decades, I am coming to the conclusion that what human-reasoning man is quick to label as disease may well be a natural evolutionary change that will ultimately lead to greater enlightening. For instance, Alzheimers. The word is well known now, and stimulates fear in the person receiving the word. Fear of losing a loved one. It is sometimes called "the long goodbye" by those who care for the person. Yet, what they experience is a freshness, a newness, living increasingly in the present moment. Their world is very different from ours, as different as a child's is.

Self Respect frees us from ego limitations. Like an internal caste system, Self Respect enables us to separate who we are from the roles we play in life. Daughter, wife, mother, entrepreneur, writer become labels to describe the activities, not my intents in those activities. It's the thought that counts.

Self Respect allows our beliefs to grow, change, alter. It enables us to move from believing into knowing from experience. For centuries beliefs have been molded through religion. In their pure form, religions helped humanity understand the world and taught principles for living together. Some beliefs after being experienced are redefined, the world being flat is a good example. For centuries the Catholic church supported this view. When Galileo used his intelligence to purport a substantiated different view, he was censored. But in time the church changed its belief, making room for the new knowing.

Such is the role science has played for the past 1500 years. The belief that the gods existed in the stars led to the physical science of astronomy. Science is a form of Self Respect for all of humanity. Science seeks to answer the great questions of life – where do we come from, why are we here, where are we going – as does religion. This Self Respect is bringing forth the whole truth, that man increasingly possesses powers once attributed to his gods.

For instance, neurologists are discovering how spiritual belief affects the brain. Buddhist monks have participated in university experiments in the hope of lending scientific evidence of effects from meditation. Scans of the Buddhists' brains were taken following meditation. The information reflected a reduction in activity of the parietal lobes of the brain. This portion of the brain classically reflects our sense of Self in time and space. Scientists concluded that this reduction could blur the boundary between Self and the outer world, promoting a sense of being at one with God and the universe. The truth is believers of many faiths describe such states of mind during meditation, trances, or prayer.

One of my spiritual beliefs is that we are all children of God, of a Creator, coming from the same Source. Philosophically, this means we are all related. The more I act on this belief in my daily life, the more my mind opens to know its validity and applications. It is personal science. In a more general scientific sense, the idea of coming from a common Source can be seen and is supported in the existence of the DNA code. The reality of man as creator comes back to us every day in the form of medical science, from heart transplants to cloning.

Taraka Yoga, a system for Self counsel, is based on the individual's ability for Self Respect. Taraka Yoga requires your resourcefulness, and the best resources available are within Self. We call these the Essential Life Skills. Self Respect is the first of these.

From the Sanskrit, taraka means "rescuing, causing to cross over" and yoga, means "union." For the student of consciousness and mind, Taraka Yoga is the process of understanding spirit into matter and matter into spirit. If we diagrammed this process in a geometric form it would be two intersecting equilateral triangles, often called the Star of David, the six-pointed star. Connect the outer vertices of the triangles and a polygon called a hexagon is created. Now we have returned to where we began – citing Dr. Emoto's research.

We have also laid the foundation for what is to come for something rests in the center of this six-pointed star that shifts the awareness from the limits of the physical world to the infinity of Spirit.•

Changing Values

Self Respect depends on self value, and self value depends on self respect. Self value is not one of the essential life skills, but it is at the very core of any effort of self improvement. In order for me to invest time, effort, will and even money into improving myself I have to deem that the effort is worth it. I have to either believe or know that the investment will pay off. A sane person will first believe that a house will be a good investment before they will buy it, and pour thousands of dollars and hours of time into fixing it up for resale. There has to be a fundamental foundation of valuing the self in order to be able to genuinely give to the Self.

How is this self value cultivated? In our culture today there is rampant self-degradation. Are we born valuing our inner self? I think so. Are we taught to not value ourselves? Yes and no. We are typically taught in our society that we are physical beings that think, and that we have some spiritual needs. In this system, self respect is unnecessary because there is nothing inside, deeper. This is a much harder base to operate from in terms of developing self-value. Self value in this system depends on what you do or become physically. Are you beautiful? Then you are valuable. Are you a high achiever? Then you are more valuable. Are you entertaining or very athletic? Then you are even more valuable. All these criteria are subjective and conditional states of value. You can lose your beauty over time, you can lose your job-position-status, you can lose your athletic ability and you can lose the public's favor with your style of music or jokes. This subjective and conditional state of self value is tremendously insecure. It continues to generate a culture of fear, greed, worry and shallowness because at any turn you could lose your base of value.

On the other hand, if you choose to invest in the system that we are thinking spiritual beings that are having a temporary physical experience, then you stand to develop solid, lasting self value based in an objective and unconditional state. When we teach our children that they are spiritual beings learning how to work the mind and the physical, it leaves the door open for them to find, firsthand, their spiritual source through self respect. In this system there is reason for self respect, looking deeper inside, because there is a deeper inside. They are free to explore the inner realms as well as the outer realms, and their point of reference, their point of identity, becomes established from the inside out, from the spiritual to the physical. When we truly accept this identification as first a spiritual being, then we can find the commonality among us all, the spiritual thread that connects us with each other, and our common source.

When we have firsthand experience with our spiritual identity, we can see through further self respect that we have an intrinsic value as a being. We can experience the divine quality that runs through everything in creation, that we are part of this divine creation, and therefore that we are also divine beings with tremendous intrinsic value in the whole. From this self respected perspective of unconditional self value we can then invest in improving our control of our minds, our hearts and our bodies, from the inside out, as it was meant to be. We will learn and master all the life skills and teach them and our common divine ancestry to our children, so they can also start with real self value.∞ –Paul Madar∞

Influence

Thought is cause. My thoughts influence and affect others around me, including all of creation. It is not so much of what I do, but how I do it and why I do it. I think of Dr. Daniel Condron (College Chancellor) as he shows students how to plant seeds in the garden. The rows are straight, the depth of the trench is given attention, the fertilizer is spread along with the potting soil. And then he carefully places or sprinkles the seeds along the ground and covers them so delicately, with care and love. When he shows students how to pick the produce from the garden he teaches them to give thanks to God and thanks to the plants for their bounty. There is a respect that is the foundation for learning, for adding to, for understanding love and creation in all that we do.

These images I add to my Self as I image me teaching and showing students how to do activities. There is a greater care that I observe in my thoughts and in my instructions to the students. What I teach and show is much greater than activity. It is a reverence for life and a love for creation that I want to add to my Self.

Self respect is also evaluating who I am in each circumstance, each learning opportunity. Asking myself am I open, am I caring, am I loving, what do I want to give, what do I want to teach? These are the questions that continue to build the image of who I want to become and it is self respecting in each moment. ∞Tad Messenger

Family of Man

Self Respect is looking at myself and others from different perspectives. It is a constant and continuous effort to know my Self and to gain a connection, an ability to place myself in another's position. It is the choice to look at people and myself from many angles. The experience of doing this develops a bond and a feeling of brotherhood and sisterhood with those I meet. Looking at myself from different perspectives is a conscious, continuous way of building my image of my Self and understanding who I am and what my relationship and influence is with other people.

When I think of family, I think of family of man. We are all on this planet together. We have different dreams and different learnings. Yet our core is that we are basically all human beings striving to know ourselves and striving to make life better. This was very apparent to me at the Human Forum in Puerto Rico. There were many different people from different parts of the world that came together and spoke of the ideas expressed in the Universal Peace Covenant. Mae Chee Sansanee, a female Buddhist Monk from Thailand, made a movie of her life's work called Walking the Path of Wisdom. In her movie she expressed the idea of our relationship with plants, with animals, with other humans and with the planet. She taught children to respect and love trees. They give us oxygen so that we may breathe and have life. We give trees carbon dioxide so that they may have life. This is an important cycle of giving and receiving that nourishes both forms. She taught children to ride elephants. She explained that the first thing one must do is to love the elephant, to show them that love, as you would your sister or brother. The elephant will be your friend as you treat it with love and respect. We must learn to love our enemies as we love each other. This is the teaching of Jesus, of Buddha, of all great masters. It is simple and true. I thought of the College of Metaphysics and planting the garden and the trees, caring for the animals. This is a point of Self respecting on how I could add her image to what and how I teach College of Metaphysics students. I envisioned myself talking to them with the plants and the animals, teaching them of our interconnectedness and that we must learn to love all of God's creatures. This also echoed in my mind as I think about "reverence for life" taught by Albert Schweitzer. The simple truths are Universal. ∞ Tad Messenger

ELS#1

A Short Class on Self Respect

Each section in MASTER LIVING includes a brief excerpt from a class I taught at the College of Metaphysics on the Essential Life Skills. Each class is a modern-day Socratic experience, stimulating new thought, dissolving prejudices, and fostering connections between the outer and inner thinker. Want to learn more? Complete transcripts of these classes are available online by contacting som@som.org

Dr. B.: Let's talk about Self Respect. What is Self Respect?

TP: Self-correction. It's being able to look at yourself and immediately embrace yourself. It's like looking into a mirror and being able to see yourself.

Dr. B: Realizing the people in your world, whether you accept them or reject them, are reflections of you. They exist there, as far as you're concerned, for your learning and growth. When learning becomes important to you then blame and guilt and other human failings become a waste of precious time.

Think of it this way, three siblings. Two get along fabulously, the other is shunned by the entire family - a black sheep, people used to call it. Everyone in the family thinks this is just the way it is and they are fairly content with the situation, except perhaps the black sheep.

"I've always been different. I can't help it," thinks the black sheep.

"S/he's always disagreed with us/been an embarrassment/gotten into trouble/not cooperated. We've tried everything," the white sheep think.

And the family continues on as it always has until someone has a bright idea, or until a white sheep finds itself a black sheep. Then comes the dawn of acceptance, allowing, forgiveness, patience, thankfulness and all the virtues of humanity. When this white sheep refuses to blame and instead thinks of his black sheep sister, magic happens. The mind opens.

I remember reading Martin Luther King's thoughts. In (the play) ***The Invitation*** he says, "Nonviolence has also meant that my people in the agonizing struggles of recent years have taken suffering upon themselves instead of inflicting it on others." This is the beginning of Self Respect, the willingness to accept full responsibility for the situations you find yourself in. This is only the beginning...•

Cyber-communication is one of the ways teachers and students of the School of Metaphysics remain connected with each other. We see it as a physical technology reflective telepathic, mind-to-mind communication. While we are developing our intuitive skill, we use technology as a means to scientifically measure that skill.

With each Essential Life Skill I have included email correspondences from people across the the United States who are learning how to be the change they would see in the world through volunteering their time and energy to pass onto others the benefits of what they have learned.

I marvel every day at how the Universal Laws work, bringing a dream question from a mother in England the same day that a request to publish **How to Raise an Indigo Child** *comes in from a publisher in Indonesia! With Shawn's email about The Silver Cord that I just sent and this one from Amy we have a male and a female, both working with what I love to call BIG EARTH! (Think Martin Luther King, Jr. who was also a Capricorn.) Both talk about the same core idea in different ways! I love how God brings us together across space and time, beyond the limits of the physical to enrich the PLANET! That's BIG EARTH!* –Dr. B

Good Morning Dr. Barbara,

Yesterday proved to be a big day of learning for me as I processed the experiences from the weeks before. As I told you yesterday on the phone we started a new class in Indianapolis on Tuesday! I was really excited and it was a wonderful experience. There were eight people there and as the week goes by it appears there will be more this coming Tuesday! I love the idea of the class still growing! This is a class I was planning on starting on a Wednesday two weeks ago. I called the people on the class list and had the ball rolling. Five people showed up and two of the five could only continue if the class was held on a different night of the week. That would have left me with a class of three. NO WAY!!! So I showed (the film) *The Silver Cord* and did a lot of looking at what was going on...

So let me rewind. When I had agreed to teach that class it was more an agreement of "yes, I should do" more than "yes, I want to." I am learning there is value in being willing to do things I do not want to do because I know they help me learn and get out of my box (oh how I love to stay in the box). In this case I also see that there has to be an adjustment in all the thoughts and not just the actions in order for the action to produce something I desire. I was pretty worried about how I was going to make teaching another night fit into my life. For the last several weeks I have been sleeping a few hours a night and still not feeling there was time for everything. I said yes to the class and then immediately started in saying to myself and to John that I could not really do this and be a director and be a mother and be a wife and learn how to be an intuitive reporter and still be a student.

How can one person possibly do all that???

So there was the first "I don't want to" thought and it was a big one.

I also had a big attachment to teaching another class ONLY on a Wednesday night. That would be a night when it was the easiest for me. I wanted to have the students fit my life if "I was going to HAVE to do this anyway" sigh...poor me. :) So, when the five students who would be three showed up I yelled really loud in my head, "SEE! This is a waste of my time!!! There are ONLY three students here!!!!"

My goodness, how self-pity can cause me to forget everything I know!!! To top it off, I was sick that first class night. Really miserably sick. AND..when I showed up to the school on Wednesday afternoon it was so messy. We were not ready to receive anyone. Could this scene become any more pathetic? :)

So...Here is where I started learning. Dr. Laurel (Clark, Amy's teacher) was helpful in pointing out that I was probably sick because of my lack of commitment. True.

Second, My attitude of having the students be there on Wednesday made it about me and not them.

Third, I still am amazed that I ever said to myself that I was wasting my time!!!!! OH MY!!! How can three students be a waste of time? Am I a waste of time too when I call up Dr. Laurel for hours? I sure hope not! Why would I say that to myself about another person?

If I have no respect for the power of one why would I draw a big class?

There are a lot more thoughts to add here but I think you get the picture.

So, I decided that I WANTED to teach. I formulated pictures in my mind of what the class would do for the people coming, what it would do for the school, what it could do for the students to have more classmates to learn from. Then I added what it would do for me to have them to give to and what we could create in Indy by opening the door to more and more people! I could see where I had been getting excited for a while about directing and creating in Indy. I think that is partly why there was a big class list (14) to begin with. I wanted lots of classes and lots and lots of people but I knew I had sabotaged my own creation in a period of self-doubt and pity. I had affected the school! Not just me but the school! OH NO!

So, what did I do?

I changed it!

I let go of the attachment to teaching on Wednesday and met the needs of the students by teaching Tuesday. I started calling people and talking to people and getting the others in Indianapolis excited. I painted the bigger picture for the other teachers and students and got them creating with me! Together we talked to all the students in the school, cleaned the building spotless, started getting really clear about what it was going to be like having a new big class of students. I was feeling my heart fill up every time we started talking! Things started working and here we are...a class of at least eight but I am thinking 12 or more is possible if I keep the energy going today!

This is so fun...

OH, one more thing about all of this. I have learned a tremendous amount about what is possible when I keep looking for ways to make something work. One of the places I kept going in my head was that I could never make a new class work because I was not going to be at the school for several weekends in a row. I think I may have spent more hours at the college in the past month than I spent in any one place here (the school or home). So, I know there is always a way to make something happen even if I am not going to be physically present! Time in a physical place is no longer an excuse.

That excuse and I have been friends for a long while, I wonder if I am going to miss her? :)

I have a lot more to share with you about the things here in Indy that are happening and a long ago promised e-mail about the seminar experience so I am sure we will "talk' soon.

Love you - Amy

Thank you Amy for learning and loving and creating the School in your image!

Some may not realize the level of self discipline required for one with Caprionic energies to even say the word "change". It is a dirty word [pun intended ;=)] for most earth signs. You are a testament to what happens when we are in our minds more than our bodies (brain pathways/habits). Learning is a choice. Self discipline enables us to look at ourselves again and again, to learn and see our learning. Those who know how to learn make great teachers. Thank you for fulfilling your part of a greater plan and being such a bright teaching light of inspiration for us all!

I love you, Dr. Barbara

Power of Self Counsel

Hi Dr. Barbara,

I wanted to share with you something that I experienced a couple of weeks ago. I had been working through some initiation stuff about commitment and responsibility with leadership. I hit a point where I was ready to give up directing feeling that now was the wrong time for me, that I don't feel ready to commit myself to all that needs to be done. I was angry with myself for allowing my present situation to be where it was, as a director and in my own personal financial situation. I was going through a bunch of ego crap, talking it through, listening to myself talk and hearing how I sounded. It was disgusting stuff but important to verbalize so I could move on.

I decided to make some lists to help me work through this issue. I first made a list entitled: **Times I have taken responsibility**. This revealed some really good things that I have done and I could see that they were filled with purpose and strong intent.

The next list was: **How I am responsible to my Self.** An okay list but there is definitely room for improvement.

Then I made this list: **Responsibilities I fear and fight.** This became a list of those things I really want to do but allow my self-imposed limitations to interfere with the follow through.

And then I made this list: **Being responsible means.** This was the big eye opener. I wasn't writing down anything positive, everything was dark and negative. Some real crazy belief systems were in there. Yuck! To see it on paper and to know the emotion I had behind it was powerful. No wonder I fight and fear commitment and responsibility when it comes to leadership. It was an eye opening exercise to do.

That night after working on this I woke up in the middle of the night with pain in my gut. I knew I had hit a core issue. The pain intensified and I eventually threw-up. I guess I had a lot of old beliefs and limitations to get out of me! After that I felt great and went back to sleep feeling very peaceful. It was a wonderful expanding experience. I thought you would enjoy hearing about this self-counseling session. It was free and very productive!

I know I have more work to do on this. It will be nice when I can get out of my own way, move beyond my limitations and firmly accept with excitement the opportunities I have to be a Leader. My intuitive reports often talk about leadership. The most recent past life reading said that Leadership and Reasoning are the understandings I have and are also what my Soul wants to gain more understandings about now. I have avoided leadership positions my whole life, so right now I am feeling like I have bitten off more than I can chew. And yet, I love the idea of being a leader and can fully imagine being a very powerful one.

I continue to peel away my layers of protection, doubt and fear that I have surrounded myself with. I'm determined to move through this so that I can finally live a life that reflects my True Self.

Thank you for listening. It was helpful to write out my experience and)talk about it with you. Have a great day Dr. Barbara. I love you.

Rhye*

Dear Rhye,

It is so rich to hear from you! Thank you so much for sharing you with me! You are such a bright light. You have the clarity to cut through the engrossing distractions fearlessly! That is so admirable and so very needed among your peers. Can you see it? It is so easy for people to become distracted and then lost in imagined fears and out of now doubts. With the first reaction, they crumble, falling prey to the dark side without ever even recognizing what is happening.

On the wall next to this computer there is a poem called **Autobiography in Five Short Chapters** *by Portia Nelson. Have you read it? It goes like this:*

"1) I walk down the steet.
There is a deep hole in the sidewalk.
I fall in.
I am lost....I am hopeless.
It isn't my fault.
It takes forever to find a way out.

"2) I walk down the same steet.
There is a deep hole in the sidewalk.
I pretend I don't see it.
I can't believe I am in the same place.
But it isn't my fault.
It takes forever to find a way out.

"3) I walk down the same steet.
There is a deep hole in the sidewalk.
I see it is there.
I still fall in....it's a habit.
It is my fault.
I get out immediately.

"4) I walk down the same steet.
There is a deep hole in the sidewalk.
I walk around it.

"5) I walk down another street."

Rhye, you are one who knows there are other streets and so you are moving to reach them. That is what fulfilling karma is all about. That is what raises us above the animal body into reasoning and propels us into Intuitive Man. Your description of the successive lists you wrote is a Taraka Yoga exercise in dyana. It is Raja yoga at its finest. You are preparing yourself now to receive! I have learned that keeping my eyes open means having no fear. I have learned to accept pain as the way I am assured of accelerating my learning, doing what I can and am capable of, going beyond limitations for certain yet more than that pain is a cleansing that can clear the vision. Leadership, is so much self discipine. Being willing to lead my aspects to fulfill the complete Law ends up serving as an example of the truth I endeavor to live. This is commitment to me. And responsibility....it is the pleasure of being secure in having something to give. It is never being empty-handed, always grateful. Ever appreciative.

Keep up the great work on the self counseling. Just imagine when we can teach even a tenth of the world how to do this!!! Wow, what changes we will see!

You have not bitten off more than you can chew. You are now responding to having eaten that fruit in the garden so many millennia ago! Give your conscious mind its due that it can't quite assimilate all that is happening right now. Well, that's why you have a subconscious mind! It makes a good partner and can certainly help in these times. Don't try to do it all alone. Getting out of your own way is in large part keeping that conscious mind where it belongs, giving it its due and encouraging it often to mature. I sometimes see my conscious mind as a child, for certainly it can still be petty and childish at times in its old brain pathway thoughts that still need cleansing. I have come to appreciate what the Buddhist call brainwashing and have freed myself from the old fear I was taught that the term meant someone else might steal my mind and do bad things to it. Brainwashing is an act of reverence, a sacred offering I practice daily, and it is freeing.

May I share some of this with other directors and perhaps in a book?

I love you and look forward to seeing you very soon. Dr. Barbara

Rhye's affirmative response enables me to share this insightful woman's story which strikes a chord common to many. Her place of learning was as a volunteer director of a not-for-profit organization, yet the challenges she faces are so typical of fast-paced, American life they could have arisen at any job. Her willingness to look at herself, even when unfavorable or unpleasant, opens the mind to see Self in a new light. This is the essence of the action that is Self Respect.

Yoga comes from the Sanskrit *yug* meaning union. Each time we exercise the power of thinking we come one step closer to becoming a mental creator. Why is that important? In every way your ability to create in your image is the key to getting what you want, fulfilling your dreams, living in harmony with others and with nature, even knowing your Maker.

The Essential Life Skills all hold a place in producing this union. Toward this end mental exercises are included for the development of each skill.

A SELF RESPECT EXERCISE

Getting out of your head so you can see the workings of your mind is easier than you might think. We teach how to move through a complete cycle in the evolution of thought. The steps can be applied to any thought and endeavor from baking a cake to opening a new business to healing a life threatening disease.

Step One: Separate

Create a chart by turning a piece of paper sideways so it is wider than long. Draw a line across the width about one inch from the top. Draw vertical lines from top to bottom about three inches apart. If you are using a standard size 81/2 x 11 inch sheet of paper you will have four columns on your paper.

Now as a heading for each column place the following numbers in sequence:

1-7, 8-14, 15-21, 22-28, 36-42, 43-49, 50-56, 57-63, 64-70
and so forth up to your present age

Step Two: Identify

Write down: My most influential experience(s) between birth and 7.

continues on page 26

Self Respect....a Magic Cure

Most situations in your life that you encounter which you see as a problem can be cured with Self Respect. A good dose of Self Respect illuminates the cause and effect in the way you see yourself and your world. Think about all the proverbial wisdoms, the enduring ones: *As a man thinketh, so is he. Thoughts are things and the physical is its manifest likeness. Nothing is either good nor bad, only thinking makes it so. It's the thought that counts. A penny for your thoughts.*

These thoughts are memorable because they hold Universal Truth. They apply to anyone, any time, anywhere in our universe. Developing the ability to think clearly brings Self Respect alive. Listen to Ivy's story, maybe you'll recognize yourself or someone you know.

Observing the Self

I'm really getting the importance of people in our lives for just this reason. I'm also getting that that is part of the reason I shied away from people for so long. I may have been found out as Dr. Barbara said. Not necessarily found out that I was wrong and bad, quite possibly I would be found out that I was capable of much more than I claimed or believed. It's time to accept the responsibility.

I remember the day that Dr. Barbara said that during classes that I sit there not saying much if anything and I would smile and look wise. My instant reaction was "I feel like I look like an idiot and everyone knows I'm an idiot because I never say anything." She said I really needed to get up outside of myself.

So I started observing myself. And she was right. I put a few things together with this as well. I learned that I don't remember a lot of what is talked about in class and therefore am unable to discuss much related, because I live in the emotional level a lot and judge things based on feeling. When I hear someone say something that feels right, I get a good sensation, sometimes Kundalini tingling up my spine and I believe what has been said is true and good. My response to this is a smile and a nod of agreement because I believe it is really true and really good. In looking at it now, I look almost cocky. Like I was the one who invented and shared that particular truth. I've been focusing on being more still, listening more attentively in classes and continuing with what I have done before, a five-day five-step reversal exercise (taught early in the SOM course) before I go into class to help me be clear and present. ∞ Ivy Norris

When this is completed write down your most influential experience(s) from 8-14. Next influential experiences from 15-21, and so forth until you reach your present age.

Now, reread what you have written, receiving the whole picture of your life up until now.

Step Three: Admit

Draw a large circle on another sheet of paper. Cut your circle out.

Read your entries once again, this time with an "eye" for the experiences with the greatest impact on who you are. Determine the age group that influenced you the most, then second, then third, and so on until you have arranged these time periods in your life from greatest influence to least.

"Something I have been doing lately is admitting out loud what I am thinking and feeling. 'I am attached to my pets', 'I feel worthless and hopeless to change', 'I am afraid of the truth', 'I love learning more', etc. With admittance of where I am, I am able to be in the truth, in the light."

Step Four: Connect

Look at your circle. Divide it into the number of sections needed to reflect all of your life periods. As you do so, determine the size of each pie piece section *according to its impact upon your consciousness*. Transfer your information onto these sections, then attach them to a piece of paper in a manner that reflects how you see your life.

This is a most amazing exercise. It always gives in accordance to what is given. Sometimes it may seem very general and nonspecific, giving a broad, if vague, picture that answers the question "Who am I?" At other times, responses are very specific and connections through life can be illuminated. Causes can be defined. One student identified how a present back injury had begun with a broken tailbone at the age of 5 and repeated itself in some form to his present age of 33. Another began to understand how the impact of a grandmother dying when she was 4 set into motion a pattern of loss and grief that is being understood more clearly with each seven year cycle.

Cycles occur in our lives as opportunities for greater Self awareness. For soul progression, we must choose that greater awareness through actions of Self Respect. Often I see this in the imagery of Jacob's ladder from the Bible. The bottom of the ladder is grounded on the Earth, in daily physical experiences of our lives. The top of the ladder reaches into Heaven, that place of full illumination. Angels, thought forms, travel up and down the ladder to assist us on our journey upward toward the light. At any time I can look down, where I have come from, look around and see where I am presently, and look up to see where I am going. This is a very strong image of Self Respect for me. I hope it will aid you as well.

The road to Self realization is paved with stones laid in the first seven years of our lives. The soul's strengths and weaknesses are made known through how we respond or react to situations in our lives. Awarenesses of these come through the people in our lives. Teresa Martin describes how Self respect, applied in the present, illumines our understanding of Self and others.

Do Unto Others

I felt very sad at dinner the other night so I went to Dr. Barbara and talked with her which helped me to gain some respect on my feelings. The whole thing centered around Dr. Pam's (Blosser) birthday dinner and the fact that we had so many leftover dishes from a busy and well-attended weekend of guests. I have come to feel very strongly about using what we have, not wasting and so forth and in some ways, that kind of thinking blankets any other type of thought process.

It seems that using everything fully is more important to me. When I was young my mother wasted a lot. Food went bad, canning was done and then not used. Sometimes food was purchased or put in the freezer and then forgotten about. She also bought all kinds of art and craft supplies, always with the intention of making lots of different things for gifts and for the house. She'd go overboard with buying 20 different kinds of ribbons instead of just what she needed.

She had kind of an entrepreneur focus and had purchased a bookstore and devoted some of the shelves to crafts that she made and others rented. Her vision was bigger than she had the will to follow through and so much of the materials that she purchased were not used.

As I grew older I found myself drawn to have things that were useful, yet I practiced the same thing. I noted this in my mid twenties and attempted to be more definitive in the choices I would make. I can't say that I made much progress until I moved to Louisville. It was at this time that I began to make choices based on use. If something wasn't going to be used, then I needed to let it go. I was very disciplined with how I used my energy always looking for ways that I could stretch my resources.

Part of my attention was on the fact that I was going to be moving to School of Metaphysics World Headquarters in Missouri and didn't want to have to give any attention to working. I became much more resourceful and creative.

I brought that consciousness with me to the College of Metaphysics and it has been valuable in terms of using the resources fully. For example, I'm pretty conscious of expenditures like having FedEx come out to pick up a box. Knowing that they add on a charge with each visit, I spoke with Dr. Pam about taking Dr. Laurel Clark's book to the printer in Illinois rather than sending it via FedEx. I combine book orders because I know it's a more effective use of FedEx as well.

When it comes to cooking, I want us to use what we have. I feel kind of lost now that the garden isn't producing like it was. I really like being able to use what we have and it's only now, at the end of the season that I really appreciate this.

But in some ways, I think this all-consuming desire has gotten in the way of simply giving because I want to give. It has been a consciously chosen practice for a while and since I did not follow through on my desire to give to Dr. Pam, I know it is time to allow more freedom of thought in generosity.

The other realization that I have regarding this is that I so easily allow myself to be swayed by others' thoughts. It's because I believe people say what they want. When Dr. Pam said it made more sense to serve the leftovers and that she would rather have that than cook a new dessert, I chose to go along, negating my own desire to give.

There were so many times when my mother would say she didn't want us to get her any gift... birthdays, holidays... I felt that I shouldn't give her gifts. It was confusing to me because then she felt hurt if we didn't give her gifts. I realize now that she was dishonest in this and I grew up being very confused about whether or not I should give. There were times I wanted to give a special gift to someone, but if there wasn't some occasion, then I didn't. I would go through all sorts of contortions in my thinking about shoulds. And now I realize that if I want to give something, then I just need to give it. When I have (do) I feel a joy in my heart that really opens me up. ∞ Teresa Martin

"Sticks in a bundle are unbreakable."
– Bondei proverb, Kenya

"The well-resolved mind is single and one-pointed."
– Bhagavad Gita, 4th BC, India

Undivided Attention

Universal Language of Mind Story

Heavy Thoughts

Two Zen monks were sent to town for weekly provisions for the monastery. It had been raining for some days and the road they traveled was muddy and slippery. Rounding a bend, they came upon a lovely woman trying and failing to negotiate a large puddle. Seeing her distress, the elder monk bowed to the woman, swept her into his arms and carried her across the puddle. He set her down on dry ground and she proceeded on her way.

As the two monks continued toward town, the younger monk was sullen and silent. They traveled many miles, over hills and down valleys. After several hours, the young monk could contain himself no longer.

"You are aware that we monks do not touch women!" he admonished the elder monk. "Why did you carry that girl?"

The elder monk slowly turned and meeting the younger's accusatory gaze, he calmly replied, "My brother, you have such heavy thoughts! I left the woman alongside the road hours ago. Why are you still carrying her?"

–a Jataka Buddhist tale

This ageless story of a disciplined mind and an undisciplined mind illustrates the power of undivided attention to sense, understand, and respond as conveyed through the actions of the elder monk and the disturbed thoughts that produce the attachment experienced by the younger. Every experience is an opportunity for discipline. We choose whether we will be focused and directed in the present moment or distracted by the past or the future. The choice is made using undivided attention.

The undisciplined mind is a sleeping mind. Some sleep through the experiences life brings them, missing what is before their eyes. A wife mourning her lost husband does not *see* the man who has been by her side for years, loving, waiting. A child who wanted a brother and receives a sister finds it difficult to embrace the truth of companionship, to *feel* happy. A man seeking approval only *tastes* the defeat in success because his mind lusts for applause that does not come. When we sleep, our minds are caught up in manifestations of what is not in our present environment. Nightmares stir our emotions grabbing our attention. Restlessness overcomes the Spirit and we are distracted from the purpose in life.

Being awake to life is a function of attention. The placement of attention – here, there, here, there – draws upon the first Essential Life Skill. Where is your attention now? Is it fully in this moment receiving the images these words describe? What happens if I write the word *yesterday*? Where is your attention now? The word *tomorrow*?

Few people realize mental attention is like an object. It can be placed where you want it. Cultivating the ability to move the attention at will is a function of a disciplined mind.

When our attention is directed consciously we become more Self aware. Self awareness changes how we see yourselves and the world, thus guiding our actions, as we learn in this Jataka tale from ancient India.

UNDIVIDED ATTENTION is
being conscious and aware
in the present moment
so we can cause the mind to be unified and whole.

> "'There is a very strong construction within this one for the capacity to attune the senses to what is before her and through that enables this one's mind to be free to experience fully." (114200BGC02)

> "When your attention is singular and consciousness aligned we are connected with others." (SOM Lesson 6)

Be Here Now.

Undivided Attention is the mental action of paying respect to one thought, person, or thing.

Why is it undivided? Isn't that negative? Wouldn't it be better to say "singular" or "focused"?

Undivided Attention pays respect to the condition of the mind at the time direction is employed. The mind is engrossed in the interactions and endeavors in the physical world. To give attention to the quality and nature of your thoughts is to think before speaking and acting. To accomplish this requires full attention in the conscious mind.

The conscious part of the whole mind exists in the physical level of consciousness only. The conscious mind is tied to the body, the physical ego, the waking mind.

The subconscious part of the whole mind exists in four inner levels of consciousness that together comprise what is often called the soul.

A third division of the whole mind, the superconscious mind, exists in the two innermost levels of consciousness.

Together, these three divisions of mind function in seven levels of consciousness. The Essential Life Skill known as Undivided Attention is the faculty that enables us to function in each of these levels. Self Respect gives us the hope that we can do so in a manner that is illuminated and evolved.

Undivided Attention pays respect to the parts of mind beyond the physical world. Undivided Attention is the open door that leads into mind. The following Dharma Profile given for a middle-aged teacher describes the ability for attention very clearly.

> This would be described as attendance. There is a very strong construction within this one of the capacity to attune the senses to what is before her and through that enable this one's mind to be free to experience fully. This has been built over many experiences.
>
> There have been a very high amount of experiences that have been geared toward refining the use of the senses. Most of these have been primarily hearing oriented. They have included experiences in Japan through that which is referred to

as geisha, through monk experiences in India through tribal experiences in South America, in Incan. There have been experiences of a variety of kinds and ways, and they have been such that this one was in attendance whether it was in attending another person, or a physical thing such as fire or being the water gatherer or attending to the needs of another such as with the geisha or in attendance to royalty.

These experiences have brought to this one a pattern of understanding that is conducive to an acceleration of this one's learning and growth and understanding. It has come together within the present time period in what can be best be described as attendance. It has been in these manners where this one has flourished the most where the most profound influence has been made, where the most profound unification of the Self has been experienced, through this kind of unity of consciousness.

This one says, "How can I cultivate my capacity to teach with my dharma?"

To become acutely aware of the difference between attending and interfering. The first does nurture the development of the giver and the receiver. The latter destroys both.

When this one becomes distracted then the solution would be for this one to see how this one can tend to or attend or be in attendance?

It is to come back into the Self. This one has come away from the Self when this occurs. It is in coming back to the self where there will be the alignment once more where the focus can be attending. (1142000BGC2)

Receiving her Dharma Profile transformed the way this woman saw the world and her place in it. It freed her to begin to unravel years of self-denying and self-defeating programming. "When I am doing my dharma, I am at peace," she said. "I don't really have to 'do' anything. I merely need to as the (Biblical) *Psalms* says, 'Be still, and know that I Am God'."

There is a relationship between attention and intention as can be seen in the Buddhist story of the two monks. Attention is the sense of the mind, enabling human man to distinguish himself from the animal body that encases his soul. When purpose is added to attention the result is the causal factor of karma – intention. Intention is the power of thought to be made manifest. The following intuitive wisdom taken from a Meditation Portrait for a sixty-year-old Colombian woman describes the uniting of undividual attention and intention. When the reporter was asked for suggestions for attuning the outer mind to superconscious mind, this was the response.

> This would be in the singularity of intention. It is most important for this one to be able to arrest the attention and be able to move it at will. This would require practice in this one's part in being able to invest the self in concentration, then there could be a greater illumination of this one's intent moment by moment. It is in this one's intention being centered and growing from a point of concern and love that this one's greatest alignment of self and with others will occur. It will open this one's capacity for connectedness and it will cause there to be a greater stream of consciousness that will be able to move through this one. As long as this one is preoccupied, as this one might identify it, or is worried, there is the dividing of the mind into segments that at times do not relate. Therefore the arresting of the attention is essential in this one to be able to cause the energies of the mind to vibrate in correspondence. This is all. (101400BGC1)

Much is made of networking and connecting in today's world. Perhaps the stimulus is technological advancement. The world has indeed become a smaller place just in the past 50 years. Even if we can "see" what is happening half a world away, what we think about what we see will always be a function of where we place the mind's attention. "Arresting" the attention as this Intuitive Report suggests directs the mind's power to the focal point of your choosing.

It is will, harnesssed with intelligence, that opens the mind.

Undivided Attention What is It?

"Barbara Condron knows this world is heading towards peace and happiness, and she knows how it's going to get there," the article in the *Columbia Missourian* begins.

It's a sensational opening the reporter chose to get people's attention.

Attention means access to everything. With it you can remember someone's name, catch a ball, add a column of figures, bake a perfect souffle, and learn a computer program. Without it you are at the mercy of brain pathways – be they productive or not.

The article for the newspaper is focused on Indigo children. I was interviewed because I wrote a book on the subject. I told the reporter that the young souls coming into the world are highly intelligent. They are quick thinkers, they have a very strong will, and they have an awareness of why they exist in the world. The Indigo child is an evolution of what twenty years ago was called a talented and gifted child.

So if that's true, why are many of these young souls being labeled and drugged?

Indigos are a result of the natural evolution of the soul. The social changes begun in the 1960's created an environment that allowed Indigos to emerge. These children have outgrown the average education system. Their unwillingness to conform to an outdated system is what causes so many of them to be diagnosed with ADHD (attention deficit hyperactivity disorder) and, subsequently, drugged. There is quite a shift from the eighties cry of "Just say No!" and television public service announcements that illustrated "your brain on drugs" as frying an egg in a hot frying pan, to nurses and teachers giving out ritalin-type drugs morning and noon, every school day. What has caused the 180° shift in the consciousness of our society?

I think our society has the attention deficit disorder. We blame the kids for it and our kids don't yet know enough to speak for themselves. Look at how we live, celebrating multi-tasking and driving down the road on cell phones eating or drinking while ignoring the passenger sitting beside us. The evidence of attention deficiency in the collective unconscious is everywhere.

In this condition we require a mental alarm clock to awaken. Loud sounds, strong odors, bold colors manifest as faster, better, more expensive. The desire for more, more, more beats in our breasts like the Tinman's hollow heart.

We can see it in our addictions. Statistics on domestic violence increase during every Superbowl game. Children can't leave home without their inhalers while mothers take Valium or Prozac to get through the day. Computer porn spam tempts some every day, enslaving them for a minute or for hours. The attitude that someone should do something about the government, education, or the environment has become commonplace, yet when asked if you voted in the most recent election or volunteer to help with kids in your community or carpool to work, how many are willing to change their lives in order to answer "Yes"? Nobody agrees with the effects of war yet our country engages in it.

People who know how to give UNDIVIDED ATTENTION in the moment live in the now.

(SOM Lesson Eight)

When we fail to direct our attention, we fail as thinkers. We are less than what we can be. Hypocrisy is one result. So is an empty shell. We get parents who arrive home after dinner from a long day working somewhere outside the home who have little energy left for each other or their children. Too many people go through the motions of life, attention divided, their thoughts somewhere else.

It is a miracle that we can think out of present time and space at all! Just think. It is a miracle that we go to sleep for hours and our hearts keep beating, our lungs continue to breathe, and we awake ready for another day. It is a miracle that we have dreams and hopes and opinions and sorrows or fears. When we take these for granted the miracle of life passes us by. In those times we are asleep to the mystery of life.

The truth is the mind *is* separate from the physical body. You, the Real You, as the *Bhagavad Gita* terms it, existed before this physical body and will exist after its time. The Real You is the thinker who lives inside the body. In dream symbols, a small vehicle, like a car symbolizes the dreamer's physical body. For instance, if the dream-car is running out of gas this is a message about needing to replenish your energy levels. The car is a vehicle, a mode of transportation from one place to another. The body is a vehicle for the thinker transporting you from birth to death.

The human body has five distinct means for receiving information from the environment. These are called senses. Watch a very young child. They see a block with their eyes. They reach for it with their hands, touching it. They smell it, taste it, and will rattle it to see if it makes sound. They are instinctively using all the body's resources to identify something in their environment.

It is the sixth sense – attention – that enables the child to determine the block's usefulness. Does it taste good? Mental attention enables the mind to say, "No." Does it smell good? Mental attention is indifferent, satisfied with the previous experience. Does it make noise? Mental attention says, "No, not until it hits the table." How does it feel? Mental attention lets the child know the block is hard, unyielding under the pressure of fingers. What does it look like? Mental attention opens the mind to the possibility of future recognition of this chunk of wood.

Mental attention at any age is the key to all the mind's abilities. It unlocks the experiences the world around us brings.

What the body gives you is an extension of your mind, a means for mind thought to express itself so the soul can learn and progress.

I have had many lessons through life in being present. From the schoolroom ritual of responding when the teacher gives roll call to being there when a friend marries to attending a woman bearing a stillborn child, I have found many applications for the skill of undivided attention. With undivided attention I built Self Respect by answering "present" instead of the usual "here". With Undivided Attention I knew the happy hearts of the newlyweds at a time when my heart was breaking with new and unwelcomed understanding. With undivided attention I could steady my mind to be an anchor in one of life's harshest experiences.

As a teacher of Mind I have seen thousands of people develop skill in using abilities they took for granted. After establishing the desire for Self Respect, each one begins with the skill we call Undivided Attention. Undivided Attention brings the mind to the present moment. You've heard about "be here now"? Undivided Attention is how you accomplish it.

Not long ago we met for a weekly PeaceMakers gathering in the Peace Dome on a Sunday morning. Dr. Daniel Condron opened the morning's lesson with a question, "What is the most important thing or things in life?"

As paper and pencils were passed around, I noted my first thoughts, "Love, wisdom, truth." Then I smiled. I had heard those same thoughts years ago on my 24th birthday. And in the same order! How much has changed, how little changes, I thought. The pairs of opposites at work again.

When the paper came to me I wrote these words and added what underlies these desires – "a relationship with God and all Creation." At the time I felt this reflected what I have learned in the past 26 years.

As we talked about what we had written I told the story of the Intuitive Report I had received that described why an emptiness existed inside me. It was a secret emptiness. I didn't flaunt it, never spoke of it, but I knew it was there and so did this intuitive reporter. Later the report would say, "That is why there is that place that isn't filled up. And you'll have to appreciate Barbara to fill it." For years, I have been learning this lesson of self-appreciation. On this day, a greater glimpse of it was mine.

A few weeks earlier, Matthew a student at the College of Metaphysics made a comment that was natural for him. I'm sure he thought little about it other than it being the truth he sees. However, it still plays in my mind as it updates previous limitations in my thinking.

The comment concerned a beautiful year and a half year old named Ella Rose who, with her sister Iris and mother Dory, visits each week. The children love interacting with our son and having the advantage of so many loving teachers. On this day, however, Ella was increasingly cranky. Her mom said she had a runny nose and was probably coming down with something. At one point, she screamed and nothing and no one could pacify her. I had heard that scream before and now knew it signified the entering of a virus into the body and the body's natural reaction to it.

I held my arms out and she came to me. I picked her up, enveloping her in my aura, and allowed healing energy to flow into my aura and through my hands. We walked for a while, I sang to her, and talked to her. She would settle for a while, then become disturbed again. Each time she was calm for longer periods as I united her senses – sight, sound, touch primarily - so her attention could be undivided.

Apparently Matthew had noted this interaction.

Later as we talked I made some statement about being with her. Matthew said, "She needed you." I said something like yes, I could offer things to help. To which Matthew said, "She needed *you,* Dr. Barbara. Just your presence." When he said this, I felt the movement of energy from my heart up to my throat and out the crown of my head. I knew instantly what he was saying and I knew how it shone a brilliant light where none had been before.

It is too easy for me to fall into ideas that it is what I do that is important. When this happens I forget to value thought as cause and so I fail to honor the Creator. I had done just that with Ella. Still chained by old childhood ideas of not being too full of myself and not being selfish with credit, this was a way I would deflect attention from myself. This was an ego lesson in honesty.

When Matthew said it was my presence that was wanted my mind went back to being with the couple through the experiencing of stillbirth. The vow I had made to their unborn child just the day before was "I will be present. Here, there, and everywhere." What I imagined that might be was far different from what our reality became. I was present for them, and in so doing was present for me in a way that forever changed me. Undivided attention gave me that ability.

Months later when I begin to pull together the varied pieces to write this book, I came across Matthew's Healer's Portrait. This Intuitive Report describes the outstanding soul patterns that support someone's healing capacity. Matthew's begins:

> This is best described as attentiveness.

I am grateful for being given the benefit of Matthew's healing presence in my life and am delighted as I realize the utility of what is given here for anyone desiring to learn more about the power of attention.

> It is of a nature of the capacity of the mind to be attending to the needs of others which this one has made a part of the self. There is much capacity within this one which is exhibited in the interactions with others in attuning this one's mind to another and then reaching to fulfill a need that is perceived. There is a faculty of clearness and precision in the use of the mental attention in this way that is quite elucidating of both needs and requirements for fulfilling those needs. In this, this one is capable of visualization and putting the mind into action in the ascertaining of need and the creation of desire. This is essential in the capacity to bring about wholeness and to be able to recognize a completeness within the existence. (3112000BGC1)

One of the results of giving Undivided Attention is the ability it gives us to recognize the specific needs of others. Those who have learned and practiced Essential Life Skills often employ them in service with others. They are known as Psi Counselors. To be effective, Psi Counselors learn to be in their minds. When you are not lost in your brain knowledge, in what you superficially "think", you realize counseling is far from having all the right answers. Psi counseling revolutionizes old paradigms of counseling, helping it to take a giant evolutionary step. The skill Psi Counselors draw upon most? Undivided Attention, for with Undivided Attention you are present - spiritually, mentally, emotionally, and physically. The *whole* you.

Undivided Attention helps us to experience all facets of our lives with greater depth and clarity, to lead a memorable and fulfilling life. The whole you is what your spouse wants, your employer/employees want, your friends want. The whole you is what Indigos of all ages need. Indigos are great souls – potential Gandhis, da Vincis, Shakespeares, and Einsteins. Their success is up to society, for that we must change ourselves.•

"Help! We're hurting!"

This story shared with me by a parent moved me to tears of joy. Her daughter, Karen, was behaving strangely. Her grades were declining rapidly and Karen refused to do her work. After the mother had tried everything she could think of, she took Karen to a tutor. The tutor noticed inconsistencies in Karen's learning behavior. She would learn very rapidly and then shut down, she was restless and unable to focus. After talking with a counselor, it was suspected that she may have had ADD/ADHD and that she needed testing. The mother withdrew Karen from tutoring; she had reached a point of despair and hopelessness.

Approximately a year later, Karen's grades had picked up and she was enthusiastic about learning. Two of Karen's relatives in her environment were constantly at odds with each other and Karen had been feeling confused about the discord. When her mother removed the stimulus, Karen began to perform well in school again. Her mother, recognizing the injury, began to nurse her daughter back to health with loving attention and encouragement. This Indigo's unexplainable behavior brought attention to a thwarting situation that needed to be healed for everyone in her environment.

Indigos are sensitive to their environment. Their uncanny ability to act out the discordant situations in our lives is their gifts to us to help us wake up and heal our lives. ∞ *Keisha Freed-Tafari*

The Cure for ADD

I spent quite a bit of time, at different instances, with two people this Christ Consciousness weekend, Rory and Lee. Both have been labeled with mental illness and attention deficit. Both are very rich souls.

Rory is a sharp, communicative, 20-year-old male who loves to be with people and to be expressive. Lee is quieter and more limited in her thinking about what she is capable of, yet there is a part of her that is eagerly seeking greater truth and purpose in life.

There is an innocent quality to both of them that I really appreciated being around. In some ways they were like small children in that they were easily excited and easily distracted. When they had their attention in present moment, focused on one topic, each were like sages full of wisdom and truth. It was at these times that I was immensely grateful that they were studying with the School and that I got the opportunity to ask questions and listen to their stories.

I found out that Rory has a desire to understand mental illness from a metaphysical perspective so he can help others to channel their energies more productively and to heal. He speaks with much passion about aiding others to be so focused on their goal or the light of their desires that the only time the past is visited is to aid them to grow in the present moment. He was so passionate about knowing how to have the attention in the present moment and teaching others to do the same. He wants the mental muscle of undivided attention developed.

When asked, Lee said her goal for the weekend was to be open for the purpose of being more connected with others. However, every twenty minutes or so she was saying she needed to go upstairs and nap because she didn't sleep much the night before. She was wanting to separate. After a few minutes of giving her undivided attention and asking questions and listening to her she opened up sharing her dreams and concerns and started to be more enthusiastic about being there. With her sharing, she got to hear her own words and the limitations they held at times. We also got to help her to see a fuller picture of the School of Metaphysics and how perfectly her studies fit with the way she desires to give to people as a healer.

I believe that undivided attention is one of the greatest gifts we can offer another. It is a necessary and "essential" skill to be a good parent, counselor, teacher, friend, lover, speaker, boss, employee, student, and minister. The skill of undivided attention enables one to be entirely focused on one thing at a time. This enhances clarity, security, stability, creativity and love.

Oftentimes we are praised in this society for having many things going on, and for having busy minds thinking about many things simultaneously. To worry about another can be thought of as being loving, multi-tasking is considered a reflection of having an employable skill, and talking on a cell phone all day a reflection of one's importance.

Undivided attention helps us to experience all facets of our lives with greater depth and clarity, to lead a memorable and fulfilling life. One of my most favorite results of it is the ability undivided attention gives us to recognize the specific needs of others. ∞ Ivy Norris

Undivided Attention

Scared of the Dark

This morning we were talking at continental breakfast about brain pathways and how you override them which is by choosing a different thought enough times. I then shared with everyone the following experience.

Last night I was making butter and it got pretty late, after midnight. I then walked to the warehouse to hang a wet bag and collect dry ones to put away and I realized that I was the only one downstairs. In the past this realization would have brought a flood of scary images from movies I have seen or scary books I have read. However, as I objectively observed my mind, I saw that none of those thoughts surfaced. I thought that was interesting and I asked myself why my experience was different this time. As I searched my mind, I came to the realization that I have thought so many light and love filled thoughts that I have closed down that uncontrollable scary image brain pathway. For someone who cannot stand to be alone at night, this was a pretty amazing and wonderful discovery. ∞ Stacy Ann Ferguson

ELS#2

A Short Class on Undivided Attention

Dr. B: So once someone has embarked upon the journey dictated by the great Oracle of Delphi to "Know Thyself", what mind ability do they need to cultivate?

TM: Mastering attention.

Dr. B: What does it mean to master attention?

JD: Holding your attention where you desire to place it.

Dr. B: Which we call Undivided Attention. Why does this follow Self Respect and why is it important?

JD: Because first you got yourself, then the first thing you produce is thoughts. Attention is the way you control your thoughts. So by being able to control where your attention is you have the power switch that controls everything. That's the root. That's the origin of the pendulum. It's where everything else starts.

Dr. B: What's the definition of attention? Who has a simple one?

MH: Moving your mind in a particular direction.

Dr. B: I thought a goal accomplished that.

PM: I've heard that it's the sense of the mind.

Dr. B: Okay, what do you think about what you've heard?

PM: I like it. *(everyone laughs)*

Dr. B: Why do you like it?

PM: Because on the one hand it demonstrates that the mind is not necessarily us, it's something that we use. The "sense of the mind" is us really using the mind. Out here with the physical senses this is how I receive nature and my environment. So the sense of the mind is how the whole mind receives knowledge.

Dr. B.: The mind sense takes you beyond knowledge.

TM: Attention means to give to. What I see with that definition is giving yourself to something is to receive what that something is. You experience it with all your senses. In latin *attendo* is "to give to."

Dr. B: That's good information to have. Root words, particularly when they go back to Latin, describe the image in mind that a word has been devised to identify. It's the closest, I think, that the Western world has to Sanskrit. The elemental component of Sanskrit is the vibration of the thing itself. That is the essence of mantram yoga and many zen practices.

TM: I'd agree with that because it's been my experience. Every time I find a Latin word it makes so much sense. It's very simple, so it must be metaphysics.

Dr. B: Right, and identifying origin is a purifier. By purifier I mean it separates and identifies all the physical conscious mind/brain misconceptions that one has placed upon a very simple, whole and positive idea. Learning origins becomes a wonderful teacher because you can realize greater truth. For instance, what do you think when I say the word "security?"

TM: Confidence.

PM: Ease.

SS: Safety.

LJ: Self-assured.

Dr. B: Yes, the common images conveyed and taught. The insurance industry is based on the illusion of security, so is the US government's social *security* program. In our current atmosphere, globally, the desire for security is dictating our thoughts and actions collectively. Security has become the absence of fear.

The Truth is the nature of the physical is change, everyone you know from your parents to your spouse to your best friend will eventually move away or die. When we realize the root of the word security, our image changes and so does our understanding. The word security comes from the Latin roots *se* meaning "apart from" and *cura* meaning "care". *Apart from care.* Think about this for a while...•

The Unconscious Mind

Undivided Attention gives us the ability to be conscious in our everyday experiences. Siddhartha Guatama, the one who became known as Buddha, taught how to be awake in mind through control of the senses and the restless thoughts the senses arouse. The ancient wisdom is as real in today's modern world, and as needed, as ever. In this email, a SOM teacher shares his experience with becoming awake in the most ordinary of American experiences – driving in a car.

Dr. Barbara,

Today I was driving down the road watching my thoughts. Going to past and future. I decided to still my mind and just be. Then, I thought about smoking a cigarete and thought with a still mind, "what will occur?" I passed through an intersection and almost got hit by an ambulance. I said, "Jeez!........wow, I just experienced unconsciounsess." So I wrote about it and it goes like this-

Unconsciousness is when one's body is functioning in the present and the conscious mind is in the past or future or going back and forth as if there is no control. Being present is nonexistent. Concentration is the ability to have undivided attention on the present. It is like two hands pulling apart the space to be still.

When a person goes too far in memory or in the future where stillness is not, the person momentarily loses the aware thinking ability and goes literally unconscious, creating karma. Karma is the unconscious energy wave pattern that keeps returning until Self has a still mind through the process. Karma occurs when self is totally unaware of the thinking and in time becomes a pttern where the self ignores it because it has pain associated with it.

Unaware of this energetic pattern, Self keeps avoiding the same situations, creating a habit or compulsion. In time, a breakdown occurs and the person wants to understand why. The need for understanding is present. The understanding is the ability to be still during the return of the karmic wave pattern and make choices with the aware thinking mind to balance the inbalance of energy. Thus creating Self awareness. The person begins to be awakened. Knowing one exists in the physical world in three ways. Past, present and future in space and time.

During the process of this awareness, Self chooses to be present more and more, releasing living in the past or future.

From this point, psychic and intuitive flashes occur. Producing clairvoyance and etc....which is sporadic because the person doesn't know the cause of it. What the person lacks is the intelligence of the power of being present, having a still mind. So what has come to me is Enlightenment is having a still mind in every area of life so reasoning and stillness dominate all of life. I could see all this in picture form of energy graphs in my mind. So what do you think about this? I know this came about by observing my thoughts for a period of time.

Love Geoffrey* *(asterisked names in this book are pseudonyms)*

So do I. It is the benefit of practicing the skills the mental exercises build. The will is the mental muscle. Just as we can build the physical muscle through repeated and intentional use, so the mind's muscle is strengthened through exercising. To be awake is the CHOICE TO KNOW. That's the diagram I am teaching in the Kundalini class here at the College. The CHOICE TO KNOW is made in the Conscious Mind through the use of the receptive and aggressive factors of concentration. Will gives us the capacity for attention. Intelligence gives us the capacity for that attention to be undivided - on mind thought rather than scattered amongst what is received through the five physical senses or related inner level senses. As intelligence chooses, concentration results.

The CHOICE TO KNOW is a present time function. It draws to it the past which is relevant and creates a relevant future. It is the action of that wonderful paragraph in the first cycle of lessons about "the Law of Duality applied to the Law of Relativity and Infinity....." This is what you are exploring in your points above. Concentration does give us the ability to identify cause in the present, from the past, into the future, and knowing this is a great step toward being a Mental Creator. You want, and intend, to be a Mental Creator and so you think in the ways you have described.

I have learned the value of describing the thoughts in my experiences so others can learn what it is like to function in more than one level of consciousness SIMULTANEOUSLY. This is why I took the time to record my thoughts for five days last winter which is shared in the first section of the book THE WISDOM OF SOLOMON. Thank you for elucidating your thoughts so others can read and learn. The more of us who do so, the faster those who want to learn can. In the process of Enlightenment, the STILL MIND calms the ego. The Still Mind establishes the Conscious Mind's dominion, it is the action of "Get behind me, Satan!" The Still Mind is then ready to make the CHOICE TO KNOW. Because it can!

It has always amazed me that awareness is present, we need only CHOOSE IT! Whether thinking about smoking a cigarette or teaching a dozen people or being interviewed on the radio, every experience is valuable in proportion to the individual's desire and willingness to BE PRESENT. It's about time Undivided Attention is taught in schools and at home, don't you agree?

Thank you for sharing your thoughts. And I have a question for you. What happened to the thought of smoking that cigarette?

Dr. Barbara

Becoming Conscious

Paul Madar describes the action of divided in an informative and humorous way. "Physically we readily split our attention between objects and sensory stimuli in our environment, called horizontal division. We can be driving down the road (one direction), listening to that new CD (two directions), fiddling with the CD cover to read the notes (three), eating our french fries (four) and would you believe, talking on the cell phone to a friend (five). Of course, the discussion with the friend is about none of this, but rather about how angry we felt about so and so when they did this and that (six). This is a recipe for disaster, not only short term because of that car we don't see pulling in front of us, but also long term because of the state that it leaves our consciousness. Our consciousness, our very state of mind, becomes fragmented in disconnected physical pieces for us to somehow fashion some meaning and relevance for our soul."

(Paul, who is completing his thesis for a Doctorate of Divinity, likens Undivided Attention symbolically to the cross.) "What happens when we choose to focus on only one thing at a time? What happens when we declare we want to experience something physical (outer) with our whole mind's attention (inner)? We focus all of our being and our power to one point, the intersection of the two bars of the cross. It is at this point that we can fully receive with our senses the object of our attention and also be fully present with all of our mind. We can fully receive the meaning and relevance of the experience. This center point, this singular point of attention is how we open the door to experience true union, interconnectedness, the divine, stillness, the silence and many other mystical descriptions of peace and love." ∞

Someone is Always Watching

I also have been spending more time being with one-year-old Alexandra. I have the tendency to be around her and then to wander off when it suits me. This is why I've been reluctant to be with her for any length of time in the absence of her parents. It's almost as if I want to keep an open door to be able to move if I desire. Since I've recognized that I have chosen to spend some time playing with her and am getting to know how she learns.

By giving her my attention and being with her, I am really getting to know how she learns through giving her attention. Since I've had a cough lately, sometimes at Dream Valley, I would cough, usually twice to clear my throat. Numerous times, she would look at me and I always explained what had just happened. Why I made the strange noise that I believed had startled her.

Soon I noticed that when I coughed, she placed her hand over her mouth. I recognized that she was imitating what I did while coughing since I'm pretty good about covering my mouth with something to contain the microparticles that can easily become airborne.

Through Alexandra I can see more clearly than ever about the sponge like absorption that occurs with children. It got me to thinking about having a still mind with the image of being connected all the way inside. This was an image that I had when I first started practicing undivided attention early on in my practices that helped me to align. Magic happened, or so it seemed. Now I know how it works! ∞ Dr. Teresa Martin

UNDIVIDED ATTENTION EXERCISE

Exercise One

Drawing upside down is a mind opener. It requires Undivided Attention to accomplish and in the process helps you to go beyond many preconceived notions you may have been holding against yourself. Try it, using the hand you usually write with and copy the upside down drawing on the following page. Complete it before turning the book around!

Exercise Two

In the growing world of science, Undivided Attention is sometimes known as synesthesia. Synesthesia is the capacity to use the senses fully. It's manifestations are in people who can taste the color purple and hear plants growing. This developed sensitivity toward wholemindedness was thought for years to be symptoms of mental illness. In reality it is the beginning of mind thought, the ability to unite the attention on a single thought and go into the mind.

You can develop synesthesia by sharpening your Undivided Attention. The next time you are oooing and ah-ing over the sight of a sunset, hold your attention still and ask, "what does this sunset taste like?" The next time you hear your favorite tune, hold your attention steady and ask, "what colors/images do I see in this music?" By asking yourself sensory questions you will train yourself to think in three, four, or more dimensions. As an added bonus, you will find your memory recall improving. You will remember your dreams as well as daytime experiences and in time you may begin drawing on subconscious experiences, commonly known as ESP, extra-sensory experience.

ESP results from the singular use of attention that is directed inward rather than outward. When you like to stroke your pet kitten because his fur is soft your attention is directed outward. When you stroke your kitten because you experienced companionship and your loneliness goes away your attention is directed inward. By deepening your level of awareness and thinking, you will refine your ability to sense someone's mood or intention before they speak or act. You might find yourself connected to others through telepathic communication lines or you might receive visions of things to come. These and other abilities are the result of a mind focused through the power of Undivided Attention.

Reproduce this drawing, as is, on a separate sheet of paper. Once completed, turn it around and see what you created. Drawing upside down causes you to use the right side of your brain as well as your left because it demands that you go beyond preconceived perimeters of thought. Thus it is a tool for developing whole brain thinking.

up to become entrainment

g the table for brunch and heard some- inside is women's work."

ium United States, those words cause ke.

ne kitchen. I knew who had uttered the ce. What I wanted to know was to whom h* at the counter preparing vegetables for the meal. and I wondered if she would let the comment pass without response. Finally she said, "It's too bad you feel that way."

We had been embarking upon a exploration of judgement – the role it plays in personal growth and development and the evolution of the soul – and so I was curious about Beth's response. I asked her why she had responded in the manner she had.

She began to explain to me in some detail that she thought Geoffrey's* (yes, the same Geoff who wrote the email) ego was in the way. She said he has a lot of attitudes about women and had made similar comments before. She wanted him to see how these affect his growth.

I asked her if she thought what she said made a difference to Geoff.

"Probably not," she replied a bit curtly.

Caring about both of them and being a teacher for both, I offered an alternative for next time. Rather than being welcome, this met with a swift quip "I said that" from Beth.

Taken aback by the defensive energy that was now present between us, I replied in mirror fashion, "Since you didn't volunteer that, I didn't know." It was a most interesting change in energy. For what had begun as a thought-provoking and enjoyable conversation that actually included two other people had changed into something a bit less attractive.

Being quite self aware, Beth knew she had escalated the conversation. "I just feel like whatever I say is not good enough," Beth was close to a moment of Self Respect.

"I'm just asking for your thoughts," I replied, hoping to encourage. Looking her in the eyes, I asked another question about Geoff, someone she supervises.

Peter, who was sitting next to Beth and who often wants to spare others the awkwardness of learning something new, offered an answer. Beth immediately turned to him and away from me.

By now I realized Beth was completely somewhere else in this conversation – other than in the present moment – and I wanted to know why. So I stayed with her. Mentally and emotionally. Without taking my eyes from Beth I acknowledged Peter's response and gave the question again to Beth saying, "I want to hear *your* answer."

We continued talking about Beth and Geoff and why his comment stung her so, and then I realized something much more important, something that relates to Beth's reason for living. This realization concerned "attending."

"Attending" is the word used in an intuitive report to describe Beth's dharma. Dharma can most easily be explained as one's purpose in life, the duty the soul is here to fulfilll. Beth's dharma is attending and she has spent much time contemplating its meaning. I understood in this moment that the actions of the mind we had employed in these few minutes were quite different. I had remained with Beth, even when it became uncomfortable for both of us. I was committed to staying with her until there was some kind of resolve.

She had received my question and allowed associated memory thoughts to be stimulated, taking her out of the present and into the past. Her attention was scattered. She had stopped attending.

I shared with her what I saw – that she was willing to drop our conversation when an open door appeared; –that I never left her, she had left me. This helped me to understand Beth more deeply. She has a high degree of faithfulness physically. She is a true friend to many and prides herself on being reliable. Yet, her thoughts are often adulterous. Self doubt is fueled by an active imagination that is often directed toward her weaknesses and lacks. Many times these are imaginary and have no real substance. As a result her conscious mind stays busy, little is accomplished, and she finds herself overwhlemed, a victim of procrastination.

This is all contrary to her dharma.

This is what infuriates her. This is how the neutral questi
had asked about her conversation with Geoff could bring about suc
extreme thoughts and emotions.

Attending requires a still mind. An open mind. An open mind holds no judgement. It determines judgement in the moment. It requires a skill – Undivided Attention.

Almost two weeks later I was cooking with Laurie, a graduate student at the College of Metaphysics. She asked, "Dr. Barbara, how have you experienced compassion?"

The question was so open that I didn't know where to start to answer her needs, so I told her this and asked if there was a way she was thinking of it.

"As it relates to our lesson and the heart chakra," she replied. "I just want an idea of how to be more compassionate with people."

"On a day-to-day basis?"

"Yes."

I began describing the thoughts that had first come to my mind. "When my mother was experiencing the final days of life, (my husband) Daniel and I were with her for the last two and a half weeks. When we arrived she was conscious enough to recognize us and know we had arrived. From then on it was a journey of letting go.

"Being with her every day was an amazing experience. Daniel and I would take turns because Hezekiah, our son, was three and one of us needed to care for him. The extremes of going from the final stages to death to the early stages of life was mind expanding, heart rendering. This was compassion itself. Being able to expand self to hold equanimity.

"The daily bedside ritual was the essence of attending. Much more mentally and emotionally than physically. I learned the boundaries of my compassion and I went beyond each one. In the end I knew it was my presence that made the difference for each of us."

I then shared stories about students and learning how to love unconditionally, about the role that patience plays for me in compassion. I told about Hezekiah and how his presence in my life has centered me in compassion. It has taught me the value of the still mind. Don't jump to conclusions. Be centered in love. Let the ears work before the brain is engaged. To be ever mindful of what being a child is.

What is it like to be ten, living with groups of people that change every six months, who speak differently, dress differently, look differently, act differently, and are at differing ages themselves? I don't need to imagine it, I need only still my mind, align my mind with his, and receive his experience. This is the height of compassion. It is Undivided Attention applied to every Essential Living Skill which produces Entrainment.

I thought about this conversation several times throughout the day. That evening I ran across a notation in a book which said compassion is from a Greek word meaning "to suffer with." My first thought was, "Oh, it is much more than suffering!" Immediately I recognized that as the thought of a busy mind.

I stilled my mind and read again, *"To suffer with."* I had been actively engaged in mentally creating a book about goodness, about equanimity, transcending polarity, and omniscient consciousness so I was capable of deep thinking with the word suffer. No longer did suffer contain its human stigma in my thinking. No longer was it a "bad" word. Rather suffer is the means by which we come to understand experience. Sometimes that experience is our own as in the classic "suffer the consequences" or "suffer the slings and arrows of outrageous fortune." The more heart we grow, the deeper our understandings, and so we can suffer with others, thus learning from their experiences. This is the beauty of ministry, of counseling, of teaching. It is why religion is highly prized throughout the world, for higher thought, deeper thought is what brings humans to compassion, and as all great Masters of consciousness have taught, love is the universal lesson for human beings.

When love is present, the mind can flourish. All Truth can be welcomed and made known. Even when it hurts, the Truth sets you free, and where there is love, hurt heals very quickly.•

"All things are complete within ourselves."
– Mencius, 350 BC, China

"I believe in the essential unity of man, and for that matter, of all lives. Therefore, I believe that if one man gains spiritually, the whole world gains with him, and if one man falls, the whole world falls to that extent."
– Mohandas K. Gandhi, 1945, India

Concentration

Universal Language of Mind Story

The Talking Turtle

Turtle was always talking.
He talked so long and so loud that all the other animals moved away when he came near. Because he moved so slowly, he often found himself alone with no one to talk to, that is, except himself.

From time to time an insect or animal foreign to the pond would wander close and Turtle learned to seize the opportunity for conversation.

One day two geese flew over the pond. Thirsty from their travels, they landed near the bank. Turtle was so excited by their arrival, he drew near to them, talking with each step of the way. "Welcome!" he exclaimed. "How wonderful for you to drop in!"

The geese felt special at this greeting.

"You must have journeyed from far away. Where did you come from? Where are you going? Your feathers are beautiful. What kind of bird are you? Are there others following you?" The questions poured from the Turtle's mouth like a river. Each time a question was asked, the geese were poised to answer. Yet there was no space as the Turtle droned on and on.

After a while, the geese drank, not really paying attention to the Turtle at all.

That didn't stop Turtle from talking. His mind raced with thoughts and his mouth tried to keep up. Finally, the geese looked at each other in dismay, their unspoken thoughts in agreement. They lifted their wings to fly to another pond.

Seeing them begin to take flight, Turtle exclaimed, "Take me with you!"

The geese paused.

"It's so lonely here, and you two have been so good to talk to," said the Turtle.

The geese looked at the turtle, all round and solid and hard-shelled. "How can you possibly come with us?" asked the female.

"You can't possibly fly," added the male.

Turtle had to admit he had no wings. Not one to give up, he used his intelligence to come up with a plan. "I know! It's simple." The geese looked his way with curiosity, eager to hear Turtle's solution. "We'll get a large stick. Each of you can take one end in your beak and I'll bite hard in the middle. When you fly, all I'll have to do is hold on with my mouth."

The geese looked at the tall trees they would have to fly over to reach another pond and said to Turtle, "What if you tire and fall from such a great height?"

"I won't fall," replied Turtle. "My mouth is strong. I've exercised it a great deal."

The geese would attest to that for in the short time they had known Turtle, he had not stopped talking. One of them said, "Your jaws have the strength, there is no doubt. But you'll only be safe if you keep your mouth closed on the stick."

The geese agreed to do their part, to take Turtle up in the air. They found the long stick, Turtle took hold of the middle of it and the geese flew up high over the tall trees.

Soon the children below saw an amazing sight in the sky – two geese carrying a turtle. "How smart those geese are!" they cried out. "They found a way to carry turtles!"

Turtle heard all this and thought, "*I'm* the one who thought this up, not the geese. I'm the one who is so smart!" He was so enraged with the children that he opened his mouth to shout at them and fell straight down to the earth.

– A Jataka Buddhist tale

The turtle talked so much because he had a busy mind. So many thoughts separated him from others, and separation breeds loneliness, fear, and despair.

When we believe we have no control of our thoughts, we have no motivation to try. Our lives are filled with chatter that drives others away. We are increasingly self-centered, ego-centric, caring only about ourselves. Have you ever been around someone who does not allow you to get a word in edgewise? What did you think of them? The answer probably depended upon your relativity to the person. For instance, if the person is a well-known speaker you paid to hear, you probably wanted them to continue past the time allotted.

Our responses to others are mental before they are emotional. Emotional before they are physical. Maybe you know someone who says no words yet the mind is continually busy. That co-worker mindlessly tapping his pen on the desk or bobbing her crossed leg to some inaudible beat is on some level experiencing something he or she is not sharing with you. Whether consciously secretive or unconsciously driven their minds are divided in some way, out of present time. Many geniuses are thought to be absent-minded by those around them. It is their present-minded moments that earn them the descriptive title.

Turtle learns to still his mind from necessity either from having no one around him, no stimuli, or from his desire for someone to listen to him. With no one to talk to, his thoughts are contained, left unspoken. When someone does arrive, he showers them with his fountain of thoughts. He has missed accepting a receiver.

Just when it looks like Turtle may be developing a disciplined mind, his ego-centered ways resurface and the relationship between identity and a restless mind is taught.

INTUITIVE RESEARCH

CONCENTRATION is
holding the mind's attention, at will, upon a chosen thought, person, place, or object for as long as desired. Concentration keeps us in the present to receive Self realization.

"...no matter what distractions have presented themselves, the urge within this one to complete, to make whole, to attain, to become has been more powerful."
(91397BGC3)

"People who know how to concentrate display a remarkable capacity to give to the universe." (SOM Lesson 1)

"What you concentrate upon is more than a reflection of you, it is you."
(SOM Lesson 20)

Intuitive Health Analyses examine the whole individual, identifying disorders and recommending possible changes to aid in health and healing. The following for a middle-aged woman describes how the busy mind pulls the attention out of present time into a future that cannot be controlled.

> There is a high degree of **anxiety** within this one. We see that there is tension within the thinking at all times. We see that this one attempts to know all that is going to occur and hold this within her thinking. We see that in an attempt to do this there is a scattering of the attention. There is the attempt to hold all details, all information simultaneously, and the experience is that this one's thoughts overflow. We see that this then causes the anxiety because there is a filling up and very little release.

This one's inability to let go was affecting her sleep cycles. She had fallen into a pattern of insomnia, and when she asked about this, reference was given concerning overworking the conscious mind.

> There is a need for movement within the thinking process. There is a need for motion. There is a need for this one to release thoughts. This one falsely believes that when this one is not thinking a thought, that it will slip away or disappear, therefore, this one holds on. We see that the amount of energy that this one expends in thinking is tremendous, and we see that there is a need for this one to relax. There is a need for this one to learn to release. There is a need for this one to learn to let go.

This type of thinking had become an addiction for this woman. She couldn't think any other way, and when she tried to, the effects increased, worsening her condition. She was like the young monk who would not let go of the young woman. How could the woman learn to release the thoughts that filled her mind, plaguing her consciousness? The best way to "let go?" **Concentration**.

> **Concentration** is essential for this one. The ability for this one to move this one's attention at will is necessary in order for this one to understand the process that is described as release....

Emotionally the report described the woman's tendency toward being "high strung" to be a "reaction to the tension and anxiety." An area of concentration was recommended specifically for her. A suggestion for her to intentionally place herself in environments and situations promoting balance was given as a means to calm the emotions.

From the mental and emotional factors, the physical body was constantly racing. The thymus and adrenal glands were directly affected as was the nervous system. Rhythmic breathing was suggested to give this one "a point of focus that will aid this one in concentration." The need for release manifested in difficulties in the digestive and eliminatory systems. Symptomatic suggestions in diet and exercise were given here to initiate physical healing immediately.

The body of the report ended in this way:

> ..... We see that there is a yearning inside this one for stillness and in this one's attempt for the stillness there is the filling of the mind up with thoughts of this. Suggest to this one that the stillness is the experience of equanimity mentally, emotionally and physically and for this one to reach for this. (782003BGC5)

Command of Concentration brings the stillness of mind. It enables the Real Self to come forward. This creates the connection between Concentration and Meditation. The ability to direct the mind at will precedes turning the attention inward for purposeful Self exploration. Mastering the stages of Concentration frees the consciousness to awaken in the inner levels of consciousness.

It may seem ironic that in order to become whole, we must first separate and identify our thoughts. It is nevertheless a Universal Truth. The desire for this begins at an early age. For the following girl, it is coming at age eight:

> This one finds the environment to be intrusive upon her and we see that this one desires very much to have a sense of what is her own. We see that often this one experiences mentally and emotionally a kind of invasion upon who she is and what she desires and what she wants to

> accomplish. We see that this one needs to learn how to create a kind of self-possession that will serve this one as a focus for her sense of identity and her sense of being able to relate to the external world.

From the pressures to conform at school to a divided family at home, this girl felt forced to live in ways she found foreign and to be someone she was not, in order to cope. As a result she was experiencing breathing problems when she felt trapped or when she would take on the thoughts and emotions of those closest to her in her environment. What was occurring between her divorced parents was affecting this child, even when they took great pains to protect her.

The suggested mental remedy for this child included developing her concentration.

> This one has difficulty distinguishing between herself and that which is outside of herself and we see that concentration exercises would be of benefit to her in being able to make this kind of distinction. We see that it would be of benefit for this one to be able to separate herself from other people, to separate her thoughts and emotions and activities from that of others for we see that they often encroach upon her, and this one becomes confused. This one does not distinguish or discriminate between what is her own and what is someone else's. Would suggest that this one take whatever steps necessary to make this kind of distinction and to recognize that she is not her environment but she is becoming her own person.
>
> We see that emotionally this one is very attached to certain people and ideas, and we see that this interferes with this one's mental drive toward independence. We see that it creates internal conflicts. We see that this one then reacts to the environment and to her own desires. Would suggest to this one that in order for this one to reach a kind of emotional equanimity this one needs to be able to develop a sense of self in the ways described and be able to express the self through the emotions, express the desires through the emotions.

Emotionally the child was "very attached to certain people and ideas." This interfered with her mental drive toward independence and created "internal conflicts". Being transported back and forth between separated parents was reflecting in her mental, emotional and physical state.

In the body endocrine imbalances foretold the onset of puberty and heightened this one's need to separate from others and to build what the report described as a sense of self-possession. The inability to separate the Self from the environment had manifested in a nervous stomach. Eating was unpleasant and difficult. She often reacted to certain foods. Physical suggestions were given, including portion size and frequency in eating. Most helpful was the following:

> It would be helpful to this one to have endeavors which she herself accomplishes alone. Something she could invest herself in and be proud of, something that she knows that she has accomplished without the constant attention or interference as it becomes, of other people. This one very much needs to create her own space and to expect it to exist and to expect it to be respected by self and others. This will take time, and it can be accomplished. This one will need to release attachments — places where this one invests false senses of security.... (22294BGC3)

One of the most valuable insights that would help this child came when the conductor of the report asked for suggestions for the parents. The response drew upon the first essential life skill – Self Respect, and in that way illuminates the link between the first and second skill.

> **This one is eight years old. Any suggestions for the parents of this one?**
>
> Would suggest to those ones that there needs to be a development of respect in them, not only in regards to themselves but more particularly in regards to this one. We see that there tends to be a misuse of this one particularly in regards to there being conflict that is actually within the parents and between the parents and actually has noth-

> ing to do with this one but these ones do not respect it as such and therefore they include this one which then causes the chain of reactions within this one that have been described in detail.
>
> Would therefore suggest to the parents that there be some distance created, that there be some space that this one is given. It would be of benefit for this one to be physically away from both of the parents for periods of time on occasion, three or four times a year so that this one can begin to develop her own sense of self away from the confines of what she is receiving at the present time period from those of the parents.
>
> The parents are more a distraction, more a detriment to the growth of this one at this time than an asset. This will only change as they are willing to become more self-aware, as they are willing to become more attentive to their own ways of thinking and emotions and to begin to learn and grow and make changes in that regard. Right now they are in an unconscious fashion projecting onto this one some of their most rejected thoughts and attitudes. Would suggest that this be changed and that there not be demands placed upon this one to change. This change needs to occur within them. This is all. (22294BGC3)

It is difficult for many people to accept the power of their influence upon the lives of others. When this is the case, it can take years before awareness that their ways of thinking, their very thoughts, influence others. Of course, most can readily admit a certain degree of conscious persuasion. This is not what is being spoken of here. This influence is the one each of us constantly emit by being who we are.

Our thoughts create the reality we live, and those thoughts are electromagnetically expressed into our energy field. As others come into contact with us, these energy fields interact. Thus it makes us happier to be around certain people while others have an unsettling effect upon us, even when there are no words exchanged. The answer is not to run away and avoid unpleasantness. The answer is, like the one given to this child, to become Self aware. Self respect gives us the motivation. Undivided Attention gives us the means to be conscious, awake. Concentration enables us to distinguish thought, emotion, and action so we can understand the whole Self.

CONCENTRATION

is the ability to sustain Undivided Attention in time and space.

Concentration
What is it?

A child sees a highly touted movie with her parents. A week later, she recounts each scene in order and in detail to a grandparent to the astonishment of her parents who run out of things to say about the film in five minutes.

A student attends a university, all expenses paid by scholarships, graduating in three years while another spends more than double the time creating debt in tens of thousands of dollars with no degree.

One server receives a $100 tip for waiting on a table of four while another – during the same shift, at the same restaurant – barely makes that amount over eight hours.

Perfume sells for $200 while cologne made from similar ingredients sells for $20.

Why?

An acumen for detail, success, and quality of service or product have common roots in one meta-physical principle: Concentration.

The child recalls the movie in detail because she lived the movie. Her attention remained undivided for the entire 90 minutes. She became the characters in the film, experiencing as they did, while the parents' attention repeatedly wandered away from the movie to work, problems, or unfulfilled desires.

The student who earns scholarships is already employing Concentration through goal setting. He has selected a target that he is aiming his time and energies toward. Weeks, maybe years, before entering university he is preparing himself mentally and physically to receive. Having demonstrated he can do the work, he applies for scholarships. He may lose out on many, yet with dedication he continues to apply until his needs are met. Concentration is fed by and feeds qualities of sustainability – dedication, commitment, devotion, integrity. It opens the mind to possibilities and demands talents be employed in the task at hand. This student may not be a better student than the other one described, meaning he may not have greater talent or intellectual capacity. What this student does have is the power a willingness to concentrate brings.

Sustained attention is often rewarded in today's world. The waiter who receives the $100 tip has earned it through his attentiveness. With mind focused, those he is serving never leave his field of concentration. He can keep many channels open, moving his attention from one to the other in response to needs. He is connected with you even when serving the next table. A look, a thought projected in his direction, is met with a response. "Is everything meeting your expectations," he asks. His co-worker is drained after his shift, filled with disatisfaction in his job and little money to show for his effort. While working he was hurried or preoccupied with thoughts of his girlfriend or increasingly tired. His channels were turning on and off and those he was attempting to serve psychically knew it.

Then there is perfume and cologne. The beauty of science now enters into our exploration of Concentration. Perfume is a distillation of ingredients, usually flowers and sometimes medicinal plants. The resulting tincture is then a concentrated form of the flower. This is why one drop of perfume is worth several sprays of cologne which may well have come from a similar flower but presents itself in a watered-down version. Often this is a function of time. The perfume process can take weeks and years, while a cologne can be manufactured in a fraction of the time. Time invested is a most valuable function of Concentration, whether for a substance like perfume or for people like you and I.

Our ability to concentrate largely determines our success in life. It will be a key factor to the relationships you have, the money you make, the quality of your health and your longevity. Your capacity to hold what you desire within your mind's eye guides your every thought and action toward the fulfillment of that desire.

Your concentration ability is more than luck or chance. Concentration is a skill, and so it can be taught and learned. In School of Metaphysics classes we teach how to practice and strengthen concentration by using an object as the focal point for the attention. The word *concentrate* comes from the Latin *com* and *centrum* which means center. The Undivided Attention is directed toward a common center or objective, in this case a flame. Extending that attention over a predetermined length of time is the act of concentration.

I learned this discipline at the School of Metaphysics at the age of 22. I had already trained myself to focus on tasks in school. The motivation was to do well since my family prized education highly. I could concentrate for long periods on people and things that interested me and almost everything did interest me. Desire plays a major part in the success of any endeavor because desire points and channels the will that produces Concentration.

After I received the first Concentration practice I couldn't wait to go home and try it. I was amazed that I had so many marks. Twelve that first time. I remembered what distracted me. The neighbor's dog barking, a car door slamming, getting tired of sitting in one position. In time I would learn that physical distractions were the first layer of Concentration exploration and development. After practicing for many weeks, each day, I began eliminating sensory distractions because I gained greater control of my attention. The number of distractions noted decreased to only 3 or 4 per practice.

During this time I started working for a lawyer at a bigger salary which enabled me to move into a duplex closer into town. These accomplishments were a direct result of a way of exercising my newly won concentration ability that I learned in the classes.

About this time we began significant energy work in our classes. My Concentration exercise experience changed. No longer a slave to the sights, sounds, smells, tastes, and feelings of the world around me, now I was awakening to internal distractions. What thoughts would take my mind from the object of concentration! Some days it seemed I thought of everything but that candle flame! I found that some days my attention would go into the past: "Why did I say that yesterday?", "Are they still mad at me?", "How can I make it better?" Other days it was the future that lured me: "I wonder if I can get off work next Friday?", "When will I have time to complete my reading assignment?", "I've got to go by the bank tomorrow". Then there were the present thoughts – like "I've got to call Mom" – that I allowed to open doors to the past or future.

At this level of practice, I clearly saw how busy I could let my mind become. As I redirected my attention to the object of concentration, again and again, I also became keenly aware that I chose to allow my concentration to slip. This was a major step in owning my thoughts, claiming them. As the creator of thought, I reached another level of practice. With my full attention on the flame I could now see when it would begin to waver. I no longer allowed my mind to be pulled away. I learned how to sustain the line of attention and allow the distraction to pass without interruption to my train of thought. The inner level image of the flame would stay with me for up to half an hour after performing the exercise. I had learned how to create a train of thought and how to follow it to the point of completion.

Through a simple daily Concentration exercise I was learning how to take control of my own mind and body. It was astounding how it affected my thinking and my relationships with others.

By the time I had practiced every day for six months, I was starting to go into mind. I could perceive the flame's aura. I realized the connection between the flame and everything else in the room. I experienced the flame through consciousness, and through the duration of this experience there were no marks of distraction to make. This was pure concentration and through experiencing it I realized the Universal truth that "Thought is cause and the physical is its manifest likeness."

My outlook on the world changed. My ideals came forward, becoming stronger. When momentary setbacks would arise and disappointment or depression would threaten to settle in, I would acknowledge these emotional thoughts for what they were – distractions. I now knew how to move my attention. All I needed to do was use this newly developed skill toward accomplishing my ideals.

I began to note that my thoughts could become scattered into "I don't know if I can do this!" "I don't have enough time." "Someone else is much better than I am." "I'll do it later." When I could catch these before I became engrossed in the thought, it was easy to center my mind back upon my ideal just as I had in so many practice periods with a flame.

I began to reach deeper and deeper levels of thought as I reached for the still, concentrated mind. It was like going through rooms in a very large mansion or passing through one veil after another. In time I realized that Concentration is the key to sustaining inner level experiences. Lucid dreams, past life recall, astral or etheric projection, perceiving chakras, and the like are rooted in the individual's command of concentration.

My colleague Dr. Laurel Clark recounts how Concentration played a major role in revealing the inner levels of consciousness. "I was studying the dream projection lessons. In these lessons the student learns 'lucid dreaming,' that is, how to be awake in dreams and eventually to control dreams. I lay down to take a nap on the couch and fell asleep longer than I had expected. Suddenly, I awoke to the sound of a horn blaring so loudly I thought that a car had driven through the plate glass and was in the living room! (I was in the St. John branch of the school, which had a huge picture window in the front room.)

"I woke up, or thought I woke up, and walked around because the horn was still so loud it sounded like it was in the room, but there was no car in the room. Then I lay back down and when I woke up completely I discovered the sound was a car horn all the way down on St. Charles Rock Road (maybe 1/4 to 1/2 a mile away). It had sounded so loud because when I "woke up" I was not in the physical level of consciousness, I was in the 6th level of mind which is the first inner level of consciousness. I had accomplished my goal which was to be awake in the inner levels of consciousness."

After studying for over three years I had a most noteworthy experience on a drive from New Orleans to Springfield. I was traveling by myself having left New Orleans at 12:30 p.m. The drive normally takes 12 hours including some interstate and lots of two lane state roads. As the sun set and the night descended, I noted the entrainment I felt with everything around me. It was a Concentration experience of being one with the darkness around me, traveling alone on the lonely highway. When I arrived the time was 10:10 p.m. I had not broken the speed limits, had not done anything out of the ordinary, no more or less stops than usual.

At the time I thought I had somehow lost over an hour. I quickly had to admit, I had gained that hour. It was my first experience in time travel, and the beginning of many exciting possibilities arising from the disciplined, directed and concentrated mind. Ivy Norris tells of a similar experience, "'Concentration removes the illusion of time,' says Dr. Dan today in our Bhagavad Gita class. I believe this is true. I remember John Harrison and I experiencing this on our drive back to Indianapolis from a weekend at the College of Metaphysics. We needed to make it to the Indianapolis School of Metaphysics before healing class, and we didn't leave enough time to do that with our eight hour drive ahead of us. So we set a goal to make it there by 7:00 and surrendered it to subconscious mind. On our way home our attention was focused and concentrated on our learning from the weekend. Time flew by. We arrived at the School well within time to attend healing class, in fact the eight hour ride took only six hours!"

On a physical level, the mental command of Concentration causes both the right and left sides of the brain to become functional. Concentration brings our whole mind to receive the essence of the experience and to bring our powers, attention and efforts toward completion of a task. With Concentration, whole thinking is made possible. Be it sustaining the commitment or marriage over decades, building a business worthy of inheriting, or becoming a well-known and respected member of the community, you will always find Concentration at the heart of any successful person.

A Mental Pioneer

I signed up to begin classes at the School of Metaphysics in Columbia, Missouri on a Monday. The first Monday of class was also the week that I was a camp counselor for a spring break camp held by Columbia's Parks and Recreation. I and another girl were in charge of twenty 5,6, & 7 year olds. I had taught swimming lessons for years at this point, but had never really spent any extended length of time with children.

Spending 10 hours a day with so many young children was definitely challenging. I had no idea how to keep them busy the whole time and I had a migraine every day by lunch. My neck and shoulders ached from the stress I stored there everyday. I had some really good moments throughout the week, but for the most part, it passed by in a painful blur.

At the end of the week, I wondered if I would be a counselor next year. I thought I probably would because I could not deny the fact that those children had given me the gift of being in the present moment. I had never spent so much time in the here and now as I did with them that week.

When spring break camp rolled around again this year, I definitely wanted to help, although as the camp approached, there was a part of me that wanted to get out of it because I thought the stress might be too much.

The first day of camp I was prepared for the worst and was pleasantly surprised. Due to all the work I had done with my thoughts and attitudes through the classes, I wasn't caught up in the stress of keeping the kids busy. I actually saw the whole experience as a big adventure. I saw the children as unconditionally loving souls, and I honored the responsibility I knew I had of the impact of my thoughts, words, and actions. The freedom I experienced from this was the ability to love and appreciate my inner authority and nurturing qualities.

That week was amazing! I felt absolutely wonderful mentally, emotionally, and physically. In fact, I couldn't remember ever feeling better. It was amazing to me because this experience was an opportunity for me to really know how much I had changed. Sometimes it's hard to see the little changes you make every day just like it's hard to see how much a baby grows every day, but a year later, when you see that baby again the difference is phenomenal. That's how I felt and that's what I saw.

Instead of waiting for the time when the kids would leave every day and looking forward to the end of the week, I didn't want the days or week to end. There were some of the same kids there the second year as the first, and the way I felt about them was also very different. There was this one boy who was really annoying to me the first year. I could hardly stand to be around him because he whined and cried so much. The second year, I loved his unique personality and laughed at the other counselor who did not want to deal with him.

One great thing that came from this experience besides the perspective it gave me on who I had become and how much I had grown, was that it totally unlocked a love of children that I never knew I possessed. I always admired people who wanted to be teachers but thought to myself, "Man, I could never do that." I realized that I love kids. Not only do I love kids, but I have understandings with children and want to teach them. I see being a parent in a totally new light and I am looking forward to teaching children of all ages in our indigo school. ∞ Stacy Ferguson

A Penny is the Thought

I was in Colorado. I had just attended a weekend Area Teacher's Meeting. It had been a very stimulating, inspiring teacher's meeting. I have always loved teacher's meetings. They are and were times where I felt most supported and a part of something big. I also knew that my awareness grew in leaps and bounds from participating in teacher's meetings. So I always made sure I was early for them and a part of hosting the teacher's meeting for all the teachers.

After this teacher's meeting was over, I laid down in a place in the school building that the sun was shining in through the window on my face. I felt warm inside and out. I was relaxed and my mind was going within. Soon I experienced the reverie state. This is a state of being where your attention is drawn within and yet you are still aware of what is going on around you. My eyes were closed. I began experiencing a stream of light shining throughout me. From within the light came a vision. First, I saw myself in the building I was in at that moment. Next thing I knew, a man gave me a penny. Then he left. As I held the penny in my hand, I imagined lots of people attending a new class I was going to teach. All of a sudden people started coming in the door. There were so many people we could teach two classes on that same night. Then I looked at the penny in my hand again, and I imagined having a new building that was much bigger than the school building we had now, so we could have many classes at one time. I now found myself standing at the entrance of a huge brick mansion, with beautiful beds of multi-colored flowers all around. Someone opened the door and I realized it was the man who had given me the penny. He invited me in and said that this building was being given to the School of Metaphysics. As I walked through, it was very familiar to me. It was exactly what I had imagined when I had held the penny in my hand. I realized at that moment that I had the ability to turn that penny into anything I could imagine. So I began imagining very big things. These were all for the School of Metaphysics. At the end of the vision, the penny in my hand had turned into a pyramid on the College of Metaphysics Campus in Windyville, MO. I was working with the chancellor of the college to build the campus. Soon there were lots of people on the college campus. I then knew it was time for me to go into the world and teach what I had learned.

I came out from my vision and sat up. At first I thought this was a dream. Then I realized that I was completely awake during the whole experience. I thought maybe I was lucid dreaming. Throughout the whole experience there was a bright light shining through. It had seemed that the experience was stimulated by the sun shining in on me through the window when I had laid down.

Up until that time, I had never had an experience like that. Since then I have had one other experience that was similar as far as the light being emanated throughout the vision. Both had to do with the School of Metaphysics and teaching. I have learned to interpret dreams in universal pictures that the mind uses to communicate with. The essence of these pictures were about a penny being turned into anything I could imagine. Each time I imagined anything, the penny was in my hand. A penny is symbolic of value. Hands represent purpose. Each time I saw value and purpose in the little things such as a penny and then added to this with my imagination, I had the ability to manifest anything and everything. There were no limits! I eventually taught this throughout the world.

The light that was emanating throughout me was light coming forth from superconscious mind. It was part of my assignment being revealed to me. Superconscious mind is the place in mind where our plan for existence is held.

During the Area Teacher's Meeting, I had been seeing purpose in every, little thing I was doing. I was giving completely. I had caused an alignment through my actions during Teacher's Meeting. Then when I relaxed and went within, I could assimilate the whole experience from the meeting.

This lifetime I have chosen to be born under the Virgo influence. Part of working with this influence is paying attention to details. I am realizing how integral this is in fulfilling my assignment this lifetime. No longer will I take for granted what I know. Thus, teaching is very important to fulfill this vision and my assignment. ∞ Dr. Teresa Padilla

Enlightenment can come Anytime, Anywhere

When I was a student at the College of Metaphysics, we cleared the land in the East Pasture of our campus. Through that winter we had already cleared the trees with axes, but the will to live was strong in the trees and the shaven stumps would send forth sprouts to continue their life. We returned many times through the spring and summer to trim the landscape of tree sprouts with machetes. Chopping tree sprouts with a machete had become pretty natural for me to do, since it was one of the major activities during my year at the college.

I remember on this particular day I happened to be out at the East Pasture chopping sprouts by myself. I reached down to clear some dry grass away from the base of a tree sprout when I saw a grub worm. Upon looking at a grub worm you might think it rather ugly, but to me at that moment something wonderful happened. Immediately I saw what seemed to be the whole universe, all of creation in this tiny creature. It was the most stupendous, beautiful specimen I could lay my consciousness upon. I felt open and spacious. I kept focused on the grub worm experiencing this wonderful connection with it. It was amazing to me how I could be connected to everything through this small creature of no consequence.

I had a similar experience when we were driving back from taking care of cattle on another property across the Niangua River. There were three of us in the cab of the truck. I was sitting next to the window watching the trees as we drove. I had the same connection with a particular tree, but because we were in motion that experience lasted only an instant as soon as the tree was out of my sight.

From that time forward I knew that enlightenment can happen at any moment in any activity or through any object, even something as mundane as a grub worm, as humble as a tree. The simple, repeated activity here at the college took on new meaning for me. The conscious mind is given a place to focus and involve itself in something you have done over and over, so it doesn't require your full and undivided attention. This frees the consciousness for insight in the subconscious mind. The minds can align and the kundalini rise. The attitude toward the activity needs to be one of enjoyment and service, for if you are resentful or wish to be somewhere else you will stay entrapped and you will get just what you bargained for. By enjoying it and giving yourself to the moment you can enter through the narrow gate and experience the eternal.

Once I returned to the college as a staff and faculty member, there have been repeated activities that became places of spiritual practice for me. One was tending the fire when we had a wood burning stove that heated the building. The hearth became my alter and a holy place where I could worship and give my best. Another place became the print shop. Through the drone of the machine and the printed sheets spurting from the printer in hypnotic fashion, I have had incredible insights, ones where I've had to stop what I'm doing to write down.

As a faculty member I have watched college students wrestle with the daily activities that populate their days. I have told them many times, especially when I see them thinking what they are doing is only physical labor. "Enlightenment can come at any moment through the simplest of activities": washing dishes, hanging laundry and folding it, gardening, milking a cow, making cheese, making butter.

Last fall Dr. Daniel Condron came to all the faculty, staff and college students. He took a few at a time out to the camp site area. There were chairs there where we sat and waited and watched in silence. And what did we see? What did we hear? I looked up and leaves were falling. Raining leaves, golden rain. As they hit the other leaves on the ground, they made a crackle sound like fire. Rain and fire were melded together through earth. It was magical, and I was very grateful to Dr. Dan for having given all of us the opportunity to experience autumn in this manner.

Yes, insight, wow experiences, can come at any time, anywhere. I'm reminded of Jesus saying, "for those with eyes to see and ears to hear." Yes, you do need special eyes and ears, and this is earned through spiritual practices like those given in the School of Metaphysics. Then you can see the truth and beauty that has been in front of you all along. ∞ Dr. Pam Blosser

ELS#3

A Short Class on Concentration

SF: This kind of goes along with what I said before like I'm concentrating on this pen or anything, an orange...

Dr. B: Use the pen. The pen's right there.

SF: Okay. If I'm concentrating on this pen, I'm going to come to deeper understandings about this pen, myself, the universe, creation, and that's a forward thing, that's an adding to. That's why I think it's "Where am I going?" because it's adding to.

Dr. B: Tell me about concentrated orange juice since you brought up oranges.

SF: Concentrated orange juice? Ummm... it's potent. You add water. Then you drink it.

Dr. B: You've already jumped ahead and altered it, haven't you? Tell me about the concentrated orange juice.

SF: Well, you take a bunch of oranges and it's like...

Dr. B: Help her out.

TM: It's the essence.

JM: You take the water out.

SS: Yea, it is the essence of the orange juice brought down to a more concentrated form.

Dr. B: Okay, Stacy, now hold that pen out there again so we can concentrate on it. Now tell me about concentrating on that pen. Tell me why the universe is in that pen.

SF: Concentrated energy?

Dr. B: Think of all the intelligence that went into producing that little thing in your hand. Think of all the people in the world who use pens and all the things they do with them.

JD: It is like the Laws, the universe and all the Universal Truths and the history of the universe and all that exists is in that object.

SF: We're all connected by it. In some way.

TM: It's the story of a guy who came to Zarathustra who thought he was a master. He was a king and wanted to be a student. Zarathustra gave him a box with a grain of rice in it. The guy went out thinking, "This guy can't teach me anything. This is ridiculous!" So, he went to the Orient and found a sage and showed him the grain of rice saying, "This is what Zarathustra gave me. Can you make anything out of it?" The sage looked at the grain of rice, meditated on it, contemplated it and then came back to him and said, "This Zarathustra is a great teacher! Everything you ever wanted to know is right here in this grain of rice."

Dr. B: So are we nodding in agreement now? Why do think so?

SS: Because we are learning to be here consciously, in direction and purpose, our minds were designed to create. So by Concentration and giving your Undivided Attention to something - really anything for an extended period of time so that it becomes a part of you - then you do see how everything intersects, in this case through a pen.

SF: It's everything from the universe it ever was, you know, all the people that went into this pen, and all the people that are using this pen right now are pens, and all the people that will use pens, and I'm really excited about the whole connectedness thing! When Jonathan said that all around the world people are using pens, it's exciting when he said that. That's also where we come from, because everything that went into this pen is there and concentrated upon it. I think concentration is both questions.

Dr. B: Yes, Jonathan.

JD: I do, too. And there's a lesson we had that says the same thing. What gives the present moment significance is when your brain will pass future into it, like concentrating everything into the present moment because concentration tells you where you're going and as you think, so you become. And it is where you are - everything that has led up to now, so it's like it all concentrates in the now.

Dr. B: Since Undivided Attention tells you where you are, and since Concentration is the extension of Undivided Attention, why would the question be any different that it answers?

JD: I don't think it would. It keeps you there, keeps you in the present.

Dr. B: It keeps you in the present.

One of my first realizations after I started classes at SOM, came to me as a result of Self Respect, and it's about Concentration. When I was in college, I repeatedly experienced an irritating phenomena. I'd be in the middle of an exam and all of a sudden this song would start going through my head. It was very distracting and I could never turn it off. It was like a musical fly buzzing round my head the entire time I'd be taking the test. I noticed it happened often, and it was not always the same song. It would however tend to be the same song during the same test.

After I'd been practicing concentration exercises for a while this memory returned and in a brilliant moment I realized what had happened and how I had caused this situation. I lived in the dorm and I when I would study, my roommate would often have the radio on, or be playing her favorite record. As I was putting the information into my brain for the test, the music was also going in, even though at the time my concentration ability filtered the music out of my conscious mind. Unconsciously, the music and info were entering my brain at the same time, on the same wavelength. So when my mind reached for the answer to place on the test, the music came with it. The programming was perfect, it came out the same way I'd put it in. Flawless!

Concentration is an amazing tool when used by an awakened mind. This realization was the first of many concerning the freedom this skill gives one for communication, efficiency, prosperity, good health, success in every endeavor, even time travel!•

The Query: "I was hoping you might answer this question and pass this around to the other schools. I am interested in finding out what insight we can give to our students on why being **commit-ted to** their **soul growth** in the form of discipline both in attending class every week and doing their exercises every day is so important. I am also interested in finding out from others what motivated them to move to that commitment....."

Response One:
I want to respond to your request regarding things to say/teach to students regarding the importance of coming to class and doing your exercises to help fulfill commitment to Self. I have an understanding with regard to this in the current lifetime embodiment of my dharma which is Fidelity. It is expressed as faithfulness and steadfastness to Truth. In other words - Commitment.

Response Two:
Commitment is a choice, and one you have to keep making. I used to use the analogy of marriage as well when I was talking to students about doing their exercises. I would have them image a beautiful wedding...lots of people..your groom waiting for you at the altar (subconscious mind) and the priest (superconscious mind)..all waiting for you, and you are standing in the doorway...I presented this as every time you commit to completing your exercises, you are choosing to walk up to the altar and get married, if not, you are just leaving your groom and the priest just waiting there...until God knows when...I also think for me, it is realizing, or maybe surrendering, to the fact that discipline and commitment are a need for me. I can dawdle around and get distracted, blah, blah, in the things I think that I want to put my attention on, but those things don't last..

I think what is hard is that everything in life is based upon what we can see with our physical eyes and senses..what we learn and teach is everything that is not physical. At first it is hard to "see" how commitment and discipline is going to benefit you, but that is why you have to stick it out, so that eventually, it does move all the way out, and you know you've changed.

Also, when I connect myself to the greater whole, why it is that I am here, of course I have to be disciplined! I always find it is those times when I only think about myself and pretend like what I do or don't do doesn't affect other people, that is when I can entertain thoughts of being undisciplined. But as soon as I think of my students, I start to build up motivation.....In one of my intuitive reports it also says that by choosing to be committed you are reaffirming your self-value. Self-value is something we have complete control over. Lucy*

Dear Lucy,
The faculty for commitment is relevant to and dependent upon one's command of Concentration. Knowing how to give the full attention of the mind engages the will with the senses - the mental senses of clairaudience, clairvoyance, telekinesis, and the like. This is the realm of meta-physics. It is the reality of our existence. To know it is to experience intentional beliefs, sometimes once, sometimes a thousand times.

Those who invest in this study are people who have been using their minds all along, ever since they were born. They have always seen auras, or dreamed dreams, or known what other people were thinking, or had an attractive quality about them, or heard voices, or the host of inner mind experiences possible. THESE are why they study. The desire to understand, to know why and what and how burns within these students. Commitment is much more than ego-motivation from a desire to please (reward) or a fear of displeasing (punishment). As teachers we learn how to ask the right questions, tell the right stories. The right ones are those rooted in Universal Truth. They exist far above personal opinion which can change in a moment or according to the company you keep.

It is most valuable, Lucy, to identify how and why you eventually became someone who was willing to put out effort for class. This insight will help you and others to know how to teach the person on lesson 1 or 8 or 16. This is most important to both you and to those you seek to serve/teach.

O Dr. Barbara

We have had a phenomenal weekend here in the Great North.

On Saturday:

We held an open house from 6-9pm. This was an expansion project led by the class I am currently teaching on Wednesday nights. There were approximately 25 people in the school with about a 50/50 student to non-student ratio. We provided tons of food, had a silent auction, and the students of the Wednesday night class gave short presentations on what they have gained, learned and added to themselves so far in their study at SOM. The three women in this class are currently studying lesson 21. All three women were glowing with the light that comes from within when one shares the gifts one has received. Each talked about how they had changed and grown, from creating inner peace, joy and happiness, to learning to overcome shyness and revealing the Self to others and learning how to overcome reaction, and instead, to not only respond with a still mind but to seek out the learning in every situation within the life.

Joy!

Over and over again it is revealed to me the power of the individual. The power to change, to evolve, to grow, to give, to be, to see, to perceive, to love, to be responsible, and in turn to be free is infinite within each individual. I am grateful for the School of Metaphysics.

The silent auction we held in conjunction with the open house had thirteen items up for bid including: a whirlpool suite at the Radisson Hotel; reflexology, palmistry, massage, and face reading sessions; a fur coat; gift baskets with gourmet foods; movie tickets; gift certificates to dinner; and much, much more! We have decided to leave the bidding open until Wednesday night. With the bidding still open, we have already earned over three hundred dollars and are expecting more.

The money we are raising will go towards paving our driveway and parking as required by the city zoning board. We have made a large graph of the square feet needed to be paved, filling them in as we earn the money needed to pave them. ***this has done wonders towards bringing the need into a workable, palpable, tangible level where we can visualize and see the fruits of our efforts on a conscious level. Prior to this the idea of actually having to raise the money and complete this project inspired fear, doubt, and unrest in many of us. It's miraculous how a simple change of perspective (a little respect) turns a monster into a puppy dog. This project now seems VERY DO-ABLE, meaning we are able to do it. Like a puppy dog it simply needs to be fed, exercised, played with, and most of all lots of love and attention!

Key Learning - Love your Creations !!!!!!!!!!!!!!!!!!

This is something I have heard many times, and have experienced many times yet I still don't always do it. Love is such an easy thing to get and such a simple thing to forget in our entrapped state. I've come to realize that love is a kind of barometer to see if you are in or out of harmony with Universal Law. If you are loving what you do, who you are, and whom you're with you tend to fall right in alignment with Universal Law. The building and dedication of the Peace Dome is evidence of this in my life and in the lives of many. I see it evident in you, Dr. B., every time I receive wisdom from you.

On Sunday:

Today Des Moines held its first session of public intuitive reports in... I believe over a decade! The excitement and buzz in the air was remarkable. The immediate movement of consciousness created by the individuals receiving and viewing reports created a field of magnetism within the school. Upon completion of the reports we served dinner, and conversation flowed. People were curious, questioning, astounded, stimulated... and LISTENING! The people here wanted to know!

After most had left Karen, Mari, Jay, and I spent some time talking about what we had experienced and learned. What I have found is that more and more within myself and my fellow teachers, we are not only looking for learning... but we are looking to build that learning into understandings.

Permanency! Security!

This followed by a couple hours of sharing vision. Our vision for

ourselves, our centers, and the School as a whole. Sharing ideas of workshops, lectures, service projects and more. It is always valuable to me to hear what people are doing and what ideas are being born in other schools. It was great spending time with Jay and sharing between Des Moines and Chicago. This is the value I get from the emails we share. Vision is such a vital ingredient to my life and consciousness.
Vision is an image... it is in mind. It is multidimensional. Vision gives me direction, inspiration, and most important to the 'big earth' - Purpose. Vision, images that are loved, is contagious.

Vision = Leadership

Sunny, one of the Students from the Wednesday night class I teach, stayed through all this discussion. She was very quiet through most of it. As Mari, Karen, Jay, and I discussed, I knew in her silence that she was absorbing all that was unfolding before her. She stayed later than she had planned and attended healing class.

Service!

Healing class was just the means to release and give that we all needed to make this weekend complete!

Prosperity!

At the conclusion of healing class, Sunny volunteered to transcribe Intuitive Reports and lead healing class next Sunday as all the teachers will be out of town for class.

And a teacher is born! Abundance!

I have marveled at this weekend thus far.... Very full and very rich. Most of all EASY! I have been aware in the past that my creations often take exceedingly long periods of time to move through the inner levels. (inertia, I know *grin*) This particular creation had been planned long ago, been pushed back, pushed back, and pushed back again. Two weeks ago in class I spoke to the students about the need to release this energy and MOVE! Everyone got behind the idea, it was clear in mind what needed to be done to make it happen, and it did! With amazing ease!

Commitment!

*** A great learning of mine I know.*** I will write more about that later. For now I will say that I have discovered that Commitment is two things: 1) It is the Concentration that aligns the conscious and subconscious minds, and 2) It is the 'glue' and the 'heat' that keeps a vision together and ushers it through the inner levels.

Throughout the weekend each of the students and teachers commented on how 'together' we all were. Every single person followed through with their responsibilities, and there were 'no last minutes!' Everything was ready and at ease because our minds were ready and at ease.

Stillness!

My learning this weekend has been on par with any weekend I have spent at COM. Since my very first all student weekend, my vision has been to make that degree of hands on learning a reality in all of the centers. I remember having wonderful discussions with my directc it in Springfield. This weekend has been the beginning of the mar tion of that vision in my life.

I would like to say that a large part of this was allowed to come into being through the seeds of wisdom in an email you sent to Karen a while back about a class that we were creating here. We were all disappointed in our lack of ability to manifest a full class within a reasonable period of time. The advice you gave Karen at that time was to recognize the creation of the class was a work in progress. You asked her to understand that the final manifestation is still to come. This was incredibly valuable to me because I often get highly disappointed when I don't get the results that I want in projects. Over time I noticed that I was poisoning my creations with doubt and fear thoughts: "What if nobody shows up?" "What if people aren't interested?" "What if someone knows more than I do?" et cetera... et cetera... et cetera... I have now come to a greater point of acceptance and allowance within myself knowing that if any of these things came to pass IT WOULD BE OK! It would be OK because it was a work in progress. In allowing it to be OK, whatever happens, I think I opened myself up to receiving the creation to greater degrees.

Ah! an OPEN MIND.

Which brings me to beautiful point of conclusion. I have much more to share... and will share soon.

I love you,
Jason

Jason, you will be at peace with what you are giving when you empty yourself. You will be the first to know you are giving completely. Until then, nothing anyone says will satisfy you because you will know you can do more, be more. It is the quest, the reach, the striving upward. "Eyes on the prize" some call it. I think of it as "Seek ye first the kingdom of Heaven and all else will be given unto you."

Just imagine when all your activities do support your image! Seek to make every thought count, then the distractions lose their power. Not everyone senses the power of destiny profoundly. Nowadays, many come by it through media rather than their own grasp of imagination-clairvoyance-realization. That is why some talk and mostly fail. You have many understandings that need to be employed. To do so you will need to build discipline in the outer mind and body.

Come to realize the power of receptivity, for receptivity enables you to receive the inner guidance or be a victim of physical-sensory engrossments. Aggressively holding your attention is what lends the ability to choose the direction you will receive from. Receiving the light emanating from who or what you give your attention to is a blessing that increases you manyfold.

The ten commandments, the eight-fold path, the tenets of Jainism, and the rest are strong codes for the conscious mind to live by.•

CONCENTRATION EXERCISES

Exercise One

Go to your local mall when you can spend a couple hours. Plant yourself in a well trafficked place. Most malls have areas where people come from all directions. Choose a place that has seating. You may even want to get something to drink.

Now watch. Carefully observe people. What do they look like? Sound like? Are they enjoying their shopping or in a hurry? Do they seem purposeful or do they not have anything better to do? Learn how to place your full attention on people by concentrating upon them. Watch for those who can sense your line of attention.

Note people's interactions. Do not judge, just observe. You are separate from that which you are concentrating upon. Make notes of what you see, then later at home review your experience looking for meaning and insight.

This exercise can be practiced anytime, anywhere. It is a great practice when interviewing for a job or going out on a date. The more you employ your psi, the better you will become in using it.

Exercise Two

Begin recording your nighttime dreams. These messages come from the inner, subconscious mind. They are invaluable feedback to the choices and actions of the previous day. Develop your concentration skill by actually writing the details of your dreams down. Do so immediately upon awakening, do not put it off, or the power of your concentration will fade and memory will take its place. Be in the moment fully for the best results.

In advanced studies, students concentrate on particular words and items for practice and for insight. For a glimpse of what can come from your effort, read Dr. Pam Blosser's Zarathustrian account which follows.

A Molecular Aha! Moment

When concentrating on the blade of grass my consciousness began to blend with it and I began to experience what it is like to be a plant. How it simply reacts to its environment. If there is light it reaches for it. If it is dark or cold the sap goes back into the roots. It responds to light and dark, heat and cold, wet and dry. It is totally dependent on its environment for its life and has an intimate relationship with its environment. Like a dance of nature the plant follows and responds to whatever is around it. As I observed its movement I had to separate my thoughts so as to fully experience. Plants don't make any judgements as to whether their experience is good or bad, right of wrong. They simply respond.

In another lesson we were to focus our attention on a red blood cell. After learning about the red blood cell, its structure and origin, I traced it through the body. As I focused on its movement, I began to experience its consciousness also. It too had a very simple agenda: to give to the body, to bring oxygen into and remove carbon dioxide from the physical body. Its one sole purpose is to cause the physical body to breathe and live. The little blood cell is so giving because all it knows to do is to serve the body. I was in awe of how busily it went about its work, serving being its only thought. I thought about how my mind would be muddled with resentment or doubt or whether I was good enough to do the job or a myriad of other thoughts when I was in the action of giving. How pure the giving of the red blood cell seemed to me. How I wanted to emulate this state of consciousness in my giving.

When I lived in Chicago, I did these exercises again. At this time I remembered reading in a book called Pilgrim at Tinker Creek by Annie Dillard where she talks about chlorophyll and hemoglobin. I went to the library to find again what was written there. She said, "If you analyze a molecule of chlorophyll itself, what you get is one hundred thirty-six atoms of hydrogen, carbon, oxygen and nitrogen arranged in an exact and complex relationship around a central ring. At the ring's center is a single atom of magnesium. Now: If you remove the atom of magnesium and in its exact place put an atom of iron, you get a molecule of hemoglobin. The iron atom combines with all the other atoms to make red blood ..."

I looked in the encyclopedia for the molecular structure of both of these molecules. Just as I had read, at the center of the hemoglobin is an atom of iron. At the center of the chlorophyll is an atom of magnesium. Next around the central atom is a ring of four atoms of nitrogen. Around the nitrogen is a ring of carbon. Beyond this are rings of combinations of carbon, hydrogen and oxygen. Even though I had read about this in a book first, when I saw for myself how these two structures are almost identical, I was amazed. Both iron and magnesium are related to light. Iron burns and magnesium produces light.

All life feeds on light whether mental or physical. Our bodies and the bodies of plants process sunlight for sustenance. What we give off is food for the plants, and what they give off is food for us. Through these cycles we are continually feeding each other. In the plant, when the chloroplast receives light, it receives an extra electron and jumps to a higher energy level --- an AHA moment --- and life begins. Does the chloroplast molecule keep this electron of light to itself? No. It begins to pass it around to fellow chloroplasts giving each a blast of energy and then returning to the one that started it. With light combined with carbon dioxide and water, the plant is able to make food for itself and have enough leftover to give to us in the form of sugar and oxygen. We eat sugars and breathe oxygen given to us by the plants. When the food substance is broken down, it is the blood, travelling across fifty miles of vessels and capillaries, that carries oxygen and sugar to the whole body bringing it the energy it needs. And what do we have left over? Water and carbon dioxide, exactly what they plant needs to combine with light.

Take a look at the chemical formula of these two processes and you will see something else very interesting:

Plant photosynthesis -- $6\ CO_2 + 6\ H_2O$ + *light energy* ----> $C_6H_{12}O_6 + 6\ O_2$

Animal respiration -- $C_6H_{12}O_6 + 6\ O_2$ ----> $6\ CO_2 + 6\ H_2O$ + *chemical energy*

It takes six molecules of carbon dioxide and water to produce sugar and six atoms of oxygen. It takes six oxygen atoms and sugar to produce six molecules of carbon dioxide and six molecules of water. Six is the number of service. We serve each other by feeding each other, and in the process keep our beautiful Gaia planet in balance.

What an incredible love story between the third (plant) and next two (fourth and fifth -- animal and human man) root races. The chloroplast and red blood cell even share the light. From the spectrum of light, the chlorophyll molecule absorbs the red rays and the hemoglobin receives the green light. That means there is enough light for both to thrive. ∞ *Dr. Pam Blosser*

"Memory
is the diary that we all carry about with us."
– Oscar Wilde, 1895

"The past is always with us,
for nothing that once was time
can ever depart."
–Rabindanath Tagore
1930, India

Memory

Universal Language of Mind Story

The Spider

When King David was a young boy he tended his father's sheep. Often he came upon spiders' webs strung across tree branches. He spent many hours watching them weave their webs by the moonlight. He was mesmerized by their skill yet could never see a use for them.

He often pondered the purpose for spiders, asking God for insight. "Why, O Lord of the earth and sky did you create such a purposeless being? We cannot even wear the webs as clothing."

The Lord's voice echoed through David's mind, "One day it will be revealed to you. One day, when you need the spider's talent the most, you will know its purpose. When you know you will give thanks."

Years later, after David slew the Philistine giant Goliath, he became a great warrior. He married the king's daughter and all the people praised him.

King Saul's heart hardened and he became jealous and in time afraid of David. Wishing to be rid of what he now saw as a threat to his throne, Saul ordered David's murder. David fled to the wilderness, hoping King Saul's wrath would fade.

The soldiers continued to pursue David, closing in on him. David took refuge in a cave as the soldiers drew near. In the dark quiet, David watched the opening of the cave. In the moonlight, just as he had seen so often in his childhood, a spider was spinning a web. This web moved across the opening of the cave.

David held his breath as the soldiers came into sight. The spider moved toward the center of her web having finished her task.

As the men started to enter the cave, the web stuck to their eyelashes and beards. "This web is unbroken!" they said. "No one has entered here. Let's go on."

And the men moved on along the ledges.

It was then that David remembered the Lord's answer to his question. The spider's purpose in his life had been revealed and he was thankful.

–a traditional Jewish story

As a child, how many times do you recall hearing, "Someday you'll understand." To the ears of the ten year old it can sound like a delay tactic. Quite often it is wisdom.

Experience is a stream of events most often forgotten as soon as they occur. The mind holds events long enough to act on them. Scientifically this is known as short-term memory. To a college freshman it becomes personal. You apply your concentration skills to memorizing tidbits of information long enough to take the test and make the grade. You may not remember all the capitals in Africa, the birthdates of classical composers, or how to conjugate verbs in Latin, what you do carry with you is the strength your mind built in placing and retrieving information from the brain.

Memory is easy to understand when you think of understanding a sentence. This highly developed level of intelligence requires that you hold in mind (concentration) the first few words until the thought is complete. This is short-term memory. Understanding the meaning of the words you have heard is a function of long-term memory and the ability of the mind to produce images. Memory is needed to carry out the simplest of actions in our daily lives – the name and number of someone you need to telephone, the items you are going to the store to buy, and where you put your car keys.

Long term memory requires more mind involvement, more experience in using the mind. As illustrated beautifully in this story of a boy who became a king, the usefulness of memory is its present time and space application.

INTUITIVE RESEARCH

MEMORY is using past experiences to add to the present and is the foundation for reasoning to occur. Memory reminds us of where we came from so that we know who we are and where we are going.

"...cease being afraid of being challenged and begin to cause the Self to rise up and out of the past and to embrace each moment as an infant with openness rather than judgement." (51500BGC4)

Drawing on past experiences and correlating them to present experiences enables you to utilize knowledge and wisdom previously gained. (SOM Lesson 5A)

...exist in the present, pausing only long enough to draw upon the past as an effective memory reference for present activities... (SOM Lesson 13)

Intuitive Health Analyses are powerful tools in the cause of Self counsel. They give us an image of where we are as intelligent beings and, to the extent that we can acknowledge our intelligence, how we can better employ that intelligence for good health. As the following woman discovered, being fully in the present is both liberating and responsible.

> This one tends to stifle the brilliance of the self. We see that this is done from memory thoughts. (12304BGC1)

What an astonishing admonition! To think this woman has denied what makes her unique and exceptional through replaying old memory scenes that do not belong in the present moment. This is the reality of prejudice in our lives.

Most people like to think they are open minded. They bristle at the thought that they might be prejudiced. Such a reaction is a certain indication that old memory thoughts are pushing their way into present-day experiences. Often with unfavorable effects.

> We see that this one allows perceptions of what has occurred previously to be present in every experience that this one has, often in a deleterious manner. This one will be in a present situation and something will occur where this one has a memory that comes forward and begins to determine the present outcome. We see that in most cases this is not drawing upon an understanding or upon something of benefit but rather is allowing a limitation or a preconceived idea - a prejudice - to rule this one's current thought. As a result there is much that this one does not offer that this one is capable of. (12304BGC1)

When I first began public speaking as a minister I battled holding back. I so wanted to share the beauty and realization in Holy scriptures yet each time I found myself face to face with memories of my grandfather, himself a preacher.

At first I just pulled back, becoming timid and even fearful in my delivery. This didn't set well with me. It left me cold and uncomfortable because I was retarding my love for Truth and my concern for others. I needed to change, and to do so meant admitting some prejudices.

I began by asking myself why the image of my grandfather would surface when giving a sermon and not when giving a lecture. This led to several trains of thought that helped me unravel my limitation. At the time I remembered my grandfather as pushing his ideas onto others. I also remembered his struggle with hypocrisy. I didn't want to be pushy and I didn't want to be a hypocrite. Not wanting was *my* limitation. My task was to transform those memories through Undivided Attention, Concentration, and Imagination. This was the only way I was going to grow into the service I wanted to give as a minister.

Like this woman I had quite a bit of cleaning house to do – mentally.

> We see there is much this one wants to accomplish that never gets done, and we see there are many associations with others that this one wants to be meaningful but which lack the kind of depth that this one would desire. It would be helpful for this one to begin to practice concentration so that this one might be able to keep the attention in the present time period. It would be helpful for this one to begin to think more deeply about the content of the consciousness, the ability for this one to think more deeply and clearly concerning the stimuli in this one's life. We see that many times this one confuses one person for another, not necessarily in a conscious fashion but in an energetic fashion. We see there are then misjudgements made and there are mistreatments of the self and others. (12304BGC1)

As a teacher sometimes students will confuse me with their mothers. Since "mother" is the first female we know, we have occasion to develop very strong prejudices. These may work in our favor or against us. This all depends upon our perception of experiences with Mom.

When students have great relationships with their mother, this reflects in the relationship they have with me. For instance, someone who learned to cook from their mother often drops into the kitchen when I am preparing food. We talk. They offer assistance. I am the beneficiary of "good" memories of mom and much is given and received between us. Another student can repeatedly avoid me. Days can go by without this person even saying hello. This student has repeatedly experienced angst in even calling her mom on the phone. I inherit "bad" memories and am denied a mutually beneficial relationship.

Through stilling the mind, the truth of present-day relationships can be seen. The past can be placed in proper perspective. This Intuitive Health Analysis gives a detailed step-by-step plan for living in the present moment.

> We see much of the time this one sees this (misjudgement/ mistreatment) as coming towards her rather than what this one is giving to others. There needs to be more **honesty** in that regard so this one can become more accountable for her own thoughts. **It is this one who puts the self into the past, it is not other people.**
>
> We see in some cases the people that this one knows in the life do not even have anything to do with the past that this one is recalling. This would be an easy place to begin to become honest – where this one could begin to become awake and alert to the reality that when this one judges someone in the present world as being similar to or like someone that this one knew previously that no longer is a part of this one's present experience. This one could very easily begin to see how the memory thoughts are operating within this one's consciousness and how they begin to shade or in some way influence that which occurs in the present.
>
> This is all within this one's thinking. It is not within this one's present experience.
>
> This is the first place to begin to separate fantasy or memory from present experience. Pursuing this process will aid this one to be freer in the associations in the present. It will enable this one to have the kinds of relationships with others that this one fantasizes about and wants to have. As long as this one allows the memory to intrude, this will not occur. We see that it will clear this one's thinking and aid this one to be able to cause there to be a freedom in the way this one does interact with others and in the way this one approaches the fulfillment of desires. (12304BGC1)

This analysis of the mental system gives insight into how memory can be transformed from hardship to productive basis for living the kind of life desired.

One of the fascinations of Intuitive Health Analyses is how they elucidate the connection between thought in the mental system and the expression of that thought through the emotions. Here is how the emotions of this woman are described.

> We see emotionally this impacts this one - the preconceived ideas or prejudices - from this one's desire for self protection. We see that this one can be very insecure emotionally and fears being hurt. As a result this one will begin to recall former experiences where this one was hurt and will then begin to judge the present by these. We see in this way this one is fighting a shadow. This one is fighting something within herself that no longer exists in this one's present life but that this one is intent upon bringing into the present. We see that this is for the purpose of understanding and it is due to karmic repercussions that this one does experience. We see however that the intellectual knowledge of this will not cause the balance that this one is seeking. It is only through this one understanding the intention in this one's consciousness that this one will find the freedom. (12304BGC1)

In my efforts to become someone who ministers to others, I came face to face with one of my shadows. My memory of my grandfather cast darkness in my mind. I was afraid of having the affect upon others that my grandfather had had on me. I did not want to cause fear or hurt in others. In order to free myself of this fear I had to admit my battle was not with my grandfather, who was no longer a part of my life, it was with my own memories of him. I began to understand what it meant to be haunted.

Because my desire to serve was greater than my insecurities I repeatedly brought myself to the present. In sermon after sermon I faced my own demon, each time casting it out. I developed ways to talk about my religious upbringing that often proved entertaining as well as enlightening to myself and others. I began to accept the freedom I had to make ministry in my own image. I became more confident as I built an understanding of Self image. The emotional charge that at one time caused me to hold back lessened each time I placed myself in the position to give in the present.

This report described how the mental and emotional attitudes affected the body by creating an *"energy difficulty is within the midportion of the body, particularly related to the solar plexus area and the other organs in the torso area itself."* The solar plexus is the physical area corresponding to a chakra, or energy transformer that recycles mental/emotional energies. The report went on to describe digestive difficulties and corrections. It also related how this woman's thinking affected the nervous system and endocrine system.

The cause of nausea was explained as *"the mental attitude that begins the process therefore it is the shutting down in the present experience by becoming lost in the memory that does set this into motion."* This affected the body in regards to the hormonal balances.

With the information gained, this woman was able to make health progress in just a few months. By practicing forgiving, she freed her attention to be in the present moment and found her creative ability improving. Her long-standing digestive problems cleared up within weeks of implementing the foods recommended in the Intuitive Report.

In the following, Memory is described in another kind of Intuitive Report, the Meditation Portrait. The Meditation Portrait is given as part of one of the weekend Spiritual Focus Sessions offered through the College of Metaphysics. The portrait explores how the individual might harmonize the inner and outer minds for greater harmony and peace.

In the latter part of the Meditation Portrait suggestions are given for resonating as Intuitive, Spiritual Man. This was the response for one woman in her sixties:

> In the present period of time this one has the advantage of being able to understand the function of memory and the ability to recognize the value of linear time. We see that as this one begins to become more aware of this, more conscious and begins to utilize reasoning applied to it this one will begin to have an ability to be present within the reasoning and to allow the intuitive faculty to operate simultaneously. We see that this was not possible in the past experiences related and we see that what was lacked in the genetic memory now exists for this one.

(Conductor question) She asks, why am I going through a detailed review of my past now?

This is in this one's effort for the reconciliation that has been noted. (102602BGC1)

In the first part of this woman's report the following reference was made to reconciliation.

It is this one's capacity to accept the self in all ways, to accept the reconciliation of that which this one has been bitter or in sorrow concerning and to reconcile this one's reality, the way that she thinks and lives with the ideals and values that this one holds. It is through this kind of reconciliation that the acceptance will blossom and through that then the harmony can expand into more areas of the self and therefore more areas of the life. (101400BGC1)

In response to her question concerning the nostalgia she had been experiencing, the report continued by identifying the purpose for her surfacing memories.

There is a real need for this one to be able to accept that which has occurred within the past and to accept it on a level of understanding that will bring this one peace rather than turmoil. Therefore it is this one's tendency to associate present experiences with past ones. This is an effort to see a fuller picture, to have a different point of view, to be able to expand the thinking to embrace more sides of what this one is able to see in the present if this one stays in the present. It is this function of memory that is quite enriching to the pursuit of consciousness and therefore this one needs to appreciate it for what it is rather than to falsely believe that it is a source of pain or of its own volition occurring to bring this one turmoil or pain.

When the turmoil exists there is division between this one's motivations concerning this one's desire and what actually occurred. When this is reconciled then there will not be turmoil. When there is pain it is because this one was inattentive in some way and did cause things to come about that this one did not want to be conscious of at the time and since that time has become conscious of. This needs to be seen as a lesson for this one to be able to integrate into the present time period a greater sense of mindfulness and full awareness and attention for when this one does so, the lesson will be learned and the pain will cease. The greater the command of assimilation of experience, the greater the command of understanding and wisdom. This is all. (101400BGC1)

MEMORY-

For animals it is instinct.

For humans it is emotion.

For the reasoner it is cause and effect.

For the intuitive person it is knowing origin, remembering where we came from.

Memory & Corporate Success

We like to think that we can separate our business and professional lives, the past from the present. Sometimes this is more difficult than at others. Amazing insight into the function of Memory and its relativity "on the job" came during a Business Mission Analysis (72505BGC1). The corporate manager of a large hotel was facing a new supervisor with very different operating ideas than her own. In light of information revealed in the report, the manager asked for suggestions to "the directing intelligence for identifying the course of mistrust in this one's past." This is the answer that was given.

> This would be in the tracing of the energy that this one is experiencing in the present time period. This would be more readily identifiable or communicated to this one as being able to remember similar situations with other people where this one felt belittled or restricted, intimidated by others where this one sacrificed what she wanted to do in lieu of what this one saw as others' power. We see that this does move back in this one's life in several different instances and these could be remembered and could be described, brought forward into the waking conscious awareness so that it could be seen for the connecting link in the energy that this one is experiencing in the present time period. This one has had some opportunities within the life to experience this energy over and over and there have been times when this one has made enemies of people who never were her enemies. We see that this is important work therefore for this one to do in order for her to be free from anxiety and worry and for this one to be free to accomplish the considerable creative ideas that this one has. There could be some benefit derived from interactive sessions, whether these be in regards to therapies or counseling that would help she shed light upon this or it could be in regards to workshops that are available that would help this one to learn to come to terms with her own creativity, her own ability to forgive, and to become a more wholistic thinker.•

Memory
What is it?

I was driving East on Highway 60 across the south part of Missouri traveling to meet my dad whose youngest brother had died. I planned to attend the funeral service, an exercise in Memory itself.

Somewhere between two little towns called Mountain Home and Birch Tree there is a small, what used to be service station that is on the North side of the highway. As I came upon it I pulled upon a vivid memory whose origin was 30 years earlier in time.

What was then a gas station was now remodeled into some kind of shop. The road was the same, even with improvements, and the way the building was situated triggered the memory of a night years ago. I was in my mid-20's, traveling alone when I was stopped by a police officer for speeding.

The anxiety and the fear came back to me. My fear of traveling alone at night motivated me to hurry to my destination. The anxiety rose because of the money I would have to pay for my indiscretion. These emotional reactions returned to mind with their accompanying physical reactions.

Then the wave of gratitude came for the leniency the officer showed me for the very cause of my offense. His paternalism spurred him to be fatherly toward me, caution me with a warning ticket, and stay with me for some miles down the rode. I was thankful for his concern.

All the memories came back as I passed that portion of road at noon on a very bright, sunny January day.

Then another memory came forward of passing this same place on another cold, very clear day some years later This time I had car trouble. I stopped for help somewhere near this area. The mechanics could do little but encourage me to go on toward Springfield which was my destination. I remember the same thought-feeling connection because I am experiencing it again. I experience fear from the trouble - the unexpected - and sense anxiety because I don't know what the outcome will be. In the present, just remembering my experience, I feel the tension in my shoulders, neck and head. The energy of the thought and emotion is expressing itself in my body now.

Stress is produced when our experience does not meet our expectations of outcome. Driving long distances on my own, I expected my car to be reliable, to safely take me from New Orleans to Springfield. In the few times this did not happen, my stress levels soared. This may sound like Essential Life Skill number six, Imagination. At the time I had car trouble it was. The stress I experienced was a function of my *reaction* to what was happening (the car engine cutting out from under me so the footfeed power would come and go) not reflecting what I imagined (sailing effortlessly down the road, pleasantly enjoying some music, all the way to my destination). However, what I experienced TODAY in real time is the memory of my experience. Today, there is no car trouble, there is only the memory of it happening here long ago.

So how can the memory of a decades old stress moment still have the power to cease my thinking, stir my emotion, and tense muscles in my body?

Memory teaches us the power of thought. It teaches us to be care-full, mind-full. Memory serves us in many ways. It can open the heart, stimulating us to love deeper, better. Two children away from home for the first time. One remembers mom and dad with greater fondness than the everyday interchanges yield. "Absence makes the heart grow fonder" goes the saying. While another relishes each moment of the new experience, in effect making memories that will be shared with mom and dad at a future time. "Out of sight, out of mind." The same physical experience, two different mental/emotional experiences.

Memory can be an escape from an unpleasant present. "The good old days" some call them. When this occurs we are living in the past, not the present. The widower forgoes present-day companionship for memories of the time with a spouse who no longer lives. The athlete dwells in thoughts of glory days to escape the effects of physical aging and a country pines for a time of innocence long past. Memory can be misused, and when it is the present suffers.

Our music reflects how we think and feel. "Yesterday, all my troubles seemed so far away/ now I need a place to hide away/Oh, I believe in yesterday" goes the Beatles' song. "Let the memory live again!" proclaims the CATS! song called – "Memory."

Sometimes Memory makes us aware of what we didn't realize we had. "I wish I'd known then what I know now" can only be thought because we remember a *then*. As we clock more years of experience, recall of everyday events begin to run together fading in a stream of images. We remember attending school yet cannot name our second grade teacher or identify the number of children in the class or even the address of the school. Yet this was our life experience day after day for months.

I have found this general whitewash of experience to be true in my existence. Yet, I can tell you my second grade teacher was Mrs. Ward and one morning she was a part of a potent lesson in self motivation for me. She was teaching phonics and spelling. I was a good student, eager to learn. Mrs. Ward was writing words on the chalkboard, encouraging us to sound them out, thus learning reading, pronunciation, and spelling all at the same time.

She wrote the letters i-s-l-a-n-d and turned to me. "Gail," she called me by my middle name which I used at the time, "what is this word?"

Immediately I recognized the word "land". Then I could separate that word from "i-s". I-s I knew was *is*. "Is-land," I replied with a smile, certain I had figured it out.

"No," Mrs. Ward corrected. "It looks like that, doesn't it?" Someone snickered, apparently knowing better than I. Yet, Mrs. Ward stayed with me. Her gentleness was encouraging. "The *s* is silent in this word."

I knew she meant you couldn't hear the *s,* it didn't make a sound. I kept turning it over in my mind and saying *i* as a short *i* sound as in the word *sit*. Others in the class were raising their hands, they had it figured out. I was being slow.

"The i sound is a long i," Mrs. Ward was staying with me.

Once I figured out the long *i*, I at first paired it with the s. Just as I was hearing it in my mind - eye - land! - Mrs. Ward called on another child who was frantically raising his hand. I was heartbroken and tears welled up that I struggled to hold back.

Emotion enhances Memory. Emotion can impress mundane details with significance creating a vivid memory. The heightened memory of emotion causes chemical changes in the brain. Intense emotion amplifies neural activity, brain pathways of long term memory. Textbooks will tell you long term Memory is created when particular patterns of nerve activity are repeated. Yet, in my second grade example, which I have recalled less than a dozen times in 40 years, repetition was not the factor. The need for soul learning is.

How I learned to spell and pronounce all the other words I no longer recall. The one I remember is the one with the emotion attached because my ego was on the line, my identity as a good student had been put in question by my tardiness in thinking. It took years to understand the depth of this experience, and every step toward understanding had been worth it.

Today, this story is pressed into service to illustrate for you the power of emotion to enhance recall. People remember weddings, births, deaths. These are milestones, important events in life because people tend to be more fully present-minded for them.

If thought and emotion create memory, what causes thoughts and emotions long past to surface in the now? In my story of driving down Hwy. 60, memories were brought forward in response to an external, physical stimulus of being at the same place but at very different times.

The function of Memory enables us to move out of present time. It enables our consciousness to be pulled towards something that has already occurred, something that has previously happened in our experience. Sometimes we remember a physical event, sometimes it is an emotion attached to that event, or an attitude. Whether we are remembering how to spell our own name or the day that we were married, Memory serves to aid us in being able to identify the cause of what we experience.

This is a developed skill. It does not happen automatically.

Habits are a function of Memory. They enable us to be able to draw upon experiences and the value of them, at will, without the necessity of taking time or effort to recall or to learn. To see this, all you need do is attend a child who is learning how to read or write.

Many times the process can be arduous and difficult. The ability to move the hand to form a circle, then add a stick on the side of it to form the letter "b" is something you probably take for granted. You have practiced it over and over, training the body to respond with ease and grace. Reading or writing then seems to happen almost by itself, we don't even need the presence of mind to make it happen.

Memory becomes more accessible as a function of Undivided Attention and Concentration. It builds upon the previous life skills. Keen attention creates nerve clusters which make Memory more accessible. Each cluster cell represents different aspect of a meaningful experience. Photographic memory is the result of mastery of the first four essential life skills.

This is indicative of the genetic code of the body. This is a kind of body memory within each of us. The fact that man can change his body memory over time and space, in a way that other animals do not seem capable of doing, is a testimony to the uniqueness of the human being. It is his reasoning capacity that enables him to excel in this manner.

The ability for genetic code to be built, for there to be particular genes that are turned on at certain times and others turned off in order to uniquely make the human species is one of the most amazing explorations that we can embark upon. Understanding genetic factors is an attempt upon humanity's part to understand the physical mechanism of Memory.

We can understand the relationship of mind to body. Intelligence can alter the genetic code. That divine spark of creativity in human beings can examine mental DNA. This is the heredity that goes beyond physical existence. It is the heredity of the soul.

This leads us into a different kind of Memory. This resonates not with the body and brain, rather it resonates with the soul as its vehicle for travel and experience. This then opens the door for the understanding of the silver cord, the ability to understand consciousness as it moves through time and space beyond the confines of a physical body. This leads to the capacity, the potential, the reality of what has been termed for centuries as reincarnation. The ability of the soul to enter and leave a physical vehicle, the ability for the soul to be "back in the flesh again".

Memory is a process of resonance with the present day experiences. My trip on Highway 60 became the stimulus for resonance to begin in my thinking. I thought of the many times I had traveled down this highway, going to see my parents. All of this owing to the way that thought manifests through the inner levels of consciousness in the creative process. Many times what we think and desire does not happen instantaneously. Sometimes it does.

The concept of instant manifestation is not a new one. It has been present within man because of his imaginative faculties for centuries. It is more a part of our existence today - with telecommunications and with technology - than ever before in humanity's existence. Technology enables us to have the world at our fingertips. We no longer have to move our physical bodies for things to happen around us.

Today while traveling on the radio I heard an advertisement for Bose radio. One of its selling points was the absence of buttons. This radio is completely controlled by a "small, convenient remote device". My mind went to all the related things in our world that are like that radio. How many remote control devices does the technologically affluent person possess? There are remote controls for televisions, dvd players, ceiling fans, timers, stereos, heaters, the list goes on and on. How does one ever keep the remotes straight?

These technological advances are illustrations of man's desire for instant manifestation: when you see it you have it, desire it and it is yours. The genius of a handful of people who create and harness technology so the rest of us can utilize it does not necessarily reflect our individual genius. Individual genius must be built, one by one, in our own time and according to our own choices.

So it is this ability of Memory to serve, to resonate, to heighten, to use the cause of the present situations in our lives. Memory enables us to see trains of thought, streams of consciousness from one point to another. Memory enables us to make the connections thus understanding the nature of ourselves and the worlds that we create.

Greeting card companies have built multi-million dollar industries in Memory. Birthdays become an occasion to memorialize individuals, to celebrate and look back over a year. It gives us a point to judge by, a point of reference.

September 11, 2001 has been a stimulus for how collective Memory can be formed and promulgated, used or misused, and the place that forgiveness holds in being able to sustain the attention in the present while remembering something unpleasant from the past. These are functions and opportunities involving Memory. They are part of the human condition evolving to something greater, to something we will eventually call Reasoning.

At its best, Memory is a tool in the mind of the reasoner to improve, learn, and grow in spirit. "Those who do not remember the past are doomed to repeat it." I've read this line in books, heard a wizard speak it in a movie about King Arthur, and seen it at Holocaust museums. It only holds truth when there is enough consciousness attached to it to understand the cause that has created that past. Just remembering the past is never enough. There must be other elements involved in our thinking for progress to be made by one person or by many.

Memory is the tool we use to make ourselves and our world stable and better. When Sir Isaac Newton wrote, "If I have seen further it is by standing on the shoulders of giants" he was talking about the foundation for all progress being the capacity to remember where we have come from as a species.

The mind works with mental pictures. We use images to associate present experiences with past events assigning value and relevance. Memory draws on images stored in the brain, which in turn have a resonance with events in the akashic record. By recalling an image memory we can tap into an akashic memory and fully re-visit an event. This gives new meaning to the "shoulders of giants" and greater responsibility in carefully choosing our thoughts of today and yesterday.

Remembering It's the thought that counts

My first memory of knowing I was a creator was at four years of age. It was Christmas time and I wanted to give my mother a present. Money was always rare in our home, and during Christmas, it was more apparent. All I wanted was to make sure my mom had a present from me under the tree to open on Christmas Eve. I remember clearly having the thought, "I know I can make something." I set out and gathered my materials. They consisted of rubber bands, scissors, shiny green wrapping paper, and string. I cut the rubber bands into tiny pieces, wrapped them in the shiny green paper and tied a string around the paper. I placed the gift under the tree. My heart was full of joy and excitement because I had made something special and my mom would have a present to open.

Came Christmas Eve night and we gathered to open our gifts. It was my mom's turn to open her presents and my sisters and I watched as she unwrapped and said thank you. When it came to my gift, excited energy burst from within. She carefully unraveled the array of string from the paper and as the paper opened out the tiny pieces of rubber bands fell to the ground.

My sisters laughed, my bubble burst and my mother said (in Spanish) "It's the thought that counts."

Concentration has everything to do with self-growth and self-awareness. From a young age, I knew who I was, and as a human, I began my struggle early in life to stay with what I knew was true. When I first found the School of Metaphysics I knew I found a place that taught with truth. My soul heard truth. My four-year-old mind held onto the truth of my identity and rejoiced when I found a great gift. Understanding the mind is a responsibility nurtured and developed by the individual. This is one reason why I have returned to study, to understand and direct my attention and concentration so that my creative nature grows bright and right.

When I heard the laughter as a child I heard "unworthy". Now when I hear it, well, it makes me laugh. Heck, I would laugh too if I saw tiny pieces of rubber bands fall to the ground. And yes, it is the thought that counts. That is the value, the beauty, and I gave with great love.

This memory has served as a point of reference toward Self identity and greater Self awareness. ∞ Capucine Chapman

Silk Cloths

Memory is using my past experiences productively. This means that I remember who I am, what I have built and draw upon those past experiences to add to my present experience. It is a key component of reasoning because it is the foundation of where we came from and what we build upon to learn and grow in the present moment. The key to having a good memory is to give each experience my full attention, to receive it completely with all the senses. Memory is a mental skill which must be used wisely to produce learning and growth.

Every year we celebrate Christmas with singing, a play, a spiritual experience to give to the students, the public, anyone who wants to enjoy the Christmas Spirit in the Peace Dome. We decided to do the same offering this year as last. Some of the props that I was responsible for last year was a long white pole with purple ribbons around it and a silk cloth. I remembered where I had put the pole because I gave it my attention. I went there and saw that it was still in place in the warehouse. Where the silk cloth was I had no idea because many people may have used it in the course of a year. I remembered what it looked like and kept my mind open throughout the week to find it.

One day I was looking for an Intuitive Report from 1999 so I went to the Dome and looked through the file cards to find the code and then the master to make a copy so it could be transcribed and used for an article Dr. Terry Martin was writing. On the shelf above the file cabinet where the cards were kept I saw the silk cloth. Two days later we practiced the play and I was prepared with both props. In this case memory was used to find something. I remembered what it looked like, felt like, smelled like and sounded like when I used it. My mind reached out from my desire and was attracted to the object and the image I remembered to find the pole and the cloth. ∞ *Tad Messenger*

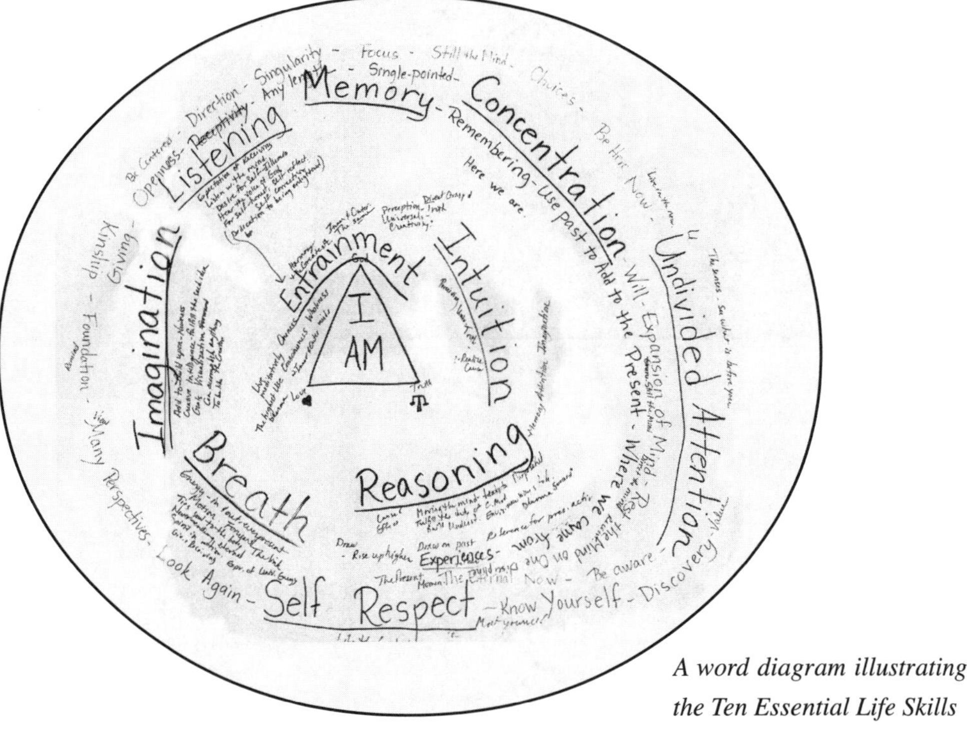

A word diagram illustrating the Ten Essential Life Skills

ELS#4

A Short Class on Memory

Dr. B: Mr. M., tell us about memory. Why is it an essential life skill, and why does it come next? There is order in the universe of disciplines in the School of Metaphysics.

PM: I'd say in order to add to anything, to build, to grow something, it has to have something to build on. Like for a drop of rain, it has to have a particle for the moisture to collect around, for a house to be built there has to be a foundation. To me, memory seems to be the foundation for future building, and then the builders come and they're the present moment, the actual process of building it on. It's a structure from which you can extend or build or to.

Dr. B: Are you talking about memory or the past? Memory is a skill of the mind. It's recall. It's not all the things.

PM: Memory is using that structure. It's referring to what has come before so that you can build and add to. You know what you've built and what has been built.

Dr. B: Think about this: the case of someone with past judgements, and opinions, and persecutions concerning her brother - you don't have to know what they are, the content is not important here. She constantly lives in the memory of things that were said or done, or things that were not said or done, which she carries around even though they hurt her. How does that fit in with what you're describing?

PM: I'd say that it's probably a misuse of memory. If you can refer with your memory back to what has happened, what has occurred, in order to do something in the present, to build something in the present, to image into the future.... This person is stuck in her memories and just kind of cycling around in the patterns.

Dr. B.: Lost in the structures she has created.

JD: One picture I have of memory is being centered in the present and bringing the past into the present. It starts with the present. The picture I get with what you're describing with this student is starting with the past. That's what I have so far.

Dr. B.: That's solid. Who can build on that? John.

JH: Memory lets us know, answers part of the question "Where do we come from?" It lets us know how we got to where we are at right now. And it helps us know our thoughts, what helped us to form our thoughts and attitudes that we currently are living with. So in a way it is bringing the past into the present, but it's saying, "This is how I got into the present."

JD: When you start with the present moment, that's what you can change. When you start with the past, that's what you cannot change. When you go from the past to the present, you're starting with something you can't change, so then you can't change the present.

Dr. B.: Excellent. Very good observation.

JD: It's like getting your orange juice and saying "Man, I wish they'd picked better oranges for this!" Then you can't really taste the orange juice because you're too busy thinking about what's wrong with it.

I had an idea I have never had before about why we teach memory starting with the present. I thought about how important it is! I always thought it was weird.

Dr. B: Well, I am glad you don't have to think that anymore. The only good reason to have a memory is how it relates to now. It's the only sane reason. The quality of a reasoner is that a memory relates to what is present in your existence. Anything less than that is rationalizing. Anything less than that is entrapment in materiality. Anything less than that is when you are engrossed in the physical.

Dr. P: I thought a lot about time and how people get stuck in the past. I've watched people be like a scared five year old. Part of them has stopped growing because there is something that happened that they didn't understand at that age. I think about some of the other things that we teach like a Secret Sin exercise. It helps the student let go of that.

I thinking of time moving in a linear fashion. Physically, it does move in a linear fashion and that if there is something that you don't understand it's like it catches a little bit of your mind substance. So time just keeps coming back to it because there's something that you need to understand. Depending on what you do with it more and more of your mind substance can get caught up in it or you can understand it and move on. With the Secret Sin, forgiveness, allowance, gratitude all those things help to let those streams of consciousness that are still in the past go, so you can bring more and more of your concentrated attention into the present which is what will bring enlightenment. So your full conscious attention is in the present which doesn't mean you disregard the past or future. When I think of enlightenment I think of that expanded attention where the present moment incorporates the past and the future.

Dr. B: Your mind can hold whole Truth....•

We did it! This past weekend of National Teachers Conference marked the final phase of "Vision Quest". Teachers from around the nation worked attentively and with love to fully realize the majesty of the energetic campus and the opening projection on the barn through the medium of latex enamel paint. In the less than two month duration of this journey I have experienced the true essence of **what life is really about**.

Here at the College of Metaphysics we practice the reality of living Spiritual Intuitive Man on a daily basis. It is through creations like this that I have come to discover my own individual purpose for existing on this planet, in this country, in our school at this time. I realized the refinement that occurs within each day, within each creation and within each choice when there is alignment of the self with giving completely to a greater purpose. Through this complete giving I came to know both my self and the School of Metaphysics on deeper levels. In the direct experience of cooperative group consciousness I learned that I am abundant. I learned that I am connected to my inner self, with other people and with the creator. I moved from believing to knowing in a way that shattered old worn out limitations within my brain. For this I am grateful.

Through the love and support of my teachers I was given the opportunity to grow and change. I am thankful for the support of the students and teachers in the School of Metaphysics who gave their time, energy, love and attention to Vision Quest. For this our school is brighter and more light filled. Having journeyed through this creation from believing to knowing I see that much more clearly the true scope of what we all are capable of as a school. Choosing purposeful change together we grow, we evolve and we truly live.

Stay attuned for another great journey through love and learning in our series of ever expansive endeavors from the College of Metaphysics. Coming soon!.....***The Best Metaphysical Jazz for Enlightenment*** goes everywhere!

I send you my circle of love
Chris Sheehan

"Vision Quest" was the term we used to describe the painting of the College Barn. On this 22,000 square foot canvas dozens of people ages 10 to 65 painted what students have been mentally imaging at the opening of SOM classes for years. Manifesting this goal was a love-inspired duty and an act of gratitude for all those who came before, those who carried the torch if only for a few weeks. Each person who spent even five minutes visualizing the dream of a futuristic campus teaching the inner secrets beyond physical life has added his or her energy to it. They have all become part of the history of SOM.

The beauty of "Vision Quest" is its openness. It will forever be a chain of experiences shared by many over 10 weeks in the fall of 2004. The College Barn is now a testimony to the benefits of group interaction for accomplishing big goals, and having been accomplished adding to the great storehouse of understandings for the soul. Too often humanity waits for a crises or trauma to unite in this way. Floods, famines, wars bring out the best in people as well as the worst. This reactionary cycle of memory leaves us at the mercy of a sometimes wrathful God.

What we endeavor to teach is the inherent birthright of each individual to be compatible with his Creator. This point of view honors what has built the present while elevating the thinking by recognizing what can be better. Creative thinking in the now is the key to using memory today and to creating useful memories for tomorrow. With experiences of the caliber of "Vision Quest", gratitude wells up from within. This gratitude is a signal for productive memory.

> I had never witnessed anything like "Vision Quest" before. It fell under the category of things that I knew existed but I had no idea how they were actually created or came about. As I watched Chris draw the outlines on the barn and then groups of students and teachers paint together, I was awestruck by the ease and beauty of it all. I will forever hold Vision Quest in my mind when I think of something big that I want to accomplish. "Vision Quest" has helped me to believe that big things really can be easy when you believe. — Stacy Ann Ferguson, Graduate Teacher COM

**Read more about Vision Quest in Section 8 on Reasoning.*

A MEMORY EXERCISE

Gratitude is a major component in making Memory beneficial in the present moment. The degree to which you are grateful for an experience is the degree to which you can have compassion and love for Self and others.

The following exercises are ways to acknowledge gratitude in your life.

Exercise One

Make a list of the people throughout your life who have helped you become the person you are today. Start at the present time with people in your life now and work your way back as long as you can remember.

Once your list is complete, read each persons name and write a few words that reflect what they gave to you.

Next, read each name aloud. Describe what this person has brought into your life. For instance, Sarah Adams was a neighbor who lived down the street from you when you were a young child. One day your bike took a tumble in front of her house. Tending her yard, she saw it all and came to your rescue. "Nasty scrapes!" you remember her saying. "Let me take the angry heat from them," as she sprinkled them with cool water from her watering can. It only took a moment for Sarah to change how you saw the world.

Sum up the lesson you learned from the person, saying something like "Sarah Adams! You were the first person to teach me that showing kindness only takes a moment."

Linger with this a moment, then conclude by saying aloud, "Sarah Adams, I am grateful for your presence in my life."

Each day follow these steps with a new person on your list. As you do, other memories may surface of people you had forgotten. When this happens add them to the bottom of your list. When you have successfully moved through your entire list you will have many new understandings of the purpose for Memory in your life.

Exercise Two

When troubled by the past, learn how to quickly defuse the charge by seeing the good in the situation. Begin by writing about your problem for a half hour nonstop. Start writing and keep writing. This stream of consciousness writing will clear your conscious mind enabling you to think cleaner and straighter. For this writing to be effective record the chatter in your head. Sometimes this will be like internal dialogue, at others a combination of ideas. Don't edit or delete in any way. Keep writing the thoughts that enter your head, even if they seem off track. They aren't. Every thought you will bring forth will have some relevance.

Leave it for three days.

On the fourth day, think of the wisest person you know. Climb into her skin, aligning your consciousness with hers. Think about your troubling situation.

Wait three more days.

On the seventh day, harmonize your mind with the wise person you selected and read what you originally wrote. As you come upon ideas you want to comment on, do so on a cassette recorder. Make sure your insights are worthy of your chosen person. Thanks to the wisdom of your friend, you now can have a more objective view of your situation.

For further exploration you can take another step. Read what you wrote again. This time identify the "bad" in the situation, highlighting these phrases or sentences in a similar way. When you have marked each one list them on another sheet of paper, actively looking for connections. Perhaps the word "I" appears in each one, or "lose" or "blame". Repetition, a function that builds memory, is a key for becoming free of restricted thinking.

Next look for positive recall in the memory using a different color or symbol to mark these sentences. Many times we see the good later, after the event has come and gone. Again look for repeated words or phrases. Now you can become more awake, more conscious of your strengths. Many people take these for granted, thus denying gratitude and chaining thoughts and emotions to injustices in the past.

Take one more step! Sometimes we learn gratitude by being in someone else's position, by putting ourselves in the other person's shoes.

Look at the situation you wrote about from others' points of view. Come up out of your shell to remember how the other people in your situation thought and felt. If you feel at a loss and think you don't know, hold your mind still and concentrate on watching the situation rather than being a participant. See it like a movie unfolding before your eyes. Sometimes you may need to practice this again and again until it becomes clear. The effort will be worth it! This can be a great eye opener and the beginning of realizing the event is neutral, we are the ones adding the color. To understand that all situations are neutral in life, that you and I are the ones choosing to make the best of them is to accept the spiritual inheritance from our Creator.

The Sacred Fire

It had been a while since the last time I prepared the chiminea. We had been on a weekly basis burning papers, documents, brochures that once served the School of Metaphysics. We started to burn these at sacred times so the energy in them could be used to the fullest. I saw it as giving to God.

The energy would return in many ways and it is always a wonder and excitement to see its return. When I lead Indigo children and their parents in planting flowers around the patio that same day someone signed up as a Dream of the Month club member beginning his new path to discovery of the meaning of his dreams. I love this time and space yet I forget and let other things get in the way of making time.

Tonight I became determined to rekindle the spark to the sacred fire.

I wanted many people to be involved, so I announced it often. As I was gathering the materials for the fire, I wondered if others were really going to join. No matter, the fire will commence, I tell myself. I begin collecting materials, placing them in a bag, then a thought comes to me, why not the whole box? What we don't burn tonight can always go toward next week.

After gathering the materials, I go upstairs to let Dr. Barbara know that I am starting. She has been one person who has been consistent in burning with me. She is the one who initiated the idea explaining how the patio area of the main building in Feng Shui language cycles prosperity. Remembering that prosperity - money - in a dream signifies value, I concentrate on this and think of my value in what I am giving and receiving, and how this is a recognition of the School's value. Dr. Barbara says, "Thanks". She is sending out emails, stirring up energy in a way she knows how.

I begin to fill the chiminea with last year's ***Thresholds*** *misprints and overprints. This issue of the magazine was on the Peace Dome. Looking at the pages I glance over at the Peace Dome. This place has such meaning for me. I was here as a college student as this building was being constructed, what an honor! I decided I would fill the entire chiminea with these sacred documents before I light it. I did this to wait for more people to gather.*

Is anyone going to come?

I decided to focus on what I was doing and enjoy this moment. It felt similar to me during the night of One Voice when we convene again and again in the Peace Dome to recite the Universal Peace Covenant as we welcome the New Year. I know what I need to do, the duty to be performed, and this allows me to release any fear or doubt.

I light the paper. It burns slowly. The top of the chiminea is stuffed full, so it smoulders creating a thin line of smoke that rises straight up. I watch this and become one with the fire. People start arriving. Chris, Stacy, Ivy, Jaqie, one by one they come. Mike, Nicholas, Dave, Jen. They begin to feed the fire. They say they are going to do a projection (of mental energies) around the fire for the next Indigo Parenting Session.

I notice the energy is scattering, playful in a way, yet different than I have experienced before. I keep people focused throughout giving them paper to burn and ways to imagine how this energy could and will return. As each piece goes into the fire people begin to voice their desires, "Dream of the Month club member", "$1000 for building Octagon", "a dozen new college students in January".

Then Talina, another student, arrives. Everyone sits in a circle for the projection. Stacy and I tend the fire, keeping it going. The energy is so calm and soothing. I feel like a sacred firekeeper from ancient times. My duty is to protect the participants.

After the projection, everyone begins to feed the fire again. Everyone is talking seemingly at once. I overhear someone talking about the different ways people have heard about the school. From lectures, radio shows, to telephone books falling on someone's head and opening to the School of Metaphysics page! I ask Jaqie, "How did you first hear about the School of Metaphysics?" It was in front of a bar.

I proceed to direct the conversation and ask everyone around the circle, "How did you first hear about the School of Metaphysics?" In this small group the diversity is great. Overhearing a conversation, dating a SOM teacher, going to a lecture when you are thirteen, in your chiropractic office desiring healing, a wife, a friend there are so many ways. I become so grateful for this moment. This moment of sharing with each other, walking into each other's life for even just a little while. I know I am surrounded by great people.

Then the box is empty. We have burned all the old energy and given completely. I stay with the fire until it is completely out. One by one the others leave. I look into the fiery embers and thank God for the experience.
∞ Laurie Biswell

"A man who listens because he has nothing to say can hardly be a source of inspiration.

The only listening that counts is that of the talker who alternately absorbs and expresses ideas."
– Agnes Repplier, 1904

Listening

Universal Language of Mind Story

Who is the Oldest?

Some time ago, a monkey, an elephant, and a parrot lived on the same mountain. Being neighbors they tried to get along but were often rude and disrespectful to each other.

One day they all seemed disagreeable and none really wanted to be, so they agreed to find a better way to treat one another. But how to accomplish this lofty ideal?

"I know," said one. "Before the death of the great lion, we heeded his judgement.

"Yes," said another. "The lion had always been."

"Let's decide to treat the oldest one of us as we did the lion," said the third, "with real respect."

Each agreed, yet how to know which was the oldest? They sat under the great Banyan tree for days pondering the question.

Finally, a way to answer became clear. "Elephant," asked the other two, "we all sit under this same Banyan tree. How old was it when you first saw it?"

Elephant thought back to his youth. "When I was very small, I walked right over this tree. The tallest branch tickled my belly. I knew the tree when it was a bush!"

Then the elephant and parrot asked the monkey the same question.

"When I was little more than a baby, I used to sit and crane my head to eat the green shoots at the top of this Banyan tree. Since it began growing, I have known this tree."

Lastly, the parrot told his story. "Once near this spot a great Banyan tree, much like this one, grew up tall and proud. I used to perch on its branches and eat its fruit, then drop its seeds around. This Banyan grew from one of those seeds. I knew this Banyan before it was even born!"

Elephant and monkey bowed in respect to the clever parrot. "You are the oldest of us in wisdom," they said, "and we will listen to you and follow your teachings."

From that time forward, elephant, monkey, and parrot were respectful to each other.

Listening is easy when the attention is directed and the mind concentrated. In this story are the keys to effective listening.

1) Establish an ideal. Martin Luther King Jr. told a story of a novelist who died leaving many outlines of future stories. One described a separated family who would inherit the family house if they lived together in it. King saw this idea as a metaphor for humanity. He said it is as if we have inherited a great world house and since we can no longer live without each other we must learn how to live with one another. Such lofty ideals become very practical when we realize how connected our world has become due to the technological advances of the past century.

Wanting something beyond what you presently have awakens the senses, we pay **attention**.

2) Respecting one another. When there is sincere regard for another the desire to attend them increases. When we **respect** someone's opinion, we listen more closely to what they have to say. When we respect another's experience, we want to hear their stories. Reading and writing are the newest forms of communication in the world. Long before the written word, histories were kept alive through storytelling. The accuracy of the stories of the ancestors rested in the hands of good listeners. Many marriages have been made on the ability to listen and they have been maintained through a continuing desire to do so.

3) Ascertain the facts. The concentrated mind, focused on receiving new data, can weigh all independent factors. By **remembering** where we have come from we can make better choices. Listening is an act of receiving information on which to base those choices.

4) Agreement. When we **listen**, we receive another completely. Beyond hearing with our ears, our minds are actively engaged in absorbing what the other has to give. This combination of giving and receiving is at the root of all agreement.

When these steps are taken, Listening becomes an Essential Life Skill anytime, anywhere, with anyone.

I N T U I T I V E R E S E A R C H

LISTENING

"...to enhance the constant awareness of this one's purpose for existence there needs to be the striving for the stillness in the outer consciousness and the alignment of the whole Self every moment. This state of being does not need to be initiated. It merely needs to be nurtured in the Self." (91199BGC7)

"Hearing occurs with the body; listening happens with the mind. Listening fuels your desire for Self-illumination. It brings awareness to a mind hungry for growth." (SOM Lesson 9)

"The capacity to listen is priceless to one desiring Self awareness for it is the open door for Self-honesty, Self-reflection, and Self-correction." (SOM Lesson 9)

Listening is stilling the mind with the expectation of receiving. Listening occurs with all six senses.

In the significance of a Past Life Profile (51696SMB7) a man learned that listening is what happens not so much in the ears as in the mind of the listener. A successful businessman with a beautiful wife and children, he had reached a point of feeling lost. He felt he had no direction in life. This was the stimulus to request a Past Life Profile in the hope that it would supply some insight into the reason for these thoughts and feelings. The significance of the report, the part that relates the relevance of the past life information to the present life, began this way:

> We see that in the present time period this one does have the ability to use this one's attention undividedly and to be very perceptive in this one's life and this one's environment. We do see for this one to have the capability of receiving the thoughts and images from other individuals however we see that this one does become quite frightened by this one's capabilities, and we see that this one does hesitate to communicate what this one feels and what this one perceives. (51696SMB7)

Although this man was no stranger to extrasensory perception and psychic experiences, he had never considered that his reality might be filled with them. At times it was easy for him to see the psi acting. Attuned to his children, he often knew when they were upset or unhappy before he would be in their physical presence. With the information given in his analysis, he realized although he received impressions from his children he was often at a loss to respond to them. When he had foreknowledge he didn't know what to do with it, so its value was lost.

His inaction led to regret which was also described in the significance as well. The man began to note how often he worked from hindsight, knowing the best course of action long after the opportunity had passed. To remedy this, the report recommended discipline, spiritual practices that might aid in guiding a "sense of confidence and trust within this one's own inner communication." One of the practices suggested was meditation, a mental science which begins with expectant listening.

Problems we encounter later in life grow from seeds planted when we are young. Consider the following health analysis (10142003BGC5) and suggestions given for a 14-year-old girl at the beginning of her creative life.

> This one wants other people to hear what she has to say and we see that this one feels that many times this is not occurring. We see that in part that this is true.

How often do we hear experts talking about the alienation of teenagers, the breakdown in communication? How often do parents hear, "You never listen to me?" The problem is not a new one, and it can be solved. This report gives insight that can be useful to many.

> We see that there is a large part that is not, in that, this one's true desire is to be accepted and understood by others, when in reality this one wants this from the Self. This gets confused with others agreeing with this one or disagreeing with her and we see that as this one turns it into a battle between the Self and others, there is a great deal of energy that is lost here and there is very little understanding that comes from its use. (10142003BGC5)

Struggles we have with others are reflections of our own inner conflicts. When meditation is practiced regularly, on a daily basis, it becomes time for the Self. Setting aside a time and place to devote attention solely to the Self is an act of healing. When concentration is applied in knowing the Highest Self, conflicts pale in comparison. Developing sensitivity to an inner voice of reason, a conscience, makes one familiar with stillness and compassion comes forward in dealings with others. This will effect a change and transference in this one's awareness of the reality of nature which the report recommends.

> .....It would be most helpful for this one to study nature, to study Native American cultures, rituals that are connected to the earth. For we see that in doing so, that this one will become much more aware of the cycles and the ability to move and to express the Self.

Listening to the Self cultivates deep thinking. The mind becomes active when there is whole brain activity, and Listening is whole brain activity. By lingering with thoughts through Concentration, one becomes aware and familiar with how one thinks. Old ways of thinking, being, doing fade. This is true for anyone at any age.

Emotionally the report describes the girl's stubborn desire for others to agree with her.

> We see that when this one even begins to sense that others are not hearing what she is saying, then this one goes into a pattern of thinking that others are not listening. We see that this is not always the case and we see that many times this one is listened to, but this one does not recognize it. **This is an internal listening problem rather than an external, and we see this one needs to own it so that this one can build the skills necessary for the mind to be still so that listening can occur.**
>
> Would suggest that this one practice listening to people when in a public place. Practice isolating different conversations or comments that people make and being able to note them fully, to acknowledge them and understand them. This would aid this one in being able to both express the Self more clearly and to understand the nature of listening. (10142003BGC5)

For this girl, the mental and emotional attitudes were manifesting in difficulty in the ears. A build up of material, largely ear wax, is impairing the function of the ears. There tends to be congestion in the head as well as difficulties in the structural system and the intestines. All of these are easily treatable and curable through diet, exercise, and specified health care.

The suggestion for the girl to become involved with groups of people who are committed to bettering themselves and their community gives her the direction she needs during adolescence. "It would also enable this one to actively listen to others and have them listen to her," the report says.

When the parents ask for suggestions, encouraging their daughter to interact with others is the first consideration. Through interacting with a variety of ages in many life conditions she will build upon the respect needed and be stimulated to interact in attentive ways. Groups that are particularly older are recommended for the wisdom that comes from experience.

> It would be helpful for this one to have the opportunity to work with others in their job, particularly ones that are creative that have a beginning, middle and end. This one can have a great affinity for something like woodworking, being able to know that this one is doing something that is important in the world is a very important part of this one's existence.
>
> **The one of the mother wants to know how she can best help this one be happy and healthy?**
>
> By affording this one space, by being willing to still the mind and listen, even when this one is tempted to talk, to trust the reasoning of this one with the information she has and to be there, be present whenever this one has a need. (10142003BGC5)

The ability to still the mind is honed with the Listening skill. Here Undivided Attention and Concentration unite to aid the listener to fully receive what is being given. Some see this as a lesson in patience, they are the ones who often build up stress and explode in anger on occasion. For the person who understands the earlier Essential Life Skills a freedon from fear brings ease and serenity, both qualities adolescents need to live with in order to learn.

When asked for suggestions in communicating her thoughts and feelings to others, the report stated the girl did not have difficulty in accomplishing this. Rather, she was being selective in who she told what. It was intentional. So why was she talking to some and not to others? The response is something worthy of everyone's consideration.

> It is a matter of whether this one feels if she will be received or not. As has been stated, this one's true desire is for acceptance. This one gets caught up in whether others agree and this one confuses agreement with listening. (10142003BGC5)

LISTENING

is the choice to allow another's thoughts into your mind.

Listening
What is It?

"Who are you talking to?" Granddad Jack asked 10-year-old Hezekiah.

Kiah paced an eight foot path, back and forth, working the raptor toy with both hands, in shamanic fashion. Often I have seen him as an Indian medicine man, healing stick in hand.

"Hezekiah quickly moved to his left as the lightning bolt barely missed him, striking the tree," Kiah emphatically chants.

He stops at the sound of Granddad Jack's voice. "Telling a story," he replies innocently without judgement, merely stating a fact. Receiving no feedback, he returns to his story.

Hezekiah's story is intended to be a trilogy called ***A Wizard's Journey.*** He has been writing it in his thoughts for two years. The first book of the three has begun to manifest on paper as he dictates the prose to a select group of scribes. I am honored to be one of them.

It is sometimes a challenge being a scribe. Accuracy is required and can be enforced because Hezekiah has a "memory like a steel trap" as he has been told and will in turn tell you whenever appropriate. Hezekiah's talent for storytelling is a testimony to the fifth Essential Life Skill and its relationship to those that come before it.

Before Hezekiah dictates a chapter, he will spend hours refining and developing the text. By the time he gives you his words he works like a tape recorder, rewinding when needed to give you the words again. When you read them back he can tell you where any unintended change may have happened due to a lapse in listening on the scribe's part. This at 10 years old from a boy who would probably never "make it" in public school in part because he has something to say.

In this moment with Granddad Jack I am pleased by Hezekiah's Self Respect. Because he is mentally and emotionally clean, he quickly tells Granddad the facts, without apology or darkness of any kind. I realize this is a product of my husband Daniel's and my efforts to insure Hezekiah has an environment where he can be open, honest, and expressive. In this moment I am pleased to see how his creativity has been fostered, encouraged, and empowered.

Listening to this interchange, my mind calls up a memory from my own youth. When I was in fifth grade, the same age as Hezekiah, I started my first book. Named for the trauma I was experiencing at the time, it was called ***The Everlasting Year***. I had many experiences and thoughts I felt strongly needed to be told. Yet my inner desire was not yet matched by physical skill and so writing was arduous. The book never got much further than the first page or two and so it was lost. This is where I learned the value of a scribe.

Now forty years later, I can be that scribe for another soul in need. His thoughts can be encouraged because someone is willing to listen.

In every culture throughout history listening has been highly valued. The urge to pray is based upon the belief that someone will be there to listen to us. This is why confession is highly prized in one of the world's largest religions – Catholicism, the universal church. For those choosing a secular path there are therapists who are paid according to the quality of their listening skill. Many relationships are forged on the willingness of those involved to listen to one another. Many wars are averted by talking and listening. Many realizations are experienced in the same way.

One of my favorite lecture topics for many years was communication. I began each lecture talking about one of my most influential teachers. When I was a freshman at the University of Missouri I took a Shakespeare class from a man named Robert Bender. His classes were filled, 350+ each semester, limited only by the size of the auditorium where he taught. He made Shakespeare accessible to me because he brought the man to life. Being in Mr. Bender's class was spending a few hours a week with the bard and his musings. I moved beyond all my prejudices about archaic language that taxed my brain to understand into the world of images so vibrant new words had to be created to describe them.

Mr. Bender embodied Shakespeare. I didn't entertain the idea of reincarnation then but having done so since then it is highly likely that this man lived in 15th century England and quite possibly performed at the Globe himself. I was so taken with this professor that I took several courses from him.

When I was a sophomore I took a literature and composition class from him. This upper level class was smaller, 40 or so, which allowed him to open the first class with a simple exercise.
He asked us to turn to the person sitting next to us and talk. He gave us about ten minutes. Then he moved from person to person, asking what each had discovered about their neighbor.

Most people said, "This is Susie and she's here at MU from Milwaukee. She's studying agriculture." Info exhausted, he would move to the next person. What an ingenious way to introduce everyone in the class to everyone else I thought.

When he got to the man I'd been talking to the man said, "This is Barbara O'Guinn, she's nineteen years old. She's from Sikeston, Missouri. She was born in New Orleans. She is majoring in Journalism here at the University of Missouri. She hopes to pursue a career in journalism when she graduates. Her favorite color is blue...." and on and on.

People began to snicker, wondering how this guy knew so much in such a short period of time.

Mr. Bender moved on to me and I said, "This is Lynn Shy. He's nineteen years old. He was born and raised in Sikeston, Missouri." When people heard that they began laughing having begun to catch on. The aha! moment. I went on and on with things I knew about Lynn, who at the time was my fiance as well. Everyone enjoyed the joke.

It was an interesting exercise in communication for more reasons than I think Mr. Bender at the time anticipated because he got the two of us together, and we shared what we knew about each other. Being a great teacher, he used this because he recognized that a great deal of communication occurs through familiarity.

Many times in our lives we are unaccustomed to, unfamiliar with those we have an opportunity to communicate with. We spend 80% of our waking time in some form of communication. This may be in conversation, in reading, in writing, in listening to the radio or watching TV. How well we communicate therefore is very important to us.

More than half of that communication time we spend in listening.

This is even more true now with technology and mass media. Perhaps you are like me, sometimes you talk back to the television. Of course the TV doesn't hear you, it doesn't listen. Most of that activity is you being able to listen and absorb the information that is being given to you.

Mastering the art of listening requires intelligently, discriminately, and effectively receiving others' thoughts for the enhancement of individual learning and growth. In a lecture (available on tape from SOM) on this topic, I explore listening through nine different individuals. This is in the hope that the audience will recognize people they've known, or maybe someone they know now, or someone they live with 24 hours a day which is – them! Here I will describe four of these. Perhaps you'll be able to see some of the pitfalls of communication and learn some ideas that can turn what is a deficit into an asset for you.

Person One: Argumentative Andy

Argumentative Andy is the kind of person who if you haven't seen him for a long time and you come up to him saying, "Oh! You're looking great!" he will say "You should have seen me an hour ago."

Argumentative Andy is always looking for a fight. Argumentative Andy is always defensive and Argumentative Andy always takes the opposite point of view.

You can want to share a beautiful sunset with "A2". You might say, "Andy, isn't this the most beautiful sunset you've ever seen in your life?"

He'll look at the colors and say, "You should see the sunsets in Phoenix. They are outstanding if you want to see a really good sunset."

It's not just the important things in life Andy argues about. It's the mundane things. The things that don't amount to much. His key words are "but". When you hear someone whose every other word is "but" you'll find they are captive in this Andy headspace.

So how do we transform Argumentative Andy into Amiable Andy? Amiable is a great word to describe the new attitude Andy can develop to neutralize his tension. As we cultivate friendliness with Self and others, the tendency to argue lessons. You find you don't have to walk around being defensive, waiting to be attacked, waiting for a fight. You can begin to be open and embrace other people and therefore their ideas.

Andy can learn how to receive others. Affirming "I hope the best for you in all situations" or "My life is enriched through knowing you" will begin transforming the nature of Andy's relationships with others.

Person Two: Bashful Beatrice

When you haven't seen Bashful Beatrice for a while she is the kind of person who, when you say "Wow! You've really changed!" will do one of two things. She'll either not say anything, staying bashful in her shell while her mind is racing, or she might say to you, "Oh, you mean you didn't like me before? There was something wrong with me before?"

Bashful Beatrice's aren't very trusting. They don't a have tendency toward believing the good, particularly about themselves. They tend to live in their own world being wrapped up in themselves. They tend to be moody. Although silent they are aggressive. They place emotional demands on others. In your willingness and gregariousness to tell them they look really great, they immediately are thinking for you, judging that this means before you didn't think they were so "hot". They demand that you keep telling them how wonderful they are. Your reassurances never seem to "sink in". They are not listening.

The key words for B2 are "I don't". I don't look so pretty/ handsome. I don't do as well as I should. There is a healthy dose of self-pity in Bashful Beatrice.

Bashful Beatrice can be transformed into a Bold Beatrice. I use the word bold not as an abrasive term but as a courageous term. A Bashful Beatrice can be transformed, learning how to be a doer. She can practice receiving compliments with a still mind. Gratitude does wonders for Beatrice.

Person Three: Closeminded Charlie

Closeminded Charlie is the kind of person who always knows what you ought to be doing. Quite often he's the person who says, "Nobody ever listens to me."

It's very interesting because as we learn to listen to our own communication we can enhance our own perspective of ourselves and life because we learn when we can hear our own thoughts. In fact many times we can learn more through listening to ourselves than to external sources. When Closeminded Charlie says "Nobody ever listens to me" he's really telling himself that he never listens to anybody else either! So of course he looks at the world and thinks nobody wants to hear what he has to say.

Closeminded Charlie tends to have his attention in the past. He's a very prejudiced person. He's attached to the old ways of doing things. His key words are "you have to".

Closeminded Charlie can easily transform into a Charismatic Charlie. By beginning to realize and embrace an openness to life. A willingness to look at things differently. A willingness to learn, a willingness to investigate. When you have that kind of openness it is just like a child and most people are very tender with children. They watch children and they enjoy watching them discover something new. They enjoy watching them express themselves. When you have this kind of open attitude it holds within itself a charisma because it is the openmindedness of innocence, the willingness and joy of discovery.

Person Four: Distracted Donna

Distracted Donna is a chatterbox. She never shuts up. She's on to another, then another and another,– quite often leaving a chain of half said phrases behind her. If you try to follow her you will find yourself being here and there and over there. It is exhausting trying to keep up with a Distracted Donna.

If she does shut her mouth you will find that when you try to say something, she is interrupting you! She's barging in right in the middle of your expressing a thought.

Distracted Donnas have scattered thinking. There's not a space for much receptivity in their communication. As a result every time D2 will miss the point of what life is bringing her. The key words are many, one of the most common being "You know." What happens in this jumping in her thinking and her communication is she will start a thought, in the middle of it she will forget what she is saying and she will insert "You know" or "You know what I mean". This seems to invite your participation yet without the receptivity to listen, she is quickly off on another tangent thought.

In order for Distracted Donna to change, she must become a Determined Donna. Determined Donnas can follow a train of thought. She can also speak a train of thought. This brings greater fulfillment in the giving of communication and in the receiving of communication. Concentration is an Essential Life Skill for Donna to master.

There are more potential listeners to explore. Egocentric Evan, Fallacious Freda, Gossiping Georgia, Hypocritical Harry, and Inferior Isaccs round out the group. Each have ways to transform their lives through honing their ability to communicate. Here four different types of people with four different problems in communication are highlighted. Each problem can be replaced with a solution.

There is a commonality with each of these people, even though they seem to express differently. The common difficulty is in the heart of listening and the ability to direct mental attention.

As long as you have physical ears and they work, you have the ability to hear. Just because you have the ability to hear does not mean you have the ability to listen. Most of us identify ourselves as either a good listener or a bad listener or somewhere in between. You weren't born a good listener and you weren't born a bad listener. Somewhere you learned whatever skill of listening you possess at this moment. Listening is a skill it can be understood, it can be taught. It can be honed and developed when you begin to develop your mind.

The sense of hearing is a physical sense that is linked to your body just as the other four senses of sight, smell, taste, and touch are. Your ability to hear is a way you can transform your ability to listen, to receive information for your mind to use. The word *attending* is often used in literature and poetry to mean listening.

It is easy to understand the relationship between listening and attention when we realize how scattered attention affects the integrity of our thoughts. Daniel, Hezekiah and I were on our way to Norman, Oklahoma for the premiere of THE SILVER CORD on the campus of the University of Oklahoma. We stopped at a welcoming station to walk outside a bit.

Hezekiah began telling a story about a four year old who drove himself to the movie store. My attention began drifting as I became distracted into other thoughts so I missed the middle of his tale.

"The little boy turned the wheel?" I asked.

"Yeah," Kie replied, "he was driving."

"He was?" I said in surprise.

"You weren't listening," Hezekiah sighed. He has been taught these skills all his life and knows how to identify them.

There was no excuse for me pretending to listen when my mind was elsewhere. So I surrendered my ego and admitted, "You're right, Hezekiah. I went somewhere else."

"Where did you get lost?" he asked, only slightly exasperated. In these prepubescent years Kiah has been learning compassion lessons in how he responds to others.

"Would you start over?" I said a bit sheepishly.

Quite generously, he did!

Attending comes from the same root word as attention. Attention is the sense of the mind. Undivided Attention is your ability to direct your mind where you want it to go so you can take in information.

There are five steps to build your ability to listen. These are:

1. ***Be an opportunist.*** This means you know your own mind. You know what you think, you know why you think the way you do, you know what you find meaningful in life and you bring that value to any communication you are involved with. You have an idea of what you want to communicate to others, and what you want to learn from the people you are communicating with. In this way you see both the giving and receiving parts of the communication. Knowing what you want to accomplish in a communication is a prerequisite for using your mind effectively.

When this occurs you can identify your own intentions and the speaker's intentions. You can know if the speaker's intention is to persuade, entertain, inform, or to unburden. You've all been in situations where a good friend just wanted to talk. They wanted to unload, get things off their chest. They wanted a sounding board. When you know your own mind well enough that you can pinpoint the purpose for that communication, you can be that willing receiver. That is being an opportunist.

2. ***The ability to direct your attention.*** When you form an ideal or goal for the communication between you and someone else, you are able to direct your attention toward the fulfillment of that goal. You know what it is you want to accomplish. You know by the end of this communication you want to know more about the person, or you want to feel closer to the person, or have an agreement with this person.

One of the ways you can hone this ability is through practicing a concentration exercise. A simple way to practice is to open a book, choose a paragraph, read the first sentence. Close the book. Now write down the sentence you read. If you find you've written that sentence down word for word so it matches what is in the book, you can open it again and read two sentences. Then write them down. When you get to the point where you can write down word for word what is already there, you extend it. Stretch your abilities. Spend 10 minutes a day doing this. This 10 minutes investment will pay off the remaining 23 hours and 50 minutes of the day. You are honing your ability to direct your attention and hold it, an essential skill for listening.

3. ***Your ability to respond.*** Respond means to take that directed attention and extend it. As this relates to listening, this is the state of expectancy. This means your mind is still. It is calm. It remains that way as long as you choose to have it that way. Some people have a hard time with expectancy. Women seem to have a bit more awareness owing to the physical body and the expectancy of the cycles their bodies experience. Think of it this way, when a woman is pregnant, what do we call this? They are "expecting". This is a state of

receptivity when the mind is completely still and open, ready to be filled. Becoming familiar with this state of mind is essential for good listening.

When the phone rings and you pick it up and say hello, that moment between your words and the other person's response is expectancy. Once you can direct your attention, you want to be able to hold it - still - expecting.

4. ***Receiving information.*** When the person on the other end of the telephone responds, you receive information. The sound goes into your ear, through the auditory nerve to your brain where information is stored that will aid you to identify the caller. It happens in a instance and you say, "Oh hi, Mom!" It seems immediate when you've done it for years. It is not just magic. It was learned and it comes from the ability to hold the mind still so you can receive.

If you answer the phone and someone is talking in the room so your attention goes to them, the caller may respond but you will have to say, "I'm sorry, who is it?" You heard their voice, but you weren't listening because your attention was directed elsewhere. Your mind was elsewhere. The ability to still your mind and hold it expectantly enables you to receive information. This is probably the biggest challenge in listening.

In receiving information we tend to become distracted. Most often what people are distracted by are their emotional reactions to what they are hearing. Argumentative Andy and the others are people who hear only part of what is given to them, then they slam the door. "You mean you didn't like me before?" "But I can't do that, I don't have enough time." Slamming the door. They lose that expectancy. Anything that was to come that could have been received is gone.

As a teacher I monitor students' progress. They will come to points where I compliment them. I may say, "You have gained great mastery of what you are doing. I can tell you enjoy doing this activity." The student who uses his mind receives this thought with honest pride.

5. ***Comprehension.*** Comprehension is the ability to receive something completely so you can understand what it is. If you only have

half the story you are Gossiping Georgia. You are carrying tales. You want the complete story. Our inner urge is to know the whole, the total. Your inner self is always striving for peace that comes from understanding. When you can extend that state of expectancy so you receive all of the information, then you can begin to realize the basis of mind to mind communication which is also called telepathy. This is your ability to not only hear words, but receive thoughts that go with those words. If you are interested in developing telepathy you know the five steps that will produce it.

Life is for learning. Because 80% of our waking existence is spent in communication we have a myriad of opportunities with people, places, and things to cultivate that learning. In the process we enrich our lives by knowing other people through the magic of giving and receiving.•

Relationship between concentration and listening

Listening is very much an acquired life skill. True, listening is absorbing what is going on in the environment, and in that way is a function of infancy. Careful listening, that is listening with the heart and with presence of mind, is a function of concentration. That's why it is presented in the Course in Mastery of Consciousness after the concentration lessons. To listen well, you have to concentrate. To listen well, you have to have a still mind, a humble and still ego, and you have to care about what you are listening to. There has to be a space made for the new information being spoken towards you, and it somehow needs to be made important enough to receive.

Many times people get antsy or fidgety when you are talking with them. This usually means they are done listening. They could not or would not hold their concentration on you. This can come from their inability, through lack of practice, to hold their mind still on one point—in this case speaking. It can also mean they have not created a reason in their mind to listen to you. It's not that you are unimportant, it's that they have not created and given to you a reason to receive you.

The highest use of concentration is to focus the mind single-pointedly on the Creator, giving value to the Creator, and expectantly listening. to the reply. The highest uses of listening are to listen to the inner self, the inner authority. Listening inward is a humbling experience, because you are, in essence, choosing to consider a higher authority than your own thinking. ∞ Paul Madar

Marlena's Story – Healing Deafness

I was born partially deaf and wore hearing aids for most of my life. I didn't have an ear drum and the ear canal was undeveloped in both ears. In my early twenties, I had started to read metaphysics, reading about being open, about [the idea that] thought is cause, and I was kind of open to ideas I hadn't considered before. Before that, I didn't want to hear, I know I didn't. I was offered the opportunity to have surgery earlier in my life; basically the doctor told me, "I could fix that," and my thought was, "What does he mean? What would be my excuse for not doing the things I wanted to do if I had this hearing?"

Reading about metaphysics helped me to be more open to change. I had the surgery to make me an eardrum and ear canal and I still had some malformities in the ear, but the doctor didn't want to mess with that any further. I started the classes in the School of Metaphysics just a week after my surgery, so I had packing in my ear from the surgery and even through that, I could hear. A month after the surgery the doctor tested my hearing and it was far better than he had hoped for. He finally told me that the percentage of the surgery even working was like 30%! So having remarkable hearing after that, just having my hearing in the normal range [which it is], well, he's writing a paper on it for a journal, it was so remarkable. I was very glad he didn't tell me the percentage before the surgery because I used a lot of visualization for that surgery!

As I was growing up, there were some sounds I couldn't hear. One of the most profound experiences for me, soon after I was able to hear, occurred when I was taking a shower and I was standing there, and thought, "What's that sound?" and it was the water! That was pretty amazing, finally hearing like what I call "in stereo." There was more to sound than I had even imagined, it was kind of hollow before. I hadn't really experienced the full experience of sound, of all of it. It was a new experience now, hearing songs on the radio that I had heard before but I never maybe heard the words. I actually understood the song, I heard the whole song through, and I thought, "oh, I didn't know that's what they were saying before."

Being an SOM student, basically I was learning how to hear in the classes, with dream interpretation and meditation on a daily basis. When I began really listening to myself, through those dreams that come from within, and taking time out every day to still my mind to listen to myself, it gave me a desire. I wanted to hear people, I wanted to connect more with people, from that experience of me connecting with myself. I wanted to hear what other people thought, I wanted to hear what they had to say, where beforehand, I did not. I recognized that I didn't have much patience. People would say something and if I couldn't hear it, and I asked them to repeat it, and they did, and I still didn't hear it, I'd just either pretend I heard it and go on with the conversation or I would physically remove myself from the environment.

Listening to my dreams gave me more compassion; I wanted to know what other people thought. Before I got in the school I remembered dreams, and now I knew more what they meant because I was able to interpret them or have them interpreted. That helped me. I would apply something every day and I had a lot of dreams about the healing process I was going through being able to hear. When my dreams were interpreted they reflected how my consciousness was open to listening or not.

When I started to meditate, I could feel my ears open up and I could hear more. Every time I meditated I could physically hear more. I heard sounds around me a lot clearer, as if someone was physically removing cotton or something from my ear each time. That was on a daily basis, during meditation and other times, too. Like in class, when I was speaking, getting my thoughts out, whenever I would give my full attention to something it would feel like my ears were opening again. It felt like the physical removing of a blockage from my ear, so I could hear more, so things would be clearer. Because before that it would be like a mumble, a muffled sound.

Just recently, I was sitting down meditating, and I had a goal for my meditation of hearing more clearly. I wanted to understand something. I was sitting in the meditation lotus position and not long after that, a few minutes of sitting there, with my attention focused on my third eye, I felt this pressure in my ear being removed, like something was being drawn out physically. And my ears felt warm, the ear canals felt warm, felt very clear, and the sound around me, it drew my attention to my ears, I was drawn to the sounds that were outside on the street, and I could hear it very sharply. I could hear people talking in the street; I was on the second level of the house, maybe 40 feet away, and there were just talking, not yelling. And before that, I would not have been able to hear that physically.

The most profound realization occurred about a year after I had this surgery to restore my hearing. I was living with my mom. I had been learning about listening, about hearing, and that what had helped me to physically hear more every day was giving my full attention to the person I would talk to or listen to.

This particular day, I was talking with my mom and she said some things to me that didn't make any sense at all. And my thought at that moment was, "she doesn't make any sense. I don't want to hear this." She walked away and I walked away and suddenly I had an experience like a vacuum, my ears cut off. I could not physically hear!

Through the exercises I was learning in the classes, I was getting really good at identifying my thoughts and what they were. So I asked myself, "what did I do?" because in class I was learning that thought is cause. I identified the thought I had, and I remembered thinking then, "I want to hear what you have to say."

I immediately sat down where I was because I was experiencing a lot of fear. I had just barely had my hearing for a year and it suddenly was gone! It really scared me. My thoughts were going, "I don't like this, I don't want this." So, through what I was learning in the classes about directing my mind, I changed my thinking really quickly. I realized I better focus on what I want! "I want to hear! I want to hear! I know what I want." It was very clear in my mind what I wanted. I wanted to physically hear, as I had those few moments beforehand.

Then I identified the thought that I didn't want to listen. So I sat down and I kind of rehashed the conversation I had with my mom. I looked at it and said to myself, well, that was a reaction of mine not wanting to hear her, and for me to hear, physically hear, I need to listen to whatever anybody says. And after that, I relaxed and I trusted myself. I trusted what I was learning that had enabled me to cause myself to hear again. I went back to my mom to hear what she had to say and within the hour, I could hear.

Since then, I've had many other instances when someone would be speaking to me and I didn't know that they were speaking to me, and I'd finally give my attention, and they'd say, "why were you ignoring me?" and I'd say, "no I wasn't," and they'd say, "I've been talking to you for the last five minutes." And it has always been a time when I didn't want to hear what they had to say. I still do that sometimes, but I am aware of it now, where I wasn't aware before of the connection between not wanting to hear and not being able to hear. It keeps me in check. Since I was born with it, I figure it's something I can use to keep me on the path.

I have an identical twin sister who has the same physical disorder. She doesn't study metaphysics. She doesn't want to take the responsibility [to admit] that it's she that has the trouble hearing. She has a lot of trouble with her ears. She had the same surgery, but her hearing is a little less. She thinks that my experience is great for me, and what she says is "that's a lot of responsibility." She still identifies herself as deaf; she belongs to different groups for deaf people. I don't, and so I hear even more because I don't even identify with the limitation. So I told her to cut that out! It's not helping.

I'm not sure if I hadn't had the surgery before I was in the classes if I would have been able to make an eardrum on my own. Having the surgery opened me up; I was ready to hear, ready for people to enter my life and for me to be in other people's lives fully. ∞ Marlena Garrison

ELS#5

A Short Class on Listening

Dr. S: We were talking in class about one of the Sutras and it says that success varies on the effort, whether weak, strong, or mild. What I presented to the students was the first experience I had with the Ten Most Wanted List wasn't so much the manifestation of the object, rather it was the awareness that this was the image in my mind. What I was describing to them was that effort was not just a physical activity. It's a continual awareness. In that moment I realized *I* create.

Dr. B: "Change is not caused by the passing of time. Change is caused by thought evolution." That's what you're talking about because that's what effort is.

There's so much in the human mind that thinks that existence is all about time. "I'll grow to love you. It will happen one of these days. It will dawn. Time will give it to us. I'll grow to be intuitive. I'll grow to know the answers. I'll grow to be successful," whatever. This thinking is a function of having been taught postponement when you are young.

In the first two years, I became very conscious of teaching Hezekiah to live out of the moment. The first time that the thought came out of my mouth of "We'll do that tomorrow" or something of that context, I heard it and I asked myself, "*What are you doing to this child?* What are you feeding this child? Why are going to teach him to have a scattered mind like you and everybody else that you know in the world? Why are you doing that?" Because I listened the questions arose in my mind, and answering them became a major lesson for me.

You have been trained, you have been taught to live out of the moment. You have been taught that something is better tomorrow. You have been taught the future is valueable because the present isn't that desireable; that whatever you can't deal with emotionally today, it's okay, it will all be over tomorrow. You've been taught all kinds of ways to scatter your attention and live out of the present. And you wonder why it's hard for you to live in the present, now. Don't wonder, accept your reality. Because it will help you to live in the present.

If your brain was wired one way, you can wire it now in another way, with effort, with devotion because you mentally see something different. The change can happen {*snap*} like that, like it did yesterday, for Laurie. That is how realization can come. All of a sudden, all of the pieces slide into place and there it is. It doesn't ever move again because you have gone to this whole new level of awareness. You know where you are and you know how you got there. That's Reasoning Man. There's no fear that you're going to backslide, "Oh God I may go back to that!" That's human thinking. You're a reasoner building on that humanity, that humanity is be-neath you. It's part of your foundation. Now you're reasoning.

So effort is not something you're doing while you're waiting to get there. You are already there. Effort is your devotion, the quality which you bring to what you have. And that's Undivided Attention. That's Self Respect. If these things are going to be beneficial for your conscious mind then the conscious mind must employ reasoning. It's essential. Reasoning is the power of the conscious mind. Do you know what reasoners do?-They ask questions, and they listen.

SF: You have to know what to listen to.

Dr. B: How do you know?

Dr. TM: Discrimination.

Dr. B: And where does a student practice discrimination?

JD: With the candle concentration.

Dr. B: Explain.

SS: You learn the difference between where you are focusing your attention and what the distractions are. What the object of your concentration is and what the distractions are.

Dr. S: The positive and negative factors of concentration.

Dr. B: Yes, and when you have identified those, what happens?

TM: You understand concentration.

JD: You know what focus is.

Dr. B: Yes, all those. And you experience something. Stillness.

SF: So that's what prepares you to listen.

Dr. B: Yes. Concentration creates the space to receive. Then listening is a further, greater, deeper level of receiving. Concentration enables you to ask questions. It is also the foundation for listening for the answers.

SF: That's why concentration precedes meditation. You have to know something about concentration before you can meditate.

Dr. B: Yes. In yogic teachings this is the difference between dhyana and samadhi. Dhyana is what we teach at SOM as concentration, the ability to extend your undivided attention beyond the sensory plane, beyond the limits of the physical conscious mind. When this is made known in your consciousness, then you can aspire to samadhi by opening your consciousness to receive the highest thought. Sound familiar?

SF: That's meditation!

Dr. B: Yes. Let's talk about meditation. How do you describe it?

JD: A means to accelerate evolution of Self....

L I S T E N I N G e m a i l s

Dear Dr. B and Family,

I have been thinking about Dr. Barbara's last question to new teachers, "...maybe it's time to ask yourselves what makes Metaphysics attractive to new people." I am currently forming my first class.

After speaking with many people I have observed that **what most people are seeking** is a way to make their lives better. Plain and simple. Many people ask questions regarding the power to create their lives in their own image. I have found that many are beginning to recognize the limitations of what they have been told to accept as their lot and want to change this. I see this as a very positive change in our culture. It shows there is willingness to change and take responsibility. Also, many ask questions regarding meditation and most come right out and say they "want to know themselves." The third thing I have come to recognize is that when you receive others and just allow them to tell you their stories or ask you many questions, they eventually come out and reveal to you, in whatever nomenclature they use, that they want to know God.

So I tell them that the School of Metaphysics will give them applicable tools that they can use immediately to create what they want in their lives. That by knowing their thoughts they will come to know themselves and by coming to know themselves they will find their relationship to the Creator. Simple.

I have found that if you really listen with patience and receive anyone that you encounter they will reveal to you what they desire or need in one way or another. We teach it all, so it's really quite easy to relate what they could learn if they choose. I allow my love of Metaphysics to radiate as I listen and answer. People will recognize it on some level, even if they are consciously unaware. You are open, they are open, truth comes out. Lovely how that works... I also appreciate and recognize that those with no specific conscious interest, per say, are still following their Soul's desire by even being drawn to you or taking the time to ask questions. And so I am extremely mindful in those moments of my gratitude for the opportunity to serve in that way. Some walk, some don't - either way a seed is planted because it has been planted with respect.

The way I see it, what the School of Metaphysics teaches is ALL attractive! People have yet to receive the information they seek. To me, it has been a matter of listening to them with my Soul to theirs and then giving what I know.

Happy and Healthy in Columbia, MO,
I send you all my Circle of Love -
Kelley

Kelley,
It is wonderful to hear your voice! So bright, so pure, so clean. It is so very easy and simple. The still mind is an illumined mind calling upon the wisdom of the ages in the present moment. That Light is the drawing power. It is the Alpha and the Omega.

Now while everyone else is thinking about attractive, I have the next step for you. What gets new people's attention?

I love you,
Dr. Barbara

The following email is from the Assistant Director of "The Chick that Took Over", concerning her involvement with a 10-year-old's first video.

Dear Dr. Barbara,

I thought I would write and tell you more of my thoughts and ideas that came to me this past weekend. "The Chick that Took Over" is cooler than I ever imagined and I am so glad I was able to be a part of it. It didn't occur to me until watching it with everyone Saturday night of how brilliant this undertaking is. I could imagine using this film (With consent from the director of course) to demonstrate what parents, teachers, caregivers can do with these young souls.

This got me to thinking of a workshop for these "ushers of indigo." What I have learned in assisting with this project is that you can teach with anything. In the beginning of creating this film it was as simple as listening to Hezekiah's idea and then imagining how we could create it. Did I know that setting up a few train set artifacts was going to work in making a city come to life? No, I simply took action on an ideal desiring to teach that you can create anything you can imagine. That is fun! That I think is the magic to aiding a child towards success. I definitely can see how the life skills that I have learned aided in assisting in this wonderful endeavor and that is what I have to give to any one who desires to teach the children of today. Any thoughts of how to present a workshop like this will be greatly appreciated and used. I have already talked to a couple of Colleges, Drury and Ozark Community College and there is a good possibility in a continuing ed course that will be for behavioral sciences. Thanks for your ideas.

I love you guys,
Laurie Jeanne

Dear Laurie,
Thank you for being your magnanimous Self! I have a strong feeling that many Indigo mothers are going to appreciate you at least as much as I do! You are awesome in our willingness to use what you have learned to aid all children. The kids in Springfield will benefit from your presence greatly. To further the college classes think in terms of how the movie was made. It might go something like this:

Week 1) Lecture on Indigos. Maybe have them take a quiz. Tell them they'll see a movie created/directed by a 10 year old Indigo next week.
Week 2) Show the movie. Discuss. Let them talk about what they see.
Week 3) Lecture on how movie was made. Steps Hezekiah took, steps you took.
Week 4) Guide participants through creative ideas they can do with the children in their lives.
Week 5) Discuss progress/show developing projects/ give feedback.
Week 6) Show results. Maybe have a festival for this, like a recital or movie marathon.

It's a possible outline. I can see it being very big at Unity churches and all the places where the Indigo Movie played a couple months ago. I didn't realize all of what we created either. As are most wonderful things in our lives, it is revealed to me in stages over time. It is good to see this through your eyes. I am very happy Hezekiah's little movie may be able to change things for other kids.

O Dr. Barbara

LISTENING EXERCISES

Exercise One

There is an energetic exchange that happens in listening. One person speaks and the other, the listener, gives value to the speaker. How do you give value? You very simply decide that you want to find something valuable in what the other person has to say. You don't have to agree with them, be persuaded, lose your identity or become like them. You just choose to welcome into your house a wealthy visitor who is going to give you a gold coin. The visitor is the speaker, and there is bound to be something they say that is useful, clarifying, cheering, illuminating, or informative to you. In that way, you give them value, you give them importance. Whenever you give your attention to someone or something, you are giving it value, importance and the tremendous energy and power of the focused mind.

Today practice giving your full and undivided attention to each person you meet. When greeting them say aloud, "I look forward to what this interchange will bring!" You may be pleasantly surprised at the way this admonition influences you and your partners in experience. Keep a journal of your encounters for later review.

Life Skill Math

Self Respect + Undivided Attention + Concentration + Memory = Listening

Following Christ Consciousness weekend at the College, one of the center directors came up to me and started talking. GZ has rarely started conversations with me. It's usually a cursory greeting, hug and then perhaps a little joke now and then. I was surprised at his attentiveness. I have heard from Matthew, a mutual friend, that GZ chooses to be around the people he believes have wisdom to offer him and chooses not to listen or be around those whom he feels do not.

I was in the midst of cooking Sunday dinner, which was a pretty simple meal and was well underway. GZ asked if there was anything he could do to help and I let him know he could carve the ham when it was done at 5:15 pm. He stayed around to talk.

At times my mind wandered and I had to bring it back. It was when I finally connected what I remembered Matthew had said, that I started trying to give him my complete attention. I assumed that he was with me for a reason and that by giving him my attention I would be better able to give to him.

It was hard for me. Through self respect, I realize that I was just as cursory as I believed him to be in the past with me. Through self respect, I realized that there was something that I could offer and gave him my attention in order to listen and receive. I never did really figure out what I could offer him specifically and became okay with just being and receiving who he is. I still felt my attention wavering at times, sometimes due to questions about what his 'motives' were, sometimes I had thoughts about dinner prep.

Then I realized that GZ really just wanted to talk about his thoughts. So I decided to just be with him and listen. At times I interjected something to think about. But mostly I just was. As a result I learned more about how GZ thinks and this brought a new appreciation for him.∞ –Teresa Martin

Exercise Two

I love music. Listening to it, producing it, moving to it, are all ways to align with vibration and allow it to fill my being. Through my years as a teacher music has been a means of teaching myself and others the power of thought. As a result I have come across many people who have been told at some point in their lives, and unfortunately believed that they "cannot carry a tune." Well, think about that! If you think you can't "carry a tune" you probably don't believe you can "carry a thought" either. That we can change when the individual is willing to practice concentration!

When I teach people to sing I tell them, "If you have a voice you can sing!" Having been told otherwise some don't believe me at first so we start with sighing. Everyone can sigh and most sighs start high and go downhill. Every notice that? Well, that's like sliding down the musical scale. Some of the fear of singing gets neutralized, right there!

Great singers are masters of listening. They can receive a vibration, embody it, and reproduce it. They can hold their attention in stillness to receive a pattern of notes then reproduce them.

Practice singing with your favorite singer. Record your duet so you can hear it later. What are you looking for? Blending. Seek to unite your voice with theirs. Listening to another sing, listening to you singing with another, are pleasurable ways to practice the art of listening and improve your command.

Voices are like instruments in an orchestra. Some are oboes others are piccolos. Some are bass drums, others violins. You can hum along with your favorite instrumental piece. Experiment. Find out which instrument your voice resonates with by singing along. When your voice seems to disappear, you've identified the instrument!

Remember the schoolteacher's dharma of attending? A couple years later, Dr. Pam Blosser wrote a song called "Be Still". The lyrics celebrate the connection between Undivided Attention, Concentration, and Listening. Listen and you may even hear the melody as you read her lyrics.

BE STILL

Be still and know that I am God.
Be still and know that I am God.
Be still and know that I am God.
Be still and know that I am God.
Yes, He speaks in the sunlight of the pink dawn so clear.
Yes, He speaks in the moonlight making shadows disappear.
And His whisper is the wind as it blows away our fear.
Yes, His voice is ev'rywhere when we can stop and hear.

Listening to Nature

Listening to nature can also be very mind opening. I enjoy listening to the animals and to the land around here. It is a really good practice ground and carries over in all areas of my life.

Last week Shanti, one of our milk cows, had a calf. On the second day Nick went out to look for her and Shanti had hidden her little one a little too well. So I took the next round of looking for her and asked Shanti to take me to her calf. I've found the importance to listening to animals while being here at the College. It has helped me understand how to work with them and understand their needs. So, with a little wack on her backside we took off walking, me, Shanti, and one of the other cow's calves who seemingly was concerned that the new calf was missing. We went deep into the woods and it was crisp and so still. Shanti mooed and waited a good 45 seconds with her ears perked up listening for a response, then the calf that joined us did the same thing. It was a wonderful example of the stillness that allows for listening (as well as being similar to a Marco Polo game). This continued for what seemed like 20 minutes until we were deep in the woods where the new calf could hear and moo back. As can be expected with these wonderful and funny animals, it was a joyful reunion.

I am amazed at what can be accomplished and the connection that can be developed through the simple act of listening. It is part of really being with someone and receiving his or her thoughts. This in itself, especially if prejudices are out of the way, can help someone tremendously to change, heal, to cross over to a new level of awareness of themselves. ∞ Ivy Norris

Listening to Your Body

A couple of years ago one of my health analyses stated that I had time set aside each day for spiritual practice yet there was a great need to listen more. The moment I heard this I saw that there was a connection with my need to listen and the difficulty with the very painful menstrual cramps that I had each month. Menstrual cramps have to do with difficulty in receiving. Listening has to do with slowing the mind down, giving the attention to someone, including the Self, or something, and letting in what is being given. I began to apply this suggestion and listen more actively.

One day here at the College of Metaphysics I had the goal of doing this. I caused it in every moment I could remember to and relished the heart opening experience it was. That night while asleep in the inner levels I experienced what I believe to be a dreamlike state of such blissful silence. There really were no images just the blissful experience. I awoke still maintaining this state, got ready to go take care of the animals and upon entering the barn I knew my world was different. I was hearing the Om sound, the sound of creation. For a moment I thought the guys who were milking the cows were chanting because there was a deep male sound to the tone. It was all happening inside of me. I caused it. Listening to the Silence is one of my most favorite and nurturing experiences I've found. ∞ Ivy Norris

Exercise Three

The highest form of listening is experienced through meditation.

Some experience meditation as contemplation. When we use the word in the School of Metaphysics we are speaking of the scientific application of the mind toward inner communion. The practice begins with undivided attention and concentration that is applied toward knowing the highest Self or the Creator. Meditation then becomes a progressive deepening of experience and awareness. As the student becomes more devoted in meditation the stages unfold the infinite nature of intelligence, energy, and manifestation. Here is the experience of one person who had been practicing this type of meditation for seven years.

Meditation Vision of the Universal Hour of Peace September 2001

I was a student at the College of Metaphysics during 1995. The College of Metaphysics is where the World Headquarters for the School of Metaphysics is based and students who have completed the first cycle of lessons are eligible to attend for a year intensive work study. As a student you live with your teachers and learn to live what you are studying. In October that year a beautiful idea was conceived and initiated - the Universal Hour of Peace. Held on the 50th Anniversary of the United Nations, we choose one hour (noon universal time) and asked people around the world to devote that hour to doing whatever brings them peace. The vision of the Universal Hour of Peace is based on the power of thought and the awesome power that a collective group consciousness can have around the world.

My wow story begins during the second Universal Hour of Peace (which is now held annually on January 1 at noon universal time). I was up early and decided to meditate on world peace. This is the vision that unfolded before me.

As I sat in meditation I was calm and focused. Gradually my perspective was from outer space looking at our planet. I perceived how noisy and loud our planet is relative to the rest of the galaxy. It reminded me of someone driving down the street with loud music blasting from their car and not caring at all about their effect on others or the environment. I was struck by how self centered our planet is. As I observed there was a shift in the energy around the planet. It seemed like things were getting more and more quiet. I watched our planet calm down and become more still. It was truly amazing to me to witness such a difference in one hour. I was certain of the power of peaceful thinking during this. I was grateful for all the souls who were dedicated to the Universal Hour of Peace.

This vision still lives in me today and brings me much comfort. One of the ways I changed after this experience was to develop a deeper devotion to a School of Metaphysics tradition called the Circle of Love. For nearly 30 years the closing of each class in metaphysics taught in any one of our schools is marked by people joining hands in a circle and visualizing light and love spreading throughout the country, world and universe. As I have practiced this both as a student and teacher for nearly seven years I have developed very clear mental images that I envelope with light. The image of our planet quiet and still is the central picture that I hold when I am part of a Circle of Love. It is awesome to me to imagine our thought form of light touching all the people in the world and literally moving throughout the galaxy and universe. A few years after my meditation during the Universal Hour of Peace I had this experience.

Eleven of us were flying from New York City to Delhi, India for two weeks of travel as ambassadors in the first delegation of Metaphysicians gathered by People to People (a not-for-profit organization promoting world peace by bringing people of different countries with like interests together). We had agreed before leaving that we would do a Circle of Love at the same time in India as our friends in the United States. This is traditionally 10:30 pm so our Circles of Love would be at 10:00 am while overseas. It had already been a big 48 hours leading up to departure with much festivity and anticipation as we left the College of Metaphysics and spent the night in New York with a whirlwind tour of Manhattan. I had fallen asleep on the plane almost as soon as we departed. Sometime later I woke up with surge of energy moving through me. I really felt energized and alert. I sat for a moment and wondered where the energy came from and my mind flashed to the Circle of Love. I asked around and found someone who knew Missouri time - sure enough, it was 10:30 pm. I realized the energy I felt came from the Circles of Love that our teachers and students were visualizing at home. My belief became knowing at that moment. The energy of our thoughts is real and tangible.

This experience brought me a sense of security that was new. I realized how powerful our thoughts are and that there never needs to be a time when I feel hopeless. I always have the power to make a difference by expanding my light and giving love to the world. I have drawn on this many times when events occur around the globe and I want to give my love and support. I send images of light to family and friends that I do not physically see often and it connects me with them. This was a solace to me in the days following the attack on the Pentagon and World Trade Center.

The night of September 11th I was at the College of Metaphysics. As was true of people around the country we had been in touch with many friends and family throughout the day and encouraged them to do Circles of Love that evening. We gathered in our main room to give our light to New York City, Washington DC and the whole world. As all of us visualized love and light encircling the globe I had the same perspective of our planet that I had seen during the Universal Hour of Peace years ago. I witnessed the most brilliant light shining strongly around our planet. I knew this was the power of thought and prayer from people everywhere and I felt assured that light and goodness is stronger than any darkness that is brought from those who live in the dark themselves.

The profound truth and meaning of these experiences continues to blossom in my awareness. The truth that we are all connected is growing from belief in my mind to a secure knowing. ∞ Dr. Christine Madar

"Imagination grows by exercise and contrary to common belief is more powerful in the mature than in the young."

– W. Somerset Maugham, 1938

"The Possible's slow fuse is lit
By the Imagination."

–Emily Dickinson, 1886, United States

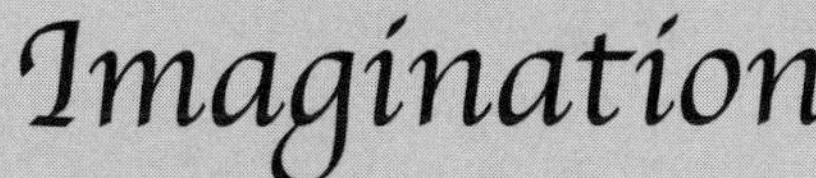

Imagination

Universal Language of Mind Story

True Arrow

Nasreddin went to the country fair to compete in the archery contest. All his students came along.

Each contestant was given three attempts to hit the target.

For his first shot, Nasreddin placed a soldier's hat on his head and stood very straight. He pulled the bow back hard and fired. The arrow sailed over the target, missing it completely and the crowd laughed.

On his second attempt, Nasreddin used less strength. His arrow flew straight toward the target yet lacked the energy to reach it. The arrow fell to the ground, many feet short of its goal.

With only one shot left, Nasreddin simply turned toward the target and fired the final arrow. Bullseye!

Everyone was stunned, then great shouts and applause rang through the countryside. The crowd was well pleased. They were astounded that the man they had laughed at could make such a perfect shot. They pressed him, wanting to know how he accomplished such a feat.

Seeing the hunger for knowledge on the faces of his students, Nasreddin said, "I will tell you. For the first attempt I imagined myself a soldier facing a terrible enemy. Fear caused the arrow to fly high over the target. With the second attempt I was thinking like a man who had missed the first shot had become so nervous that he could not concentrate. Weak with worry, his shot was too."

Nasreddin stopped.

Finally a student asked, "What about your third shot? Who fired that arrow?"

"That was me!" was Nasreddin's reply.

–a Sufi story

Imagination is a powerful tool for Self realization in the hands of one who knows who they are. Those who know themselves, trust their choices because they are willing to complete what they start. At peace with their own abilities they do not strive to be something they are not. They image being a better individual.

Nasreddin's lesson in imagination teaches the most important elements. First, when we pretend that we are something we are not the mind fills with fear causing us to overdo, feel overwhelmed, or exaggerate our situations. Second, once fear is allowed to take root it colors the Self image, dividing the attention and weakening the will. Third, when the disciplined mind is directing all thoughts toward the object of its desire, success is assured. The teacher had such control of his imagination that he could overshoot, undershoot, and perfectly shoot in order to teach his students a valuable lesson.

Imagination is the Essential Life Skill that insures progress of ourselves as individuals and as a race of people. Imagination enables us to become better tomorrow than we are today.

IMAGINATION

is using our creative intelligence to think in pictures in order to fulfill our needs and manifest our desires. Imagination is the ability to fulfill the seed idea. Ideals and goals give us guidance for what to do and who to be in the present moment.

"...a capacity for seeing and perceiving microcosms and macrocosms in ways that are far beyond what is common."
(91397BGC1)

"An effective imagination teamed with will, can accomplish anything including enlightenment." (SOM Lesson 5A)

"Imagination is the expression of our desire to be like our mental Creator. The desire to learn is a manifestation of imagination." (SOM Lesson 23)

Imagination is one of the faculties that made William Shakespeare describe man as "the paragon of animals." When imagination is used the right side of the brain "lights up" in wave activity. Imagination gives desire wings and hope the will to manifest.

Imagination is behind every child's daydreams, in front of every great leader. It is the inner desire to make a difference in the world and, in its highest manifestation, the desire to make the world a better place because we have lived.

Imagination is what is needed for any evolution of the spirit. Left to physical laws, evolution will continue through the DNA code. Imagination is the factor reasoning man possesses that can accelerate this evolution. This is much more practical than it may sound. Consider Tom and Dick. Born a year apart they have the same parents, live in the same house, have many of the same teachers in school. Most of their environmental influences are similar. Yet Tom and Dick are individuals.

Tom is the perfect child. Well mannered, quick and intelligent, he charms his teachers and makes the grades getting into the college of his choice. Dick is seen as different, a rebel, a problem child, a daydreamer, depending upon who you talk to. His teachers say he functions way below his capacity, and not being interested in college he follows what he is passionate about – computers.

Tom graduates with a MBA, gets a high level corporate career, marries a great gal and makes a family of his own in the mold of his own parents. Dick becomes a web designer, postpones the marriage thing, begins networking with others and finds he can make as much money as his university-trained brother. He sends his parents to Europe. Tom buys his family a house.

Tom and Dick are creating their own lives according to their images. "There is not right or wrong, only thinking makes it so," as that imaginative genius Will observed.

The reality that we make different choices is a function of imagination. So is the ability to see options.

LT is a blend of Tom and Dick. This 60-year-old male has served others all his life. His public service has included over twenty years in law enforcement followed by almost as many years in state government. Now as he enters this latter third of his life he is seeking a different kind of life. His love for people has driven him to help those in need, yet the ways he has served has tended to make interpersonal relationships difficult to sustain. In his earlier years when he might have married, he didn't think it fair to insist that a woman wait as he answered distress calls in the middle of the night. So he never married or had children. His experience has earned him wisdom yet he does not know how to share it.

This is what prompted LT to attend a Superconscious Meditation weekend at the College of Metaphysics. Hoping for intuitive insight into the direction his life might take, he received that and much more. His intuitive report (10999BGC3) highlights many of the same motivations and actions of his entire generation giving us keys to better understand that those approaching retirement have actually yet to begin their most important work.

LT's report first addresses how he focuses his attention. This is described as "quite powerful," the "crux of how the inner and outer minds are harmonized." The stimulus for LT to direct his attention has been "disparaging energies" meaning crises or conflicts. Being a sheriff, you can imagine what he may have seen and experienced over 20 years. LT was drawn to this profession, even when unpleasant, from an impulse "to right, to make things right, to aright, to actively move toward the resolve."

Injuries drove him to seek other means of filling his need. With encouragement from others, he ran for state office and won. He thought he would experience a reprieve from the stress of constant crises. What he found was the level of violence ceased and the crises were of a mental/emotional nature. Now his health was leading him to seek a different way to make things right.

> It has been fostered for a long period of time and it is very pronounced within him to the point that **this one has difficulty imagining other ways of being.** There is a very strong need for this one to be needed and it has been this underlying need that has produced within this one the kind of configuration of attitudes that have pushed this one in the directions that he has moved. It has also in that way furthered this one's growth and development in terms of soul progression and in terms of willingness to serve others. **(10999BGC3)**

Learning what the underlying, largely unconscious motivation of his life has been helped LT to put his life in perspective. He had always thought it was others who had the need and he was trying to be there to fill it. This information put a new perspective on the choices he had made in his life.

Most people go through life largely unconscious of the soul urge. They make choices largely upon external stimulus, what looks attractive, what sounds good, what feels right. Their conscious desires arise from outer world sensory experience. Wanting to love becomes wanting a significant other. Wanting self value becomes wanting money. Wanting to influence becomes wanting position or fame.

For the conscious mind to become aware of inner drives requires all the Essential Life Skills leading up to imagination. Responding to that drive requires conscious imagination.

> There has come a point, however, where this one no longer wants to continue in the same vein that he has become accustomed to and there is a desire for a very different way of experiencing this same inner sense. There is some reticence concerning this for there is not the imagining of the way and therefore there is some anxiety attached to making a change where there is not direction. **(10999BGC3)**

LT's report speaks to anyone who has experienced being at a fork in the road. There is a moment of openness where self-doubt can arise. What changes anxiety to anticipation? The capacity to image an intended destination.

LT's report told him that his reticence came from wisdom, from his considerable experience. It advised him not to see this as a problem. It states that he has a great capacity to "transfer the alignment of Self" into any endeavor. In other words, he need not be attached to the career. Who he is, how he thinks, and what he has to offer is not limited to any profession.

The report continues giving detailed suggestions on how the imagination can be used to affect the change he is desiring.

> First, he must recognize that this is true that the capacity within the Self is not limited to the means by which they

> have been used previously. Once this is realized then there can be the opening of the imagination to realize that the motivations that previously served this one well no longer will suffice and this one needs to pursue a different motivation that would be more directed toward a vision or an expected outcome not based upon something being wrong or disharmonious or ill, diseased in some way, but rather based upon the wisdom that this one has accumulated in terms of what can be and ought to be according to this one's determination. **(10999BGC3)**

When the reporter was asked for suggestions for attuning the conscious and subconscious minds to the superconscious mind for greater enlightenment and Self awareness, the purpose for LT's life choices were illuminated.

> It would greatly behoove this one to consciously direct the thoughts toward wisdom. To be more attentive to the wisdom that this one possesses. In his actions, in his mental actions, include the betterment of others, the passing on of the wisdom to others. It is something that will aid this one in expanding the consciousness so that it can be attuned to that which is present within the superconscious mind. As long as this one remains more physically dominant, in terms of thinking and action, this will be missing in this one's life. Therefore it is the expanding of the consciousness, even in the outer endeavors, that will aid this one for the attunement. **(10999BGC3)**

Few people realize or entertain the connection between imagination and wisdom. Most believe imagination is being different from others, or standing out in a crowd. Some deny their imagination with "I can't" attitudes. Spend ten minutes a day thinking about what will happen when more people see the connection between imagination and wisdom as described in this intuitive report. It makes for an exciting and attractive world!

The responsibility of society - the adults in our world - is clear. As we become more awake to the fact that we determine whether we see hope, love, joy, promise in the world, we can become worthy teachers and role models for young souls. When a child is told he is intelligent, energetic, and charming, he imagines himself in this image. He builds a belief in himself in accordance with the feedback he receives.

When an adult encourages a child to try new things then reprimands the child for turning over a plant or breaking a dish or cutting his clothes, what happens to that child's imagination.

When a child tells a parent they have seen this house before and the parent, knowing the child has never been taken to this place says, "No, you haven't." When the child insists, even to the point of accuracy, and the adults silence the child with, "Stop making up stories!" What happens to the child?

Who is the child in your life imagining himself or herself to be like? For children to create a different world, they need people who can imagine what that world can be and live it "as though." This is imagination in action.

How long does it take for a child to learn fear? An Intuitive Health Analysis (1797LJC4) for a six-year-old boy describes the effects of the undisciplined imagination, giving considerable insight for those who want to provide wholesome direction for young souls.

> We see that there are many fears that populate this one's thinking. We see that this one has a very strong imagination and that there has been some incomplete reception and understanding of experiences that have occurred in this one's life. Therefore, there are gaps that this one has filled in with the imagination. We see that there is an extreme sensitivity within this one and that there is not an accompanying discrimination. Therefore this one does absorb thoughts of others, particularly those who this one loves, and when this one does not understand the full implication of these thoughts this one fills in with his own imagination the remainder of this and is left with fear. (1797LJC4)

The report gave three recommendations for aiding this boy to value and direct his thoughts. First: "Would suggest to this one that it is important for this one to communicate." A combination of Self Respect and Undivided Attention are in order here. Self Respect will build this one's sense of self importance and encourage this one's willingness to learn.

Undivided Attention will teach him the value of each experience. Second: "Would suggest to this one to learn how to verbalize what this one is thinking." This requires others who are willing to listen to what this one has to say and give feedback that will aid him in developing his ideas. Third: "Would suggest to this one to also ask questions and to attempt to complete the kinds of thoughts that are incomplete." Again a good listener can aid this one to understand the fine art of concentration as it applies to carrying a train of thought. Although specific to this child, these suggestions can apply to anyone controlled by their fears.

The report goes on to describe this one's need for security and how it can be taught. Suggestions for building self-confidence and self-esteem are given. "Any type of creative project that has a physical outcome such as painting or drawing or making sculptures, anything that this one could make with the hands, cooking, would be of benefit."

This child is "highly sensitive emotionally", reacting to others' emotions. He does not yet know how to discriminate his own emotions for theirs. When mom is scared because he disappears in a store, his excitement of finding a toy he wanted is mixed with her emotions of panic and relief. She may be able to sort it all out, but he is left with mixed emotions he can neither explain or resolve. This affects the stomach and nervous system creating irritability.

The parents believed their child needed more independence, so they asked for suggestions on teaching this. The surprising answer proved to be an exercise in Self Respect for them.

> This one does not really need to learn independence. This one is independent. This one needs to learn security. Would suggest therefore that this one be taught how to trust the self, through speaking the thoughts. Would suggest that this one be given daily goals that are enjoyable to this one, that this one desires to accomplish and to note what this one has accomplished with praise that is genuine. Would suggest that this one exercise the creativity in ways that have demonstrable physical effects so that this one can understand the power of himself and to know that what he causes does produce effects. (1797LJC4)

The suggestion for daily goals gives both the parents and their child a direction to move in – mentally and physically. Through using attention to image something desired, the child can learn to discipline his imagination. With discipline he will have a powerful tool to use throughout his life.

Although it doesn't suggest it, concentration and meditation practices for the parents could give them the peacefulness *they* are lacking. If the child is absorbing fears and emotions from those closest to him, the greatest way these individuals can show their love is to change their own way of thinking, to improve the influence they have. Being able to discipline their own minds will eliminate many fears. It will also build a stillness that will calm the emotions. It will also provide a living example of how to use the imagination productively.

The report mentions that the boy has learned to cry to get what he wants. What he wants is attention, and suggestions are given for being more honest in this rather than pretending something is wrong when it is not. This is a misuse of imagination that the boy has learned. It can be changed, and is much easier to change when the ego is more moldable.

The focused and centered mind needed by children is addressed in LT's intuitive report. A meditator for a number of years, LT experienced difficulty keeping centered in the meditative state. The source of his difficulty and its remedy gives insight into using imagination to produce inner peace for us all.

> This (the difficulty) is noted and it does arise because there have been very strong habitual brain patterns established concerning problems or crisis as has been given. Therefore this one has trained the outer mind to rely upon this state in order for there to be the harmony spoken of. Therefore it is difficult for this one to seek harmony in a different frame of mind in a different state where the outer mind is no longer active or called upon to work.
>
> Would suggest that to see the two as completely different would aid. They are not the same. To then be able to envelope the mind with a still image that is very personal to this one. It could either be of his own acquaintance or

of his own making, but a place that is his and his alone where he experiences peace and stillness and calmness. This would be the place to cultivate, to go to, to learn to live there, to learn to exist there, to learn to be there, and to experience the Self there, would be the unfolding process that would aid this one greatly. This is all. **(10999BGC3)**

IMAGINATION

is the process by which people arrive at new and useful ideas.

Imagination
What is It?

Imagination is the spark of potential creativity that exists within every individual.

I was traveling on Interstate 44 one time from Springfield to St. Louis, where Schools of Metaphysics are located. I was about halfway there and all of a sudden the thought of chocolate chip ice cream entered my mind. There was no physical stimulus for it, no ads on the radio or Dairy Queens off the side of the road. I wasn't even hungry. I hadn't had ice cream for quite a while, and it wasn't even something I would normally choose to eat.

It seemed to appear from nowhere. That was probably why I noted it. It was so odd and out of character. The image however was very clear and I had to laugh.

I arrived in St. Louis in late afternoon. After visiting with the director and a few teachers, I decided to shop for groceries while they prepared for class that night. I went to the grocery store, and the memory surfaced of the ice cream thought. "This will be a great treat for everyone!" I thought.

I stopped at an ice cream shop on the way back to school and looked at all the many flavors. I smiled when I saw the chocolate chip ice cream because I remembered that crazy thought earlier. Although chocolate chip was okay, it wasn't my favorite and not something I would choose. I opted for chocolate almond fudge which more people enjoy.

When it came time to share the surprise, I opened the container and what was before me was one gallon of white ice cream with black chuncks of chocolate in it. For whatever reason, the company had put chocolate chip ice cream in a container labeled Chocolate Almond.

It's been a long time since I thought that coincidence rules the universe. Just as I do not believe that chance controls our destiny. Before me was evidence of the power of thought, the power of mind, the power of the image making faculty. The statistical probability of this happening is something like 1 to the 1 gazillion power. It doesn't even compute. Other forces beyond the physical had to be operating for me to be at this place at this time.

Had some unseen person been traveling with me that day and known about my thought of chocolate chip ice cream? Then had that person known that chocolate chip ice cream was in that one chocolate almond container that I chose? I don't think so! Something was obviously at work and some connection was happening. It's only the ability to image that enables us even to enter into this realm of reality.

Imagination is the world of dreams. The ability to create the man or woman of your dreams and believe that someday you will find him or her and someday you will create a life with them is a faculty, not of memory, rather of imagination. The ability to experience something and believe it can be different, to believe it can be better, it can have an outcome which is more whole, more complete, happier and healthier, is a function of imagination.

Imagination enables man to know Self as a creator. Imagination is what separates us from animals. By imaging, we create. With intelligence we can create anything we conjure up in our minds. Inventions, problem creating and solving, making things better, changing habits, becoming enlightened are all possible because we are mental creators.

Employing imagination opens us to the possibilities of a different way to look (think diet), speak (think foreign language or public speaking), live (think new job, house, position), or be (think self-reliant, self-disciplined, healthy). Imagination is how we humans express our differences.

Imagination is so important to us that we even give great credence to it. We call this fame, celebrity, and the image can sometimes be far from the truth. This is the challenge of humanity.

The ability to image is the ability to receive facts, information as it exists, and to begin to entertain new lines of thinking "if".

All of imagination which moves humanity into reasoning is based upon what follows that one word: "If".

The ability for compassion, for kindness, to love your neighbor as yourself, is a function of imagination. It is a function of your ability to place yourself in someone else's position. I remember as a single child, growing up I would travel with my parents. I would occupy the backseat of the car, often turning around to watch the parade of buildings and cars behind us. More than once I can remember looking over as we were stopped at an intersection at a car traveling perpendicular to ours. If I saw children I wondered, "What is your life like? Where have you been and where are you going? Are you happy? Sad?" I wondered what these kids were learning, what their teachers were like. I wondered what that kind of life would be like. I wondered.

The ability for wonder opens the mind to imagine. The ability to put yourself in someone else's shoes is the beginning of expanding beyond the limits of yourself and being able to recognize the kinship with all of humanity, the reality that we are all, in spirit, brothers and sisters.

I was raised to have an open mind, to realize that all people are related. We are all sons and daughters of a Creator. So it didn't matter to me the color of your skin, the accent in your speech, the level of your education. I wanted to know about YOU. The open mind, free of prejudice and undisturbed by memory thoughts, accelerates learning. Eventually, with imagination applied to produce reasoning, it no longer mattered to me if you recognize no god or hundreds. Imagination opens the mind to possibilities, and it opens the heart to magnanimous love.

Imagination enabled me to abide conscious thinking that enables me to embrace many people. My husband Daniel and I are raising our son with the experience of this reality. For him, it is not just a dream that all people can live together, all people can sit down at a meal together, all people can learn to get along, all people can learn how to coexist without fighting and hurting each other. The reality we are choosing to give to him by living at the College of

Metaphysics is the atmosphere of learning, growth, love, concern, truth, honesty, and change.

His ability to imagine will be sparked from this reality, where in my existence the desire or image of people being able to live in this way from choice was until the last decade of my life merely that – an image, a dream existing in the imagination only.

My experience is to dream and cause it to happen in all levels of consciousness. My life is about learning how to make those dreams a reality in my life and in the lives of others. My son's experience will be how to live the dream.

When I think of imagination and dreaming, the words of Martin Luther King Jr.'s "I have a dream" speech always resonates in my mind. This is a function of memory, yes, *and* it is a function of imagination because his image of all children living together in harmony is alive in my mind. It is one I strive to live daily.

It is this impetus that has served well in being able to cause creativity in the Self which is much more a function of the next Essential Life Skill: Breath.

Many believe they are not very good at imaging. They say, "I can't see things in my mind." Yet if you ask them to describe the house they live in, they can tell you its shape, size, color, and texture. They use their senses to describe the image they hold in their mind which feeds our minds the information it needs to receive and/or create that image.

There is an entire science that is presently being explored called synesthesia. This is one of the key sciences for using the imagination effectively. To be able to separate the five physical senses of sight, sound, taste, smell, and touch is to realize their subtleness in thought. This gives us the power to describe someone or something through the faculty of all senses. So when you think of your favorite pet you can tell someone what it feels like, looks like, smells like, sounds like and maybe even what it tastes like!

Because of our mental faculty we can taste success. We can smell danger. We can hear a choir of angels. We can feel excitement. We can see "it" coming. Image is all about what can be.

U.S. Senator Robert Kennedy once said, "Some people see things as they are and ask 'Why?' I dream of things that never were and ask 'Why not?'" I first heard this when I was a young teenager. At the time, because I was pretty much a negative thinker, a bit of a pessimist you might say, his phrasing appealed to me. My ego was stimulated by being able to see things that others didn't. In the ensuing years while studying and applying Universal Truth I began to understand the power of positive thinking, the ability to mold consciousness to transform the consciousness of lack or have-not to the consciousness of want and do. Making "it" happen is a function of positive thinking, and positive thinking is an expression of imaging that which *can be*.

So I have learned to think of Kennedy's idea as thinking of things that can be and making them happen.

This can be achieved through goal setting or idealism. I see them as related and different. Goal setting is a conscious action of the mind, a response to desire stimulated from our environment. In other words we want to be healthier so we set a goal of losing weight or we want to raise our standard of living so we set a goal of earning a raise or applying for a higher paying job or going to night school at a local university.

Idealism springs from the inner mind. It is more a product of subconscious understanding and dharma. For this reason it can be ignored or denied by the conscious mind. This may sound like cynicism or look like apathy. Idealism, respected, changes the inner and outer worlds. It captures the power of belief and mobilizes the will to experience, thus producing knowing in our lives. We live our ideals.

It was a combination of ideal and goal which brought to me the experience of serving as president of the School of Metaphysics at the age of 27. My ideal was to embody the teachings of the School of Metaphysics, to be a whole, functioning Self and accelerate evolution. My goal was to serve greater and greater numbers of people, personally and collectively, through that organization. In what position that might be did not matter. Perpetual growth did, and having a place to serve did.

At the time this took the form of watching and learning from the existing president. I noted what I and others learned from his thoughts and actions. This is how I had formed the ideal of serving through giving Intuitive Reports. I never gave much attention to being an intuitive reporter. My attention was directed toward how the reports aided people, eased their minds, stimulated hope, answered long standing questions. I wanted to help more people have access to intuitive wisdom, and I wanted more people to have access to knowledge of Universal Laws and Truths. This imaged thought, living and acting this conviction, shaped my future in harmony with my assumption that I can be a whole, functioning Self. This caliber of thinking is real to me and it continues to guide my life choices.

Today I do not know where I will be in ten years or what specifically I will be doing in the world. I do know that wherever and whatever, I will be more awake and therefore more able to embody cosmic consciousness.

I remember a specific moment when I was almost six months pregnant. I walked out of the main buildling on our campus to feed Sir, our college mascot dog. Standing up I looked around me and the thought came to me, "My life is about to change." It was a simple. all-encompassing thought that nothing would ever be the same again. It was in that moment that I realized the depth, with clarity, of what was about to occur. I had no idea in my conscious mind of what having a child would entail, what the changes would be. I only knew I was willing to respond, to do whatever it might require of me. I had the most profound sense at that moment that the change would pick me up and literally move me to an entirely different state of being.

Now ten years later that memory, that moment of imagination, comes back to me again and again as I live it, as it unfolds before me.

Imagination in the outer conscious mind is the beginning of what subconsciously is clairvoyance, the ability to see lines of probability. Probability is based upon all factors remaining the same. In physics this is akin to laws of inertia, that an object at rest tends to remain that way unless acted upon by some external force. What causes a change, what causes the outcome to be different, is the faculty of will.

Will is what engages humanity's potential. Will is what causes the memory and imagination to meet in the present moment to initiate something new. In that moment a new thought is illumined in the mind of the creator. Has every expectant parent had a similar moment of realization as mine? Perhaps. What makes the difference is when the experience occurs in your own consciousness. The concept of free will does not mean we can do whatever we please. Free will means our thoughts are creative!

We are all blessed by the brilliance of many. We ride in airplanes invented by someone who knows much more than we do about aerodynamics. The houses we live in are temperature controlled by a flick of a switch connected to machinery most of us will never see, much less understand. The miracle of birth astounds each one who experiences it. What makes the difference is how we use our imaginations to better ourselves and our world.

The power of imagination is perhaps best described in *Genesis* from the *Bible*. In the description of the creation of the world, God creates man "in his image and after his likeness. Male and female he created them." When you study that word, "image", you realize that what it's saying is that God, our Creator, our Maker, the One that brought us into existence, has the capacity to image, to bring forth with thought. This is the truth of the influence of imagination in our lives.

We are made in That image so we are an expression of God. We are also made after the Creator's "likeness" and to be like means to have similar attributes. We have that capacity to image and to express. So anytime that we are in the act of doing that – whether we're a child playing on a beach with sandcastles, or whether we're a 50-year-old corporate person drawing mind maps, or 98-year-old Grandma Moses working with canvas and paint – we are aligning and connecting our consciousness with that God image, that creative energy from the Source. This is profoundly healing.

It puts the life our thoughts create in an entirely new perspective when seen from the soul's point of view. Imagination is our vehicle to get there. •

The Mind Works in Pictures

When I was in the first series of lessons I learned to use a tool for visualizing called a Treasure Map. I had been taught that the mind works in pictures, and that the conscious mind plants seeds in the subconscious mind by imaging specifically what is desired. I had been a student for about 3 months, and wanted to move to a new place. I was living at the time in Ann Arbor, Michigan which is a college town. It was known for high rental prices and landlords who do not take care of the places they rent.

I had been accustomed to living in houses with 5 or 6 roommates, with somewhat crowded rooms and shabby furnishings. This time I decided that I was going to experiment with what I was learning about visualization and image exactly what I wanted. I wanted to live on a quiet street, with trees and a yard. I wanted a garden. I wanted a fireplace (there's nothing more comforting than sitting in front of a fire on a snowy Michigan evening!) And I wanted a piano. I also wanted to pay $125 a month rent. That's what I had been paying in the house I was sharing with 5 other people.

When I told my friends what I wanted they told me I was crazy. "You cannot find a place with all of that for that amount of rent. It's impossible!" they said.

I decided I would see how this imaging worked. I drew a picture of my final goal: a drawing of me playing the piano in a room with a blazing fire in the fireplace. Outside, through the window, you could see a flower garden and trees all around. Then, I drew 30 pictures in order leading to the goal. One picture showed me looking in the newspaper for housing ads. One showed me riding my bicycle to look at prospective places. One showed me talking to people to let them know what I wanted. One picture showed the notice board at the Student Union, where people advertised places for rent. And so on.

I did each of the activities pictured. On the 10th day, I rode my bicycle to the Student Union and looked at the bulletin board with places to rent. There was a notice from a professor who was going on sabbatical and wanted to rent her house. I called her up and she said to come over. I found the street, a lovely tree-lined street with huge mansion-style houses. At first I could not locate the address, and then I saw that there was a kind of arbor with a street number on it, but no visible house. I walked through the arch, covered with vines, and there was a little house that looked like it could have been in a fairy tale. A beautiful flower garden surrounded it. As I approached the house I noticed a vegetable garden growing by the side of the house.

I rang the bell, and a kind woman answered the door. She invited me into the living room and the first thing I saw was a piano! I looked around and there was a stone fireplace. She showed me around the house, which had three bedrooms, a living and dining room, and a kitchen. It was perfect! I asked her how much she wanted for rent, and she said $400. I quickly calculated, $400 divided by 3, which meant $133 per month for each person if I had 2 roommates. That was just slightly higher than the $125 I had intended to pay. It never occurred to me I might ask her if she would lower the rent to $375. I took the place, easily found two friends to share it with me, and soon moved into my dream house on a quiet street, with piano, fireplace, and two gardens! Picturing exactly what I wanted had worked like a charm.

Soon after this I started teaching metaphysics. I was so grateful for the teachers who had come before me, who gave me such simple step-by-step practices, that I wanted everyone in the world to have what I had. I often used treasure maps to aid my students to visualize a school full of people who were joyfully learning. ∞ Dr. Laurel Clark

Teresa Martin is governor of SOM Productions, the development of media for the promotion of consciousness. We collaborated on what became an amazing film about the quest to answer "Who am I?" called THE SILVER CORD. Based upon intuitive research, the movie is a product of permanent memory. The way we are sharing this movie with others, and the use we intend to make of it, is pure imagination! Teresa's story conveys how using resources is the result of ingenuity.

Wealth Comes from Using what you Have to the Fullest

I wanted to have better packaging for THE SILVER CORD dvd. We were using what appeared to be cd double disk cases for dvds, which was okay, but, for some of the people we would be sending them to, I wasn't really happy with it. I also wanted anyone who purchased it to be able to recognize immediately that it was a dvd.

I first accessed all of the materials that we had. We had the slimline cases, which at first seemed to be too flimsy. We had the cases that had been donated from Blockbuster stores through the efforts of Jason and Keisha, two students. We had printed covers for all possible sizes and labels that would work on the dvds, no matter what kind of packaging we had.

I recalled the kind of packaging that videos come in and the few

VHS's that were long enough to require two tapes. I haven't had much experience with renting dvds, but assumed the style of packaging would be similar. Then, I thought of simple ways to connect two dvd cases together and still be attractive.

Two of the slimline packages would be a good size. One by itself seemed kind of flimsy, but two seemed to be a good size in terms of looking nice on a shelf without requiring a lot of space. It opens like a book, so by taping two together it would be like reading a hardcover book although there would be no pages.

So then it was a matter of putting them together. The first thought was tape. I wasn't sure if the packing tape would be strong enough. When I tried it, I found that it was. It took some effort to pull the packages apart, so I figured that it would work just fine.

Then when I showed it to Dr. Barbara Condron, she added to it by suggesting that the inside covers could be useful in providing information for someone wanting to find out more about the school, SIR, intuitive reports and the website. I think between the two of us we have come up with a really good package that I would be happy to put in anyone's hands.

So now the next step is to get it into the hands of people who can distribute it throughout the country. Sending letters to distributors such as New Leaf and Ingram will insure its movement. There will always be a place that people can purchase this.

I am picturing it moving very quickly. As all of the centers come on board with the movement of THE SILVER CORD premieres next spring, with publicity going on in all of the cities, there are likely to be many people being introduced to THE SILVER CORD through the posters placed around town. It is likely that many more people will see it than will come to the premiere. So this means, that with the internet website, we will likely have lots of sales. This is important because we need to raise two million dollars for the construction of a building for our world headquarters. Receiving funds for this film can help us achieve this goal.

Through this movement of imagination, I realized something people need to know. Need, followed by the disciplined movement of mind, promotes creativity. For me, having a still mind enabled me to separate and identify components that resulted in something we were all happy with! ∞ Dr. Teresa Martin

Can someone who spent years obtaining a Masters degree in business administration leave the material world behind for spiritual heights? This great story written by one such person integrates several life skills, describing how they are applied to developing the skill of imagination. I call it....

BUDDHA COMES OUT OF THE CLOSET

The only one good use of imagination is to imagine being enlightened. Everything else is secondary. Really. All other uses of the imagination are for less than full illumination of the Self. Some may very well lead to enlightenment, like imaging teaching thousands of people. Other imaginings are entirely physical wants and are oh so temporary. More and more I'm reigning in my stray imaginings and choosing to image being an enlightened being, like Buddha.

Just recently, I settled on a most marvelous thought. I was out early one morning, walking, doing pranic breathing, spinning my chakras, and inviting in my highest self when all of a sudden I had the thought: maybe I could be a Buddha. I had entertained the idea a long time ago but it was not serious. It was intellectual and I had dismissed it pretty easily, citing so many attachments, distractions, and compulsions that it would never work.

This time, though, it was different. This time I was in the midst of doing spiritual disciplines and the idea went in and sat there. I turned it around in my mind. I held it there and considered that it will probably take many lifetimes of devotion, discipline and selflessness. I will require a lot of ego flexibility. I was excited at the prospect this time, I was using my imagination to image being an enlightened being, and it was working. I had emotional investment as well.∞ Paul Madar

"Imagine all the people living life in peace." – John Lennon

In 2004, College grad teacher Tad Messenger was among a delegation of metaphysicians who traveled to Puerto Rico for the second Alliance for a New Humanity conference. This experience with imagination arose during that conference.

Imaging World Peace

Imagination is the skill which makes gives us the opportunity to progress with awareness and on purpose. Whatever we can picture in our mind we can make happen. Whatever I imagine is real. The substance and energy has always been there. Nothing is new. The way we put different things together with our creative intelligence may be new.

Before I went to Puerto Rico, I imagined myself talking and being with people from all over the world who were united in a common purpose, to bring peace to the planet, to cause the reign of peace to exist throughout the world. One of my first experiences the first night, Wednesday night of the conference was Deepak Chopra talking about unifying to reach a critical mass where there would be world peace caused by the consciousness and the action of many individuals. I saw how the expression of the Universal Peace Covenant and the thoughts that have been imagined in the School of Metaphysics was in all the presentations. The thought of peace is becoming more and more a life's work for many people.

I remembered the images I created in my mind during Peace marches in 1969 and 1970 were an embracing of the family of man to live together peaceably. That image has been cultivated and nurtured for many years by many people. One Voice, the Universal Hour for Peace, the planting of Peace Poles throughout the world are a few among the many actions that have moved humanity toward the coming of an age where Peace will rule the nations.

The experience I received at the conference in Puerto Rico was the energy and the work that has been going on that all relate to images that each of us have created. The power of thought and the imagination can bring about tremendous transformations. It can transform the world.

I imagine myself becoming more loving, becoming more compassionate and caring. I imagine myself being an example of peace. This image has transformed me. I am no longer a mean, strict, uncaring, separate, selfish person. I am moving in the direction of my goal to be like Christ. To gain and build qualities of acceptance, gratitude, forgiveness, love, and compassion. ∞ Tad Messenger

ELS#6

A Short Class on IMAgiNatIoN

Dr. B: Where did we leave off last time?

TM: With expectant listening.

Dr. B: What makes listening "expectant"?

Dr. L The still mind.

LJ: Hope for a response.

JD: Imagination.

Dr. B: Yes, the still mind is both receptive and aggressive. In its receptive existence it draws to it. Absorbing stimuli. In its aggressive existence it changes according to what has been received. It is responding. Which leads us into the sixth life skill.

Let's first stay with what the first five skills produce for a moment. We teach listening through teaching meditation, and we teach meditation as a natural evolution of the skill of concentration. What are you listening for in meditation?

TM: Your teacher, your inner self.

Dr. B: Your inner self, your teacher, the Creator. The Creator is the Source of creation. So it is natural that listening to your Creator would unlock for you what creation is all about. Expectant listening cues you into your creativity. I have been consciously evolving, for the last ten years, how I view and therefore teach the First Cycle lesson material.

By the time I was in my early 20's I was wrestling with the programming of public schooling. Public schooling is supposed to teach you your place in society. It is to socialize you so you know where you can best serve. Upon graduating from the University of Missouri I was expected to create a life. Nobody taught me how to do that, but that's what I and everyone else around my age was supposed to do. It is a shared experience because the programming is similar. See the analogy to computer programs being the content for the brain?

PM: The computer-brain will only work according to the programs because the programs link the operator to the machine where the info is stored.

Dr. B: Exactly. You, the thinker, are the operator of the brain-computer. Let's keep exploring this line of thinking. So you're out here thinking, "I have to find my purpose in life, what I'm supposed to do." Your mind's very busy trying to figure all this out, because you're a decent human being and you want to do good. Because you have been programmed to fulfill a function in life and society, be it factory worker or physician, then that's what you're aching to do. Then that inner urge, the inner drive to fulfill your mission in life, speaks in a way that captures your attention. You hear it and you listen. Your imagination of "what could be" is sparked.

Now you go to a new level of thinking because you are opening your mind. You are beginning to think beyond what you have been taught, what the existing program says. The new program says you have unlimited potential, you create your own reality with the quality of your thoughts, you can be anything you imagine. Now you must digest this new information in the presence of the previous program. Sometimes this means you wrestle with thoughts like, "Should I get a better job? Should I have more money? Should I get married and have kids? Should I do all these things that I've been told all my life that I should do?" The old programming includes others who live by it - this may be family, friends, employers - telling you, you really should. "Yes, yes, yes. That's what I taught you. You better do what I taught you. You should, should, should. That's what life's about. You'll be sorry if you don't...." Dot-dot-dot, deet-deet-deet, and your brain's like a little computer and your mind is in there somewhere going "Whoa!" in the middle of all of it.

LJ: You're trapped in the box trying to live someone else's life.

Dr. B: Yes. How many people do you know who are trying to live out their mother or father's fantasy life. All well intended and well meaning, "I want you to have it better than I did. This is for your own good," some parents say. Only to wake up one day to realize what they have done may have been wonderful on the outside, but it is causing them heart problems, cancer, or diabetes on the inside.

TM: So there is a need to use creativity to heal.

Dr. B: The need to imagine something different. Henry Ford said, "There's a better way to do it. Find it." And a popular saying is "If you do what you've always done, you will get what you've always gotten." That's drawing on the same program over and over without ever programming something new. Using your programs creatively requires what?

JD: Imagination.

Dr. B: Asking the question, "What if." Throughout the years I have had occasion to aid many people in learning how to get a better job. Most of this is helping them to become aware of the beliefs they hold about themselves and the world. It is difficult to make $4000 or more a month;- *if* you believe you can only hold a minimum wage job. *If* you believe you have to have a college degree in something to make over $4000 a month. *If* you believe you have no skills. When you begin opening your mind to possibilities, your beliefs can change. What if a vibrant personality is worth more than minimum wage to an employer? What if a knack for writing poems can be harnessed into song lyrics or greeting cards or clever ad campaigns? What if a person you already know in your environment needs someone like you to housesit while they are out of the country for three months? There are infinite possibilities in finite experiences when you go outside the box, outside the confines of the programming that says "you are to do this", "you can't do that."

Dr. L: It is the ability to see differently, to see what your teacher sees in you, to admit the resources available to you. Many people think imagination is living in the future so they don't get anything done in the present.

Dr. B: The secret of imagination is that it only works well in the present. When imagination works out of the now. we, being so cleverly human, have lots of labels for what imagination produces. We have anxiety, we have worry, we have panic. We make up medical terms about it to describe it: paranoia, phobias; we create all kinds of apparitions when the imagination is operating in the future.

LJ: And we stay in the present through control of our attention.

JH: And concentration.....•

Hi Dr. Barbara,
Here is an experience my student had recently. She has been very successful at manifesting her desires! It is a joy watching her in action. This might be a good story to put in the (school newsletter) *Vibrations*.
O Rhye*

Picture Your Goals

When I first came to The School of Metaphysics, I was struggling with my ability to envision the financial success of my business. As the sole owner of an independent coffeehouse, I have seen tremendous success in nearly every endeavor, every piece of my dream but the financial reward for all of my hard work just would not come.

Before long, I learned that I am blocking my own financial success. The dream of creating a meaningful and strong community within my coffeehouse was my primary focus. While I handle the finances in a responsible manner, the money was not a definition of my success, it would naturally follow as my dream fell into place. But it did not.

I had spent 2 years of accomplishing goal upon goal, growing my business nearly 25%, yet I found myself owing $10,000 to my suppliers. While my studies with Rhye were helping me to understand my self-imposed limitations, I could not seem to learn fast enough. My business was in trouble and even my 10 Most Wanted List was not doing the trick. Why? Because I kept blocking the image of financial gain, it could not be associated with all of the goodness that my business was bringing to the community.

While visiting the Bolingbrook school, Paul Blosser suggested that I create a picture book to capture the desires outlined in my 10 Most Wanted List. Feeling like a 1st grader again, I accepted Paul's colored pencils and created a rudimentary drawing of each of my desires, including the $10,000 I would need to keep my shop open.

Sketching a manicured female hand gifting me with a $10,000 check did not necessarily increase my faith. But, without fail, several times a day I would thumb through my little book and believe the best I could. With this daily routine my faith increased. 10 days later a female customer (who is well manicured, by the way) approached me with an offer. Would I like a partner in the business? She LOVES this coffee shop and it can,t cease to exist. What would I need to keep it open? $10,000? No Problem. 4 days after that, she handed me a check for exactly $10,000.

We love our business, we WILL make it a financial success and we are achieving my (our) mission at twice the speed! Now, where are those colored pencils you had in first grade?

Mary*

Email 2

Hi Dr. Barbara,
I'm sending you an e-mail about moving from Louisville, Kentucky to Palatine, Illinois and sharing my experience and what's it like moving to a new place as a student.
Love,
Jessica

Why Move?

To some people moving to a new city, a new state might seem like a huge, dramatic thing to do. For my parents it was stressful and traumatic. To others, they didn't understand why you would want to leave your friends and family. A few were excited for me, craving the adventure and the change themselves. For me I was split down the middle, quivering, holding onto uncertainty, and deep down I wanted the change, the opportunity to manifest my ideals. So I left. I threw everything I thought I needed at the time into my 4 door Elantra, shut the door on what I had previously been for twenty-two years and was on the road towards something new, something different.

When I was younger, I always had dreams of being fearless, embracing continuous change and motion. Moving through experiences, not holding on to them. Living for the adventure. Then I find myself scared, vulnerable, wanting the comfort. My subconscious has given me what I wanted, because I'm here, now, in Palatine, with the opportunity to be who I always imagined being.

It's time to change. Am I ready? (aspects of me quiver with uncertainty) (other ones jumping around, excited, wanting to scream "Hell ya!") Go ahead, push me off the edge! No, wait a minute, I'll jump! Honestly, I should probably say that I miss Louisville, but I don,t. Actually, I don't miss parts of my self, that I'm going to graciously give to Louisville or at least leave there. My limitations, my doubts, my oh...so many fear thoughts. Well, at least as much as I allow myself to leave behind for now. I'm going to breathe. Accept. Surrender to what is and what will be. Trying to stay in the realm of gratitude. Dr. Paul has already given me so much, patience, acceptance, and understanding. Not to mention wonderful cooking! Thank you so much!

When I arrived at Palatine, that night I was in my new bedroom, putting my clothes away. I had a big goofy grin on my face, because I felt different. I didn't feel like me, the me I was use to. It felt strange, like I was putting away somebody else's clothes, somebody else's things.

Since I've been here and everything in my environment is new (trust me I've gotten lost a few times), I've had people ask me, "So how do you like Chicago?" I pause for a moment and think, "I haven't figured out I'm in a different state yet." I've thought about this some and I didn't know if I haven't really opened my eyes yet or if living at the school has something to do with it. The school has the same type of welcoming, loving presence that I've grown to know and appreciate.

So why move? Have I answered the question yet? I was hoping I could just gracefully move around the subject. I'm learning more and more that all I ever wanted, needed, and was looking for is inside me. That home is where you are, even if at times it's the roughest, most unloving one (maybe that's a scorpio thing). Every time I've been dissatisfied, it's always because I wanted more from me. I wanted to be able to give more, to be more. What matters more is the movement in your consciousness. Physical moving can help you look at things differently, it can support you in moving past your limitations and creating something new. I'm learning moving to a new physical location is not going to magically change you, that you change you. That change is a choice. I have to choose to be different, I have to choose to think differently. Moving may support that decision, that transformation, but it's up to me to move and change my state of consciousness and build more productive, expansive thoughts and habits.

During teacher's meeting, Dr. Paul Blosser gave a Bible study session on Chapter 22 of Matthew. By interpreting it in the Universal Language of Mind the story talked about commitment and how at times your thoughts and actions can waiver from that. And to me that resonated with me, because I feel like commitment to my self and even outward situations is definitely something I want and need to learn.

I made a commitment to come to Palatine and teach. I made a commitment to my ideals and my soul development. I wanted to make choices and decisions with my thoughts and actions that would align with that commitment. At times I have the doubting thoughts of "Do I really want this?", "Can I even do this?" I feel the animal instinct run through my thoughts, through my body, "Run now!", "Hide!", "Get away!" And that's where the reasoning and mental discipline I'm learning comes in. I'm learning to surrender and want to do whatever I can to teach and build a class of 10 students. And honestly deep down I'm excited, for the adventure, the discovery of really knowing who I am and why I am here.
-Jessica

Dear Jessica,
For anyone thinking of moving, you have just given them every reason to follow through. Thank you. For anyone who has moved, you have reminded them to revisit their own experience, update, and realize. Thank you. For anyone in a position to stimulate and offer others the opportunity to move "in the school", you have stimulated an inner urge toward generosity. Thank you.

I understand that you may be unaware of what you are being thanked for, your attention is on you and your learning -- as it should be. You are learning a very important lesson right now: how to use the 7th Level of Consciousness for soul growth and progression. This is the biggest lesson a student learns. It is the most challenging because it directly involves the transformation of the conscious ego. As the conscious mind moves forward, its intelligence receives the motivation and aggressively determines its direction. This is what you are practicing every day, and that is why you are growing stronger. Just by doing this, you are making quite a few people proud to know you, and in turn I believe that will include your parents. This kind of growth can be difficult for them to understand, so you will grow an amazing amount of compassion because of them. Cooperate and be willing to grow that huge heart. I know from experience it is worth it.

Now that you are settled in, teach as many people metaphysics as you can. Double and triple the size of the student body there in Palatine. It is a good time for Scorpios. Draw on the greatest power in our universe - thought controlled by intelligence to teach dozens. You'll love your experiences and they will remind you daily why you moved to Palatine!

I send my circle of love,
Dr. Barbara

IMAGINATION EXERCISES

Exercise One

A simple and very practical way to exercise your imagination each day is when giving or receiving directions. If you are asking how to get from the convenience store to the library, begin to realize how your success is dependent upon the following steps.

Step 1: Clear your mind with undivided attention.

Step 2: Hold your attention on the individual giving you directions.

Step 3: Listen with your mind so you can receive his or her images.

Step 4: Recall what you saw in your mind and heard with your ears to verify the directions.

Step 5: Now imagine how YOU will travel to your destination.

We enact these with little awareness, so when we need a skill in another area of life we don't think we know a thing about it. Yet, we do and we can improve. This can be practiced when telling someone how to bake a cake, balance a checkbook, or relaying and interpreting a dream. And it is particularly handy for students who must prove their knowledge on tests! Mental picturing is one of the most economical assets you have, and it is a common factor in all successful, wealthy people.

Exercise Two

Imaging Your Day

Most people are prejudiced against imagination. They hold onto early ideas that their day and night time dreams have little or no value. Maybe a class of 8 year olds laughed at their drawing and the wounded ego said, "Never again! I will not place myself in this position again." So the person has lived through 9, 12, 18, 25, 38, and upwards refusing to put the self on the line. For this person, the risk of using imagination has led him to refuse life. He or she "lost the love of their life" because the risk of being hurt, of being laughed at again was greater than the desire for love or companionship. Such a person ends up settling for the sales job, the desk job, the management job, when they could have been the inventor, the explorer, the CEO of the company. The truth is, when we spend our lives backing out of situations, what we lose are opportunities.

This is an exercise that will build your skill in visualization.

Choices.

You will need a notepad that you will carry with you throughout your day for a week.

First, write for 15 minutes answering the question "How imaginative am I?" Write in a continual flow, keeping your pen to the paper throughout the 15 minutes. Do not be concerned with ideas, memories or thoughts that may spring from nowhere surprising you. Likewise, don't be distracted by misspellings, poor grammar or other left-brain distractions. Your objective here is to continue writing your thoughts for the duration of the time set aside. Let it go. Do not reread it.

Day One

As you go through your normal day, note and record those activities you do daily. For instance, wake up, go to bathroom, get dressed, grab a cup of coffee, drive myself to work might be your first entries.

Day Two

As you go through your normal day, note the activities you do daily. Choose to describe them using adjectives and adverbs. For example,

"I awake easily before the alarm goes off." Or "I wake slowly after the snooze alarm sounds." Or "I get up before everyone else in the household." Whatever describes your activities, this is what you write for entries on Day Two.

Day Three

As you go through your normal day, note the activities you do daily. Choose to describe YOU in these activities. "I am happy in the morning." "I am grumpy when I get up."

Day Four

As you go through your normal day, note the activities you do daily. Think about how you usually are in each of these. See the patterns you have established. In today's notation, you determine if this is a pattern you want or do not want. Perhaps its usefulness has been served. Today you will determine this by a notation like this: "Waking up late and grumpy: Yes." Or "Waking up late and grumpy: No."

Day Five

As you go through your normal day, note the activities you do daily. As each arises, draw on your thoughts from yesterday. When an activity you said yes to arises, note the reason this is valuable to you. For instance, "Waking up early and happy usually makes for a good day. I think a positive attitude pays off." When an activity you said no to arises, think of what you might do differently in order to produce a new outcome. "Waking up late makes me grumpy because I have to rush" may lead to "If I choose what I'll wear and have what I need in the car before I go to bed I'll pick up ten minutes" or "If I leave my blinds open, the sun will come in and maybe the light and heat will help me wake up earlier" or even "I don't like my job, that's why I oversleep, and it's time I did something different!"

Let it all rest until Monday.

On Monday as you go through your normal day, note the activities mentally that you do daily. Before they arise, make a choice to either do the same thing you have been doing or to do something different. Write about each. The positive thinker might write: "Got up early. I am happy, looking forward to...." The thinker who wants change might write: "Decided before I went to bed that if I got up late again, I would get out of bed on the other side. I woke up late so I did this thinking this new action will change my attitude and therefore my day."

Practice this each day. Creating the kind of life you want and the kind of person you want to be in that life. At the end of this week write for a half hour on "How imaginative am I?" Now reread what you wrote this past week.. You'll be amazed at the change in YOU.

> *The most powerful way I use imagination is in daily practice of imaging my day. This includes my intention for my activities, the way I'd like to become and be as I do whatever activity, and the emotional picture of how I want to be, and then the specific activities. Using imagination in this way involves my whole mind. ∞ Paul Madar*

A Dharmic Lesson

Remember the excerpt from the Dharma Profile from the Undivided Attention chapter? It describes how attending became one woman's soul duty. That report goes on to answer several questions, one of which is most enlightening for the relationship between attention and imagination. Her question, in the form of statements about herself, concerns a desire to bring something new to those around her.

> At times this one feels like there are things in her environment that are not in harmony or disharmony within her environment. She tries to create harmony and is not always capable of doing this and would like to know what she can do to build an understanding of this also how to create harmony within the self.
>
> Harmony is not this one's dharma. Attending is this one's dharma. At times when this one becomes distracted other thoughts or ideas

> become important and therefore divert this one's attention from the essence that is attempting to come forward through that which has been described as attending. Therefore in regards to what has been queried, this pattern or constellation of thinking can be most easily recognized as a distraction away from that which will bring this one the greatest sense of comfort, power, security and aliveness. (1142000BGC2)

This response was mind opening for this woman who was about to experience her second Saturn return (an astrological phenomenon linked to an individual purpose and life mission). For years she had confused two of the Essential Life Skills: Undivided Attention and Imagination. This in turn led to fears for her adequacy in bringing to others something valuable or helpful, which is her greatest desire.

As you create in your image, keep in mind where that power begins – within. Turn your attention inward drawing upon your ability for Self Respect then direct your mind using Undivided Attention, Concentration, Memory, and Listening. In this way wishful thinking will be transformed into wish fulfillment, daydreaming into visualization. Whatever you create will be more whole.

> **This entity says, "How can I enrich my devotion to God through attendance?"**
>
> It would be of greater benefit for this one, greater help for this one to entertain broader images of God, images that are active through her rather than separate from her. When this one is in attendance there is the completeness. It is whole. The experience is profound. To think in the manners in which the self is separate from God or from any one or thing that this one is attending is to move away from the dharma itself. This is all. (1142000BGC2)

"To go fishing is the chance to wash one's soul with pure air, with the rush of the brook, or with the shimmer of the sun on blue water. It brings meekness and inspiration from decency of nature, charity toward tackle-makers, patience toward fish, a mockery of profits and egos, a quieting of hate, a rejoicing that you do not have to decide a darned thing until next week. And it is discipline in the equality of men – for all men are equal before fish.

–Herbert Hoover, 1920

from Egypt

The creator of the world was the sun god Ra-Atum. The priests of Heliopolis told how Ra-Atum emerged from the chaos and gave himself human shape. He then sneezed into the space around him, and from this action he created the air god Shu and the moisture goddess Tefnut, the ancestors of the other gods.

from India

Ancient scriptures known as Vedas speak of Vayu, the god of air and wind. Vayu is present when the warrior leader Indra fights battles against evil demons.

from the Middle East

After the first great creation, the Lord God began making the earth and heavens. Before there was any rain, a stream welled up from the earth, watering the surface of the ground. The Lord God formed man out of the clay of the ground and blew into his nostrils the breath of life, and so man became a living being. –*Genesis 2:4-7*

Breath ties the soul to the body.

Inbreath is the first action of the newly incarned soul, and the outbreath is the last action of a lifetime. All the breaths inbetween are opportunities to experience the depth of life-giving connection from the Source of Being. The spirit of God moves through breath and forever gives energy to the whole system, mentally, emotionally and physically. As these quotes reflect, such understanding has pervaded our planet for millennia.

When we focus on breath we cause the physical body to be relaxed. We cause emotions to be calm. We cause mind to be still. When all of the attention is focused on breath, the mind cannot think other thoughts that might disturb its peace. Each individual can choose to breathe rather than argue. Breathe in place of fighting. Breathe instead of recoil.

Breath connects us with the Earth and with the Universe. It both grounds us and frees us to the heavens. Breath enables us to "refresh, to heal, to inspire" as the ***Universal Peace Covenant*** eloquently describes.

If breath does indeed tie the soul to the body, how does that occur, and why is it so? This is what we will explore with the seventh Essential Life Skill – Breath.

BREATH

is spirit in motion, continuous giving and receiving.

INTUITIVE RESEARCH

BREATH ties our soul to our physical body. Infinite energy moves through us at all times. Breath is spirit in motion, continuous giving and receiving.

> "It is through the complete giving of energies, be they time or money or possession, or love or wisdom, or creativity--through the complete giving of energies this one will find a complete return." (913994BGC)

"By learning to breathe intentionally, consciously, you learn how to draw upon cosmic energy directly, energizing mind and body." (SOM Lesson 12)

"Breathing is the expression of universal energy as it manifests itself through your individual physical form." (SOM Lesson 17)

Ivy Norris has endured physical pain much of her life. It has led her to investigate, learn and develop her own healing potential. She recognizes the power of breath to place us in the present moment and sees breath as a powerful discipline for facilitating change, growth, alignment, healing and connection.

"When I wanted to go without anesthesia for the dental work I had done last year," she says, "I used breath to ride through the pain and remain relaxed."

"When I want greater insight into my state of consciousness, I observe my breath. Am I giving and receiving with fluidly, are my mind and my heart open, am I being honest? All of these I can see with observing my breath."

One health analysis recommended breathing techniques to help calm and balance Ivy's nervous system.

> "This one tends to hold the breath, and therefore there are many times when there is a lack of oxygen ,and this is part of the difficulty with the energy. There are times when this also produces a kind of fogginess within the thinking. Deep breathing as a regular practice and causing the breathing itself to be rhythmic rather than this occurring only at times of crisis would be of benefit." (090720041LJC)

Intuitive Health Analysis is a tool every health practitioner needs to use. Each report offers insight into the mental and emotional factors affecting the individual's physical health. Breathing serves many purposes in this pursuit. Often breathing patterns will be recommended to stimulate thinking, to help blocked energy move, to oxygenate the blood, to cleanse the cells.

A man with lungs weakened by smoking tobacco and work environments finds among the suggestions given is a particular breathing pattern and aroma therapy designed to cleanse and strengthen his respiratory system.

A woman with digestive problems discovers how diaphragm breathing will cure chronic constipation. Another is taught deacelerated breathing to ease a racing heart.

One analysis reveals how an infant is moving away from connected breathing patterns and toward holding the breath.

Breastfeeding is recommended for its close connection with the mother as well as physical health benefits for the child.

A woman in her mid-20's discovers the headaches she has suffered since her teenage years are related to an unconscious attitude of shutting down. Since she prides herself on being open this is a surprise to her initially. She is aware of feeling separated from her real desires asking, "Why do I feel disconnected from my inner Self, and how can I change this?" The report says, *"This is due to the shutting down or clamping down that has been spoken of primarily with how this one receives the stimulus and then shuts it off."* Here is the description of this woman's mental system during the time this analysis was given.

> We see within the mental system that there is frustration at times that this one does entertain and play with. We do see that there is a kind of clamping down of this one's thinking and thought processes at times.... This one does have the ability to be very gregarious. This one does have the ability to cause there to be a great movement in short periods of time. However, this one does use the ability against the Self at times where this one does clamp down as this one would see it on things, and then the thinking is affected by this movement. We do see that when this occurs the thinking slows down, the thinking processes become unclear to this one. We do see that this one then becomes irritated and annoyed, and then this does lead to the frustration that this one does experience within the mental system. (5252003TAP1)

This report describes in detail how the restriction of energy in the mental system – the thoughts and attitudes – is present in the emotions and physical body as well. In the emotions this registers as frustration. Far from a negative "bad" feeling, the frustration is what allows this woman to slow her thinking. In other words when she is frustrated she wants her mind to be still, she wants everything to be still. Her body then tenses, restricting respiration, then blood flow. Tightening in the nerves and even the bone plates that comprise the skull create the feeling that her head is in a vise, typical of migraine headaches. This repeated physical restriction is producing anemia in the body as well as fatigue.

Suggestions for care of the body include:

•Diet: Water. Green leafy vegetables. Red meat, particularly liver. Carrots, especially eaten with the red meat.

•Therapies: Accupressure along the boundaries of the head plates.

•Exercise (movement): Swimming, yoga.

Both recommendations for the type of exercise employ conscious breathing. Hatha Yoga, the system most familiar in the West, is a system of union based upon postures and breathing working together. The focus is mental and emotional movement as much as physical movement. Mental posturing of focus and concentration employ the initial Life Skills. This enables the person to listen to the body, giving it new images of health and updating cellular memory. When breath is used properly the imaged change is enthused throughout mental, emotional, and physical systems of the whole person.

The suggestion for swimming made a lot of sense to this woman. Swimming had been part of her life all along. She even managed a swimming pool for a period of time. The insight the report gave her concerning her need for perpetual motion is a key to longevity and immortality. This inner drive is appearing in more people as our race evolves. It can be seen particularly in children and is often feared and labeled as attention deficit hyperactivity disorder (ADHD). The label exists so a diagnosis can be made and drugs can be administered. With the capacity for breath at her command, this woman need not fear becoming dependent upon pills or mechanical devices.

Moreover, great insight into the causal factors at work in the compulsive need for movement is described here. This wisdom has universal import for all of us who are ready to make that evolutionary leap into identifying Self as energy:

> We do see that this body is very prone to movement because of this one's ability to receive stimulus and therefore this one's body has a pattern of energy that does exist within the body that is ready for motion. Therefore when this one ceases motion and stops motion

> in any capacity there is the backing up primarily within the area of the head and the nervous system. This does tend to affect all other areas within this body when this does occur.
>
> Therefore, any kind of perpetual movement that can be endured with the body would be of benefit for this one such as swimming, such as yoga, such as this one utilizing this one's goals individually and collective or common goals to make choices, to follow through on movement of this one's ideals. (5252003TAP1)

So why is this need so strong in this woman? Why was this happening to her? Upon hearing the report she didn't grasp the cause of the problem and said, "I don't have a picture of what clamping down in the mental system means. Could this be explained?"

Here is the answer given.

> We do see that this one receives the stimulus into the Self with much light, and then this one allows the thinking to move very quickly to something else. This one loses the train of thought, and then this one needs to go back in order to connect with what the original stimulus was. When this one goes back to the original stimulus then this one clamps down on the thought, tries to remember it, tries to capture it, tries to receive it again, and these attempts are failed for this one is trying to recapture something that has been lost. That is what this one is seeking. It is this one's natural ability to receive in any moment in any movement with every breath. Would suggest to this one that this one simply allow (Self) to receive stimulus. (5252003TAP1)

Additional suggestions for the mental system taught this woman the steps she could take for giving self and others "breathing space".

> Would suggest to this one that (the frustration) is a choice for this one to allow. It is a choice for this one to allow any energy, any thought, any movement of any thought in any order to exist within this one's consciousness, within this one's energy or energy field and within this one's life.

> Would suggest that this one take greater care with this as if this one was tending a garden. For we do see that this one does have experience with this, and this picture would aid this one to be able to cause there to be greater care with allowance. When this does occur for this one the frustration will not be there. This one's natural ability to be able to receive a stimulus and cause it to move through her will shine. (5252003TAP1)

A year before receiving this Intuitive Health Analysis, this woman attended the Spiritual Focus Session on the Life Skills and wholeness. The intuitive report given during this weekend is called the Healer's Portrait. The Healer's Portrait describes the outstanding pattern of soul understanding related to health and healing. This can be applied to self and others. It is a phenomenal tool in the hands of any parent, care giver, and health practitioner, anyone who interacts with others who trust and rely upon them.

The information in this woman's Healer's Portrait sheds light upon the health analysis we just discussed. It explains the driving force within her for perpetual motion in ways that can useful instead of debilitating. The Healer's Portrait (3902BGC6) opens with "This (pattern of soul understanding) would be curiosity." It then describes the mental action.

> The availability of receptivity in its most open and fertile form is essential for wholeness and for healing. In order for there to be something whole, there must be a receptor for it, and we see that the capacity for curiosity is that which does mobilize the receptivity into action. Therefore, there can be the aggressive and receptive principles at work to form something that is whole and complete. We see that this one has brought to the Self an interesting and incomparable cluster of understandings which does cause there to be intense scrutiny and discernment. This then is expressed through this one's curiosity and desire to know. We see that it is when this one acts upon this that the greatest ability for wholeness is experienced in herself and with others. (3902BGC6)

The source of this woman's pain is described here as doubt. Through eliminating the second-guessing, the feeling that she has missed something or lost something, she will free herself of the pain of self-doubt.

> It is this movement (eliminating doubt) that will then open this one to the wholeness within the Self and this one's influence with others in regards to the wholeness. This one tends to only give pieces of the Self, and this is not compatible with her being, therefore, there is pain associated with this. When this one gives completely, there will be no pain. (3902BGC6)

This woman asked for and received suggestions for stopping her headaches. Contrasting the response in the Healer's Portrait with the information given in the Intuitive Health Analysis is a demonstration of how the two work together. Given by two different conductor/ reporter teams, a year apart, the connection – the breath if you will – between the two is intriguing.

> **This entity says, "How can I use this quality of curiosity to permanently heal myself of migraine headaches?"**
>
> By exploring and sinking into the receptive nature of the Self. By understanding and exploring the ability to draw to the Self that which is desired, to elevate this one's thinking toward purity and goodness so that this one becomes confident that this one will only draw to the Self that which is compatible. It is when this one doubts this that there is difficulty, and when the doubt begins then there is conflict and fighting in this one being torn between the limitations of the physical beliefs and the inner sense of knowing that does make itself pronounced within this one. Therefore, it is through the stilling of the outer mind, so that the minds can be aligned, that there can be the embracing of the condition of receptivity, the expectancy. By becoming more mindful of how this one is aggressive and becoming more purposeful with this as well as using reasoning as the foundation for it, there would be a much greater sense of freedom in being able to expand and to begin to cooperate with the Self. Where there is cooperation there is not room for conflict. (3902BGC6)

In Oriental forms of movement from sacred dance to tai chi, breath is the way to understand and unite with universal forces. The reception of cosmic energy into the Self enlivens the mind and provides the life force for the body. Yes, as evidenced in some martial arts, breath can be a powerful weapon that can cause destruction. That is owing to the individual wielding the breath, not the breath itself. How much we respect breath, how attentive we are to its movement is the beginning of knowing the unity of all life and an act of homage to a Force greater than ourselves.

In a Meditation Portrait (101400BGC6) done some years ago, a woman asked for suggestions for attuning the conscious and subconscious minds to the superconscious mind. Here is the answer she received.

> As there is the flourishing of the embracing of movement in the consciousness there would be the tapping of energies that this one has yet to experience. It would give this one a sense of aliveness that this one has been unaware of heretofore. It is through the receiving of superconscious energies that this one will find expression of the motion that is life itself. In order for the alignment to occur this one must be willing to move. Would suggest that this one seek the rhythm to utilize the intake and exhale of breath as a point of focus to become aware of motion and rhythm. This would greatly aid this one in the alignment. This is all.

Breath
What is It?

What light is for the intelligence of humanity, breath is for its energy.

Yogis can direct their breathing in such a way to slow down their internal organs and to increase their brain wave activity. The breathing almost ceases entirely in the deepest of meditation as the body essentially switches over to a suspended state of animation and sustenance from pure energy rather than internal combustion. As the yogi comes up from this deep meditative state, the breathing begins increasing and the body's internal combustion engines begin again.

These ideas seem foreign to the Western, more materially-oriented mind. We would rather stimulate brain activity through a movie or video game than through meaningful discourse and days alone with nature. When hungry, our first thought is chemical rather than electrical. We think of ourselves as matter beings when it is our destiny and within our power to think of ourselves as energy beings.

Breath is the way the body drives its energy system, just as a air feeds a fire. Its importance to us is everywhere in our lives. The reason why aerobic exercise is health-producing is not because the heart has to pump harder, thus moving blood through the circulatory system for cleansing. It is because we breathe more deeper and completely when the body is taxed. It is the breath that stimulates the cleansing that brings health. It can also bring miraculous healing.

I have experienced this many times throughout my life. In my childhood I lived with a Christian faith healer who helped many to be free of their afflictions. His hands-on healing enabled the deaf to hear, the lame to walk, and many to be freed from the slavery of chronic pain. I didn't understand how he did this, nor did he other than to attribute it to a Higher Power. I did feel the energy in the room when he would heal. I remember the dynamo and hypnotic effect of the cadence of his speech. I remember breath.

In those early years I appreciated breath according to my activity. Its relevance to my performance, my ability to do something in the outer world, became apparent when I would try to swim long distances underwater or when I would want to hold a note for several measures while singing. The expression of the self through speech is a function of breath, as is the staggered gasps arising from fear or emotional distress.

In my studies with the School of Metaphysics I became aware of breathing patterns, practicing different ones for specific purposes. Through these I experienced the power of mental breath, the breath of God. By far it is intuitive breathing which has produced the greatest depth of wholistic healing. Is breathing an alternative healing method? I suppose to some it probably is. Since it is something we all do every minute of every day of our lives, it seems silly for me to think of it as "alternative". Afterall, the alternative to breathing is not breathing, and we all know where that leads.

I have experienced and witnesssed some instances of miraculous healing owing to how the breath is directed. One involved someone who became very dear to me. His name was John and in the Universal Language of Mind, the symbolic language used by the inner mind, his namesake, fittingly to our interaction, represents the quality of believing. The story of what intuitive breathing brought to us both begins with something I wrote some time ago. It describes how knowing John helped me to understand the meaning of "breathing space."

SPIRITUAL BEINGS HAVING A PHYSICAL EXPERIENCE

It has been a long journey for John, and the rest of us who have grown to love him like a brother. A journey that has led to his twilight of blindness and failing kidneys, both the natural progression of medically treated diabetes. I know that John's life story could have been different, and it is only in the past several years since disease has entered my life through family members that I have been visited with an ever-increasing comprehension of health.

We all wanted John to change. Because he had the power. With each successive examination of his mind and body, the answers were there. John refused to see.

Eventually we had to, each in our own time, admit that no matter what we could see in John – the charming manner, the multifaceted talents, the comfort-producing wit – John did not share our perception. To the degree this was true, John was power-less.

And so his physical disease, juvenile onset diabetes, followed its "natural course" all the way to dialysis and the impending kidney transplant.

For John it is probably his siblings' offer of their kidneys that has jolted his consciousness out of denial. Gratitude is dawning in his consciousness as never before. As another healer observed about John, "He's arrogant. I have rarely met anyone more in need of humbleness."

The Lord works in mysterious ways, I was taught as a child. And He has worked perfectly for John, the little hurt boy who didn't get to do what he wanted and vowed to never let anyone hurt him again. John the man who built such a tough shell it became an impermeable barrier when he wanted out, when he wanted to give. When life was easier, he would not surrender his ego. As life gets harder, it is more difficult for him to stay the same.

That's one of the lessons you can learn from having a John in your life. Anything you can change for the better, do it now. The rest prepare yourself so when the opportunity arises you are ready to respond.

I know John's brother's willingness to give "the gift of life" has impressed John's consciousness as nothing else has. It is the heighth of unconditional love, a love John could not even imagine before now. John's brother is doing what he believes is right. He has uncompromising faith that it is God's will and whatever happens to him, his wife and children, his brother, and the rest of the family is truly in God's hands.

The difference is John sees it all as a matter of winning and losing; John's brother believes it is providence that can only foretell good.

One way of viewing the world looks at the flesh only, taking its pleasure from the moment without thought of payment. It produces a dying life, a physical engrossment that leads to dependency, neediness, hopelessness, and fear.

The other is the material world viewed through spiritual eyes lifted upward toward God's grace. The power of faith to do all we can while the opportunity is present, and leaving what we may not see to He who is greater than any of us.

I believe I have become a better person because John Clark is in my life. I know I have come to understand much of what puzzled me, personally, before. He has helped me ease my pain of the space between knowing what "can be" and accepting "what is". That has made me better able to minister to others. He has brought a grace into my

> life, that helps me give more completely, more freely.
>
> I have a new understanding of healing I didn't know before. A fuller understanding of being in the present and the place faith holds. The more intellectual, brain-oriented among us say faith is denying the facts. There is a difference between "facts" and "truth". The first depends upon time passing, an assessment of what has occurred; the second is timeless.
>
> Perhaps the misunderstanding arises because believing for many is an intellectual idea.. *Faith requires action.* Mind action. I can buy $200 worth of groceries, if I only believe I can eat the food, I will die. That's the difference between believing and faith. Faith carries us upward and forward, in harmony with the natural rhythm of spiritual progression. It evolves us into knowing. Where there is knowing there is peace. Where there is peace there is love and beauty and balance and wholeness and integrity and honor and communion. All that comprises well-being that we think of as health.∞

Two years later, I found myself in the position of teaching John how to breathe connectedly over an extended period of time. This type of breathing is known by many names, rebirthing being the most famous in the West. It also produces many effects. I have found that breath reflects what we bring to it. It gives in accordance to how we give, so for some breathing practices can bring physical relief. For others, emotional release is the reward. A few experience freedom from the body enabling the soul to come forward and the spirit to experience ectasy. For those familiar with Biblical teachings this is what it means to be born of spirit or reborn.

For John, breathing was arduous. If you haven't experienced connected breathing, you may think, "What's so hard about watching yourself breathe for an hour?" That is a good question, and one you will only answer by experiencing it for yourself. By this point in his life everything having to do with his body took effort – the dialysis three times a week, the blindness, the nerve degeneration desensitizing his body. What happened to him because of his efforts to consciously breathe and what I learned in the process is an inspiring story of ancient science meeting modern technology. The following excerpts from notations in the scientific journal I keep on pranayama research explain.

May 2000

JC is consumed by the condition of his physical body. Even when he wants to think of other things, his physical limitations are always in his consciousness. Diagnosed at the age of 15, JC has sustained his physical body on external sources of insulin for almost twice as long as his body worked independently. As a result he is blind and his kidneys no longer function. Every other day he must spend three hours or so tethered to a machine that filters the waste from his body.

JC had had one rebirthing session before coming to me. The first session left him exhausted. He had concluded this was because the rebirthing followed a dialysis treatment, which at this point, because of its unnatural means of purification, drains JC of energy. JC was putting out energy from already depleted stores. I concluded the draining did not occur from the amount of energy expended, for when breathing becomes metaphysical it replenishes owing to its cyclical nature. My conclusion was that what happened to JC in the first session was an incomplete breathing cycle. Like sexual activity without orgasm, there was a lot of heat and little light produced.

This was not a negative thing. It was not punishment from some unseen God. It was not a sign to never breathe like this again because it made him feel bad. It was not because the rebirther did not know what he or she was doing. The beauty about the breath and mind is they are both subject to the laws that govern our universe. Therefore, each of us brings to us that which we have full capability of responding to and understanding. We can always handle what life/karma/God brings us. How we choose to respond tells us everything we need to know at any given moment. JC's first session was the manifestation of JC - his thoughts and attitudes about himself, his life, his condition.

I had counseled JC for over two years, since the blindness started manifesting. I had known him for over a decade and had even officiated at his wedding. I knew him well. I also knew that rebirthing, working in this manner with breath, could open doors for him that at best would lead to improved health and at its weakest might lead to illuminating experiences to assist him in separating from the physical body thus making his transition of death easier.

I learned from this first session with JC that people with a strong death urge, as Leonard Orr (father of rebirthing) calls it, have unconsciously and consciously accepted the inevitability of an end to physical life and because this is true they have accepted a death sentence. JC was given his at the age of 15. His parents accepted it, from their beliefs, seeing turning their son into a drug addict the only alternative to his death. When that's all you are willing to see, all you are willing to investigate, it limits the information you can believe. The imagination is left barren, and memory takes over in the form of other family members who "shared" this condition or strangers who have managed to extend the days of their lives if sacrificing the quality.

All of us grapple with this belief for it is without doubt the most predominant belief in the collective consciousness of humanity. At least as strong as the belief that you must mate and reproduce the species. The animal drives of the body are still predominant. Survival remains a potent one, and so we fight what we believe threatens our survival. So JC became a legalized and socially-accepted teenage drug addict. Reasoning man in the form of medical chemists had extended his death sentence without ever addressing the cause: JC's consciousness. It was my hope that through using breath in the form of rebirthing JC would be able to come to awarenesses and answers that had eluded him for years.

Since the rebirthing is an engrossingly personal experience, here might be the actual engagement of JC's mind. Rebirthing might just figuratively and literally pick JC up and deposit him in a completely new place of enlightenment. His own breath might be the missing link to a transformation that nothing else had been able to bring about.

Hearing about JC's first session was an eye opener for me. I had expected more. I had expected him to experience more, to receive more from the experience. When I separated my expectation and hope for JC, I could clearly see how his experience was the expression of JC's thoughts. ***JC had JC's experience****, not the one I could imagine for him or one like all others I knew of to this point. Of those rebirthing, JC was my first contact with someone who possesses - literally - a prolonged illness. Realizing these truths was important in order for me to assist JC without interfering in his process. This was my mental preparation before this psi counseling session.*

I was pleased with JC's willingness to work. Based on what he told me about his first rebirthing session we decided to use two pillows to help elevate his upper body. In the first session one of his discomforts was the tendency for fluid to back up in his lungs, a chronic condition JC accepted as the result of dialysis treatments. This action, combined with his expectation that it would make a difference, did help, relieving the problem. JC knows I care about him, and by caring for him now, this set the tone for this connected breathing session.

With help he breathed continually for one half hour. His breaths were strong and for the most part connected. There was considerable movement in his feet and legs for most of the duration and I knew he was expe-

riencing energy in these extremities. At a half hour he suddenly bolted upright, sitting, eyes still closed. I encouraged him to continue breathing, giving him a pattern of breath to imitate. He at first made feeble attempts to breathe in rhythm. After about five minutes they were stronger and I asked him if he wanted to lie down. He did, on his side.

This would turn out to be a learning experience for me for within minutes JC was losing consciousness, falling asleep. Three times I brought him back when he would lose the thread of aware consciousness, and finally I just allowed him to sleep for about 20 minutes.

After his rest JC described his experience. He said his feet felt like they were burning the whole time. It would be after I talked with his wife that I would learn how significant this was. She told me JC had been losing sensation in his feet and calves for years. I had thought this a more recent development of the last few years, but she said, "No, in fact it was because he had lost sensation that the sole of his foot had become infected without him even knowing," which led to surgery and a cast some ten years earlier. She saw the return of feeling in his lower legs and feet as a very positive sign even if JC described it as being uncomfortable.

I thought about this for days. I knew from researching rebirther's accounts that diabetes was a difficult disease to counteract. The years of abuse of external chemicals shuts down the body's natural ability to produce and distribute insulin. It's like tying your right arm to your side and never using it, after a while it atrophies and is useless. JC's daily insulin shots had killed his pancreas, the every-other-day dialysis was killing what was left of his kidneys, and other drugs had killed his eyesight. He was dying piece by piece.

I also knew the potential healing power of breath. Being that which ties the soul to the body, the breath is more than life force. It is ultimately the breath of life from our Creator. There is no limit to what this divine energy can do. The only limits exist within the mind of the breather. JC's experience gave him an experience he hadn't had for a dozen years - sensation, feeling, in his feet and legs. He just kept saying in amazement, "It was like a burning." With deeper thought, I realized how big a step this was for JC.

His words reminded me of what I'd learned about purification. The breath does purify the body. In fact, 70% of unused energy exits the body through breathing. (20% through perspiration, 8% urination, and 2% defecation.) Connected breathing was burning away JC's disease, one breath at a time.

Tuesday, July 11, 2000

JC was restless. Tried to separate from the body, let the body relax and still breathe but it was difficult. I suggested he let his body sink into the bed so his mind can go anywhere it wants to go. He tried and quickly returned to moving, twitching his feet, moving his arms and hands.

After the session, he reported his body didn't hurt as much yet as he talked he told of sensations in his hands, neck, face, head, ear, rib, legs. Places he hadn't had sensations in months and even years. Awareness of the energy had spread this time, progress was being made.

He was reminded of the first time he was to receive a kidney transplant. (The surgery was postponed because JC's lungs were filling with fluid.) What brought this to mind were the pockets of fluid, more fluid came out. Dialysis, extra water out, something hidden in there. He felt weight he hadn't felt before. Then the water in left lung which was what kept him from getting the transplant the first time. What brought this to his mind was his rib hurting.

Assigned him to practice continually breathing. Upping the minutes starting with five when he could attain that with awareness three times go to six minutes.

John missed several session appointments through the summer. This was mostly due to nausea brought on by the dialysis treatments. We didn't meet again to breathe until the latter part of August. Notation of this session and the aftermath follow.

August 17, 2000

JC's session lasted just short of an hour. Breathing was inconsistent no matter what I tried. But within the week he had a miraculous experience.

JC worked at MCI. The computer telephone sales was a perfect pairing for they allowed JC to go beyond his physical limitations. Friday afternoon, three days after the session, he was sitting at his terminal when all of a sudden he could see the computer in front of him. The shape and lights, for several seconds, then slowly it narrowed as if going farther from the light in a tunnel until his world was dark again.

JC was so shocked he didn't tell anyone for days. In fact it was at our next appointment, without rebirthing, that he shared this secret. This meeting was when I shared with JC the truth from my perspective. I asked him to what he attributed the recent health improvements. He mentioned the vitamins, herbs, being most conscientious with his insulin, acupuncture, but he said, "You know I think it's the change in attitude."

Certainly, John had adjusted his mind in many ways. He was praying daily, affirming a high power. He was accepting his physical condition, learning from it rather than resenting it in self pity. He was as inde-

pendent as he knew how to be. He expected this to please me, but whether I was pleased or not had little to do with John's capacity to recover.

I said, "Now, let's see, Leonard Orr and Marcia Roismann came to the College of Metaphysics a couple of days before Easter, so it was the second or third week of May when you had your first session with Marcia. Then we have had how many sessions since then?"

"Four."

"Four. All the things you mention you were doing before the breathing sessions. The breathing is the only new factor, and yet you don't even mention it. Why is that?"

He was hard pressed for an answer, trying to pass it off as, "Well, it's a combination of all of it."

He needed to know.

"John," I began, "I know without doubt that what has caused the sensation in your feet and legs and then other body parts and now changes in your eyesight is the bringing into your body of Divine Energy. I am certain of it. All the other things do not harm you, but they have not caused the change. The bringing in of prana has.

"I understand the healing potential of Inifnite Energy. I have experienced it personally and seen it happen with my grandfather, an evangelical faith healer. I understand how the energy flows into the mind and body and am learning daily about its power.

"You have thought about miraculous healing. Now you have evidence that it is possible, and it is shaking your belief systems.

"You will need to update those beliefs in order for healing to transpire.

"There will come a time when you will need to decide that you are willing to heal, to live."

That was the last time John and I met in counsel. Although he talked about breathing again, something always came up. Within three weeks, he was gone.

The place that breath holds in John's story is an inspiration to us all because it shows the wellspring of Spirit that is available to us right now. We do not need to be put on a waiting list to receive breath. We do not have to have insurance or a lot of money to breathe. It doesn't require that we are hooked up to a machine, although inhalers and oxygen tanks are beginning – as His Holiness the Dalai Lama and other spiritual teachers have noted – to turn human beings into machines.

Breathing requires awareness. When performed in harmony with universal principles it holds many benefits. Just as pregnant women learn breathing techniques to ease childbirth, so you can be taught the many expressions of pranayama for health, happiness, and success in life.

People who hold their breath are afraid. Those with airy voices are dependent, often feigning weakness. People who are out of breath are driven by their emotions. How we breathe tells us a lot about ourselves. Learning how to breathe rhythmically and in conjunction to mindful states of consciousness builds confidence, security, and peace within Self.

Remember the six-year-old living in fear? His parents wanted to know why he had difficulty breathing in some situations. The answer was simple and direct, "This one becomes emotionally agitated."

Almost a third of the children in the United States have some kind of breathing problem. We can do better than helping them become addicted to an aerosol can.

Recently one of the children who came for summer camp brought her inhaler with her. I had seen her on many occasions and never knew she owned such a device. All the times I had been with her she had never seen a need to use it.

She told me on the second day about a conversation with her dad the night before. He had asked about if she had needed her inhaler, and she had told him she had used it only once. I noted the information, not saying anything one way or another.

In the later afternoon we walked out to a field, the future site of the SOM World Headquarters building. She grabbed her inhaler before we left. I merely looked at her and smiled. "I don't think I'll need it. It's just in case."

I wondered "in case of what". I knew several scenarios and they all had imagined fear attached to them.

We walked the quarter mile and talked about being in nature, the expansiveness of creation. We talked about freedom, and I taught her a breathing exercise. Then we came back and created a relief sculpture of our experience.

The next day I heard her tell her dad she hadn't used her inhaler since talking with him. That meant she had gone almost two days without feeling the need.

The following afternoon a large group of 50 or more had gathered under the outdoor tarp for a cookout. I saw the girl reach into her pocket, pull out the inhaler, like a medical cigarette and inhale. Her dad, who is not in favor of the habit, said something to her as did a few others around.

"I don't need it often," she said. "It's just so I don't faint."

A light went off in the head. Fainting! Allopathic practitioners are giving inhalers to 12-year-old girls because they are feeling light-headed. I was shocked for the concept had never occurred to me. Physically speaking, the light-headedness comes from hormonal changes that come and go in the youthful body as genetics does its work of maturing the body. I've been there, and I've also experienced it of late in the exiting from the reproductive cycle commonly called menopause. This is 40 or so year cycle is the Kundalini energy working through humanity's consciousness toward higher reasoning.

I was compelled by an inner voice to speak up on behalf of this young soul. "It's natural for 12-year-old young ladies to swoon!" I said with a knowing smile. The girl looked over, and her face lit up. I heard her breathe a sigh of relief. Someone had told her she is not abnormal, impaired, or diseased. Now she had a different way of looking at her experience. The other women present knew what I was talking about. "It's all part of becoming a woman, of being appealing." Some of the men in our company nodded as well.

How quick we are to create a problem where there is none. This tendency in humanity holds us back in old beliefs that are largely physical only. As we begin to embrace the possibilities that imagination brings, new realities will make themselves known to us. A hundred years ago man wasn't flying around the world, or seeing what is happening there on 32" screens. Just imagine what will happen as the creative drive that fuels technology is turned inward!

Breath Free

Lesson 24 (in the School of Metaphysics course of study) is about the second stage of meditation taught in the School of Metaphysics, expectant observation. Much of this lesson teaches expectant observation through the student's practice of observing his or her own breath during meditation and employing Hong Sau. Hong Sau aids the student to make a shift from watching the physical breath to experiencing the mental or cosmic breath coming in the medulla oblongata.

I had been studying this lesson for about a week and practicing the Hong Sau everyday just as my teacher had taught me in class. At the end of the week, I traveled with other teachers from my school in Norman Oklahoma and teachers from Oklahoma City to our area teacher's meeting in Tulsa. We began teacher's meeting workshops on Friday evening and then continued with more on Saturday morning. After lunch we divided into groups to venture into the Tulsa business community to talk to people and pass out literature about the School of Metaphysics. Each group went to a different area of the city, and we all agreed to meet at a particular time at the Visitor's Center at Oral Robert University which is located in Tulsa. This university has some notoriety because this was where the evangelical minister Oral Roberts reported talking with a 700 foot tall Jesus. Of course, all the teachers were aware of this recent 'happening'. We were also excited about visiting the campus because it is known for its teachings and the healing prayers that go out all over the world from there. Most of us had never seen the university campus or the famous praying hands in front of the university.

At the appointed time, we all met at the Visitor's Center, a tower that permitted a bird's eye view of the campus, as you walked around the circular top floor. As we looked we talked about the difference in vibration we experienced in this part of town. I arrived with another teacher, and we drove up a hill, seemingly through an entry way between two hills and into a valley where the university is located. We talked about the intensity of the vibration that was here as one of great love and dedication. We also noted that this part of Tulsa seemed to be more light-filled with many of the buildings gleaming white in the afternoon sun.

After we left the visitor's center, several of us walked over to the main campus building. This was the building with a statue of praying hands in front. We all sat down for a few minutes, and I thought 'I wonder what it would be like to be inside the praying hands?'. I had heard jokes about the praying hands statue, but here in front of them I realized what these symbolized and the great presence this bronze statue represented to humanity.

With this question in my mind, I sat quietly and began my Hong Sau practice. I figured this would help me calm my mind and body and help me to place my attention in the space between the two hands. Within a few minutes, I noticed a change, what I would later learn to call a shift in my attention because the change was that my body became lighter, almost as if I had no physical body. I also lost the sensation of breathing although I was hearing my incoming breath. My breathing seemed much louder, as if I was breathing in my own ear. I could not feel my body breathing. It was as if I was detached because I still knew there was a physical body, but my physical body was not moving. The detachment I experienced was like watching or observing some action or activity in front of me but being totally separate from it, perhaps distant.

I became lighter and lighter and I felt myself drawn towards the praying hands. I was aware enough to realize that my physical body was not floating and was still where I had 'left it'. I was in amazement because I was noticing how my mental attention was being drawn towards the praying hands. Pretty immediately I had the sensation of my attention being inside the hollow of the praying hands, not quite as if I was physically sitting there, nor from the perspective of 'being there' and looking out from the hands. I would describe it as a mental sensation of being there because I was not where my physical body was and there was a kind of surety, security or peace in what I was experiencing.

This is what I now describe to my students as a 'click' that occurs when there is a mental connection. This click occurs within the mind as a complete shift in consciousness and attention occurs, for example in thought projection.

This was a very valuable experience for me because it was one of my first conscious astral projection experiences. This experience also illustrated the central point of the Hong Sau lesson, that I am a soul and not a physical body. I learned that I truly am where my attention is. The whole experience whet my appetite for astral projection practices in the second cycle of lessons and to deeper and deeper experiences in meditation. –Dr. Paul Blosser

When our son was young he began learning about anger. He would get mad when he feared someone was going to take something from him and he would want to strike back. He had heard the instructions from many about "Not nice", "How would you like it if...." and "Stop that!" None of these were helping. Being a thinker he knew he didn't want to be angry, and he wanted to know what he could do instead.

I thought about it. At first I offered the Thomas Jefferson method of counting to 10. When he told me that didn't work for him, it pushed me further. This turned out to be a very good thing. "Okay," I said, "then this is what I want you to do. The next time you feel yourself getting angry, I want you to sit down right then and there. Put your hands in this position." I showed him a mudra that calms the mind. "And take ten breaths. Make sure you count them. Big breath in and big breath out."

"Okay," he said.

This has stuck with our son. He knows it works from experience. He does not yet understand the mechanics of how and why it works. He will in time, when he asks for more instruction.

When we breathe, we are committing ourselves to being fully present in our physical experiences. We are in effect uniting the soul part of us with the physical part so the mind and the body can coordinate in the same place.

When we don't breathe well, shallowly or haltingly, we are to one degree or another keeping ourselves, our soul, from fully experiencing what is going on with our body, with the environment that we have created, with our thoughts and choices. This was apparent in John's experiences and in the experiences of a young student I will call Pia. This is her story of learning how to *be here now*.

Pia's third rebirthing session proved to exemplify how rebirthing in the hands of a psi counselor, an individual learned in using the inner mind, can be assuring, encouraging, and revelatory.

The intention of our meeting was for me to teach Pia, a student at the College of Metaphysics, how to breathe intuitively. She had come to the United States in her mid-teenage years. Open to learn and willful, she had breathed well during her first two sessions with good results. I had learned from my rebirther that each session is different, this had been my personal experience and the experience of everyone I had assisted in intuitive breathing as well, so I passed this wisdom on to each person I had the privilege to attend.

This breathing session would indeed be different for Pia.

Prior to beginning we talked of her previous experiences, and of events happening in her life. Family problems back in Chile had arisen and while she was felt pulled in several directions emotionally she also felt quite certain she was making the choice her parents would want her to make in working to contribute something worthwhile to the world. Pia spoke of her tendency to separate herself from others, figuratively as well as literally. This was on her mind as she began breathing.

Very soon evidence that this would be a different session than previous ones became apparent. In previous sessions Pia breathed full-bodied. She received physical breath as if out in the open, clean air. She would move herself to drink of the divine nectar, the cosmic energy, nearing points of surrender. This time was different.

Pia breathed for less than five minutes before beginning to drift, letting her breath move away from her awareness and control. I would speak to her softly, encouraging her to breathe again, and she would immediately respond. This went on for a half hour. Pia would breathe anywhere from six to twenty breaths and then allow the breathing to become disconnected and shallow until her consciousness all but let go. She would have fallen into sleep were it not for our combined resolve to sustain awareness.

About thirty-five minutes into the session, I asked her how she was doing. "I keep drifting," she replied.

"Yes," I affirmed. "Do you want to keep breathing?"

"Yes."

I supported her, breathing with her, more confident that she would harness the will I knew her to possess and place fuller effort into her breathing. Indeed she did. For the next twenty-five minutes or so Pia breathed connectedly. During this time her hands moved into a prayer position which she would later comment had been difficult from the tetany that she settled into them. But indeed she did free them and they expressed unity and connectedness at the area of her heart.

Finally she fell into a breathless state for several minutes. She came back to the breath in a more shallow way, fading off easily. I asked her how she felt. "Good" was her reply. "You've done well," I replied, "Let's roll over and you can rest a while."

Upon returning to the room. Pia began to talk about how scattered she seemed in the beginning. "I just couldn't stay with it. I don't know if I was going to sleep or not, but I couldn't keep it going."

When I reminded her that each session is different, this was little comfort. Pia was disappointed in her performance, starting to judge this session as not as good as the previous ones, as a waste of time.

To help her put the experience in perspective I described how the session progressed, how the first half hour she would lose track of what she was doing easily. Through talking she began to reveal the thoughts that had come to her mind. "They were moving so quickly. First I thought of Dane (an aquaintance), then Kay (her first metaphysics teacher), then Cecille (a college classmate)."

I asked Pia, from her viewpoint, what these people had in common.

Pulling away, was her response. Dane had just quit classes a few days before declaring his intent to go to California to become a musician. "And I can feel Kay slipping away, becoming more distant. And Cecille gets that way sometimes."

When I asked if she could see how these thoughts related to the way Pia had breathed today, she at first was puzzled. "You mean scattered?"

"In part. Remember what you were talking about before you began breathing?"

"Emotions?"

"Yes, and more importantly the separation that you are not always aware of. These people represent that separation to you. Obviously Dane because he's moving and you may never see him again. Kay because you once lived with her, seeing her every day, and now she lives elsewhere. And Cecille, who you physically live with every day but often feel disconnected from. Three different,perhaps progressive, examples of separation."

Pia was thinking now.

After a few minutes of silence I asked if she remembered moving her hands. "Yes," she replied.

"It looked like you were trying to pray."

Pia lifted her hands into the position she had wanted to move them into. "It was hard because my fingers were cramped, but I kept moving them back together. I remembered my grandmother and I thought of love, and connectedness." Emotion welled up into her eyes. The bittersweet joy of love and pain of physical separation.

"Maybe that's your answer."

"To what?"

"To what to do when you feel separate."

Pia thought about this a few moments. "Yes, my grandmother was very loving to me as a child. We have a special relationship. Maybe I should call her."

"Yes, you need to express how you feel, the love you experience. Not just with your grandmother but with everyone. That is how you will 'feel connected'."

It was a stretch because Pia placed such emphasis on love being attached to a particular person. This emotional tie struggled with the broader mental scope reasoning offered, the unconditional love that exists beyond blood ties and physical realities. She offered words to this affect to which I replied, "Maybe that's why the first part of your session was so different and so difficult."

She cocked her head. "Maybe your first half hour's experience was to expand your capacity for love and compassion for it gave you the experience of what it is like to be Dane or Kay or Cecille. To be disconnected, distant, separated."

Pia thought about that for a while.

"It's the karmic opportunity for more complete understanding. When we can experience as others do, we can understand."

As we left the building it occurred to me more deeply than ever what a wonderful pairing Psi counseling and intuitive breathing are. We spoke about the depth of the session, how at first it seemed like a struggle for Pia. Without the interaction between us, it would have taken days and maybe weeks to put into perspective. With interaction we were able to explore the experience in several levels of consciousness.

With rebirthing the potential to heal is limitless, for whatever the individual needs at the time is what is highlighted. Having someone attending you who knows how to interpret the mind's energies is a consciousness-raising asset.

Since my first few intuitive breathing sessions, I fully accepted the idea of assisting others during extended periods of connected breathing as spiritual midwifery. This day I had reached another level of understanding in just what that meant. •

ELS#7

A Short Class on Breath

Dr. B: The most undervalued life skill is breath. We can live weeks without food, days without water, how long can you live without breath?

TM: Not too long.

JD: Although some yogis reportedly can for some time.

Dr. B: Yes, anything is possible with God consciousness. For those who believe in their mortality, breath becomes priceless. When adults learn the value of breath and pass this on to their children then the consciousness of the planet will begin to change. This is what Leonard (Orr) has been working toward for years.

Each time he visits the College of Metaphysics I am stimulated to learn many lessons. One of them from his most recent visit was a Self-Respect lesson. In my admiration for him, I began to think about what he has done in his life. How he seemingly is willing to drop everything and go anywhere on the planet to teach any number of people about connected breathing, what he calls rebirthing. In this way I think of him as an ambassador for pranayama, the practice of the power of energy. His ideas are innovative and bold. Controversial for some. Although at different times in his life he has been received by hundreds, including doctors and heads of state, most of his work is people to people over time. I could see the geometric movement of what he has done and I realized that is exactly the same way that the School of Metaphysics is moving through the world. Self respecting I realized that the incredible amount of people who have been touched by the school is truly awesome *because of the longevity of it.* Endurance.

The amount of people who you can touch over time is proportionately aggregate.

I deepened my understanding of the power of One through our son, Hezekiah. In the first few years I reflected on the difference between teaching dozens, hundreds of people above the age of 15 and spending hours with a single child. Something my parents would often remind me of, surfaced. When I was very young my grandmother asked how many children I was going to have when I grew up. My reply was 15. For years I thought this was a solution to the loneliness of being the only child in the family. When I started teaching, the ideal class size was 15. As I passed on to others what I valued as truth, I understood this childhood memory in a new way.

One of the many realizations receiving a child into my life has brought to me is revisiting the power of One. As an adult. I experienced the power of One many times as a counselor. None of us know who we will become or what we will end up doing throughout life. Yes, we can interpret inner level signs and we can come up with conscious desires and creations. We can receive indications of our destiny from many sources. In all of it the Truth is, all we have is the present, this moment. In the beginning of *Revelation* the Lord God says, "I am the alpha and omega, the first and the last, the one who is, who was, and who is to come."

Because you never know where the present moment is going to go, you never know what it will produce in you or in another person, or in the world, in the universe. This moment with the One can be just as powerful as talking to a thousand people all at the same time. Jesus taught, "Where two or more are gathered, there I AM in their midst." This is the power of breath. The energy invested, the alignment experienced in the giving and receiving can be the same, and over time the many moments create something greater. You keep breathing in and breathing out every day. Being with one, being with a thousand. A whole functioning self does one and the other, both.

JM: What I really see is in order to really use the breath you have to have the foundation, what has come before it. To be aware, you have to be able to hold your attention. You respect yourself enough to recognize the importance and power of the breath. In using it consciously with awareness, it aids you to be in the Presence. It is a circle. Everything that comes before it leads up to being able to use your breath with awareness then you recognize that you are the breath, not the body.

LJ: I was thinking about breath, and thinking that it is the connection. Through breath you know that you are connected to God, your Creator and so everything that leads up to it is building that knowing that you are a Creator, to being like your Creator. It is like knowing where you come from.

Dr. B: In the second chapter of Genesis, the second story of creation, after the universe and the world have been formed, the early root races, the Lord God makes man from the ground. Then what does he do?

LJ: Gives him life.

TM: Breathes the breath of life into him.

Dr. B: Yes! The breath of God is in man, in the thinker. Leonard calls connected breathing "the biological experience of God." It is. Breath ties the soul to the body. The intake of breath is the first action of the body when separated from the womb. The outgo of breath is the final action of the body when leaving the physical. In one final exhalation the flesh is left behind as the soul, withdraws its mental attention. Jesus calls this the Holy Spirit.

When we look at all the manifestations of Holy Spirit people experience: miraculous healings, speaking in tongues, lights going off, moments of illumination and brilliance insight, a wide variety can occur, the common denominator is an altering of the consciousness in the moment. Learning to extend that moment *over time* is one of the reasons for attending the breath. In religious practice, for instance in Christianity, this is the importance in going to church every Sunday and repenting so you might "be saved". Look at that a moment. The essence of "being saved" is allowing Jesus into your heart. It is a moment of purity, aligning with the Christ. You practice this enough Sundays and pretty soon you *are* that new person! You don't do those old lustful, greedy, murderous, sensuous things anymore, they leave you because your consciousness is different. Or the Hindu journeys to be in the presence of his guru so he might receive a darshan, a blessing. Receiving a darshan from the guru is similar to Christians going to faith healers and receiving a miraculous healing. Modern-day shamans. Every culture has an expression of the Truth of breath.

TM: So the shaman is channeling the God energy into their patients.

Dr. B: Breathing the breath of life. What we endeavor to do here is study it through both observation and direct experience. In this way we become our own experiment. That is what the stage of adolescence is to be that you become your own experiment. All great scientists, great thinkers do this. Sometimes they end up giving the body more than it can handle. Pierre Curie is a good example. His hands were inflamed and raw from handling radium during the time he and his wife Marie were experimenting to uncover its potential healing powers. Visionaries are known for the risks they take. Theirs is not the average, normal existence.

Dr. B.,
Just wanted to share a thrilling experience from yesterday.

My 10-year old son has occasional bouts of asthma. He started having trouble on Monday. My first reaction was to grab the albuterol, a steroid that accelerates the heart rate among other side effects that any reasonable parent would not like. After a shot of albuterol and a nap the trouble did not go away and even worse he had a fever. Now I'm giving him a shot of Motrin. Finally, I realized that this was an opportunity to put into practice what I've been learning. (OK, I was allopathically unconscious and on automatic).

Trying to discern the cause, I thought that perhaps an earlier experience of rushing around had caused the problem, but my son said that it wasn't the problem. I took him in my arms, stilled my mind and did some deep breathing to guide him into relaxation. I visualized the mercury in the thermometer slowly dropping, I visualized his bronchioles relaxing, and his racing heart slowing to its normal pace. Gradually the fever subsided and his racing heart returned to its normal pace. However, his breathing improved, but there was still some wheezing.

The wheezing continued through the night and two more doses of albuterol still hadn't worked. I began to really worry. Suddenly, he told me that he had had a dream. The dream reflected worry and agitation and frustration. Because of the dream interpretation skills I've gained, we were able to trace back to the thought that caused the problem. Boy was I excited! We talked about the incident and I showered him with much love and acceptance so that he would not be afraid or worry. This was the beginning of **my son's recovery** to full breathing.

Although my intention to help my son to learn some new ways of thinking through reading a book I checked out at the library, he had begun to judge himself harshly for past mistakes! He was not inspired by the book! I helped him to see that he was having a learning experience. With lots of love, attention, visualization, a healing projection, and WATER!!!! he recovered and was ready to ride his bike to the park and play with friends!

O Keisha

Peace Dome Presentation Spans 50 Years of Humanity's Potential

The Invitation spans the development of peace consciousness around the world from Sweden to Tibet, the Congo to Alabama. The hour and fifteen minute presentation unites eight Nobel Peace Prize winners, encompassing 50 years of peace consciousness.

"It is like being in the presence of some of the greatest minds in the modern world," said Barbara Condron, The Invitation's creator and director. "Hearing Albert Schweitzer's words that we are becoming inhuman to the extent that we become supermen are heard in tandem with Dr. Martin Luther King's admonition that man has learned to fly the air like birds and swim the sea like fish, but not learned the simple art of living together as brothers pricks the conscience and opens the mind."

Starting in 1954 with medical humanitarian and musical genius Albert Schweitzer, The Invitation highlights the evolution of man's search to live in a peaceful world over the past five decades. Dr. Martin Luther King and scientist Linus Pauling from the United States in the 1960's, Betty Williams from Northern Ireland and Mother Teresa from India in the 1970's, Alva Myrdal from Sweden and his Holiness the Dalai Lama from Tibet in the 1990's, and last year's honoree Shirin Ebadi from Iran come to life before your eyes. Their thoughts of peace stretch the limits of the imagination, often challenging the way we live. "When Mother Teresa says she was shocked to see so many young children given to drugs in the West, you believe her," Condron says. "When she says she wanted to know why, you agree with her. When she tells you it is because there is no one in the family to receive them, you come face to face with how you conduct your own life."

The Invitation is presented only at the Peace Dome on the campus of the College of Metaphysics in Windyville, Missouri near Bennett Springs. The dome was dedicated in October last year as a universal site for peace. On that day people from all seven continents participated in a synchronized reading of the Universal Peace Covenant, the document that serves as part of the script. The remainder of the presentation is comprised of excerpts from speeches made by Nobel Peace Prize laureates. Condron sought and received permission from the Nobel Foundation in Sweden to quote the laureates' speeches and from the Board of Governors of the School of Metaphysics to use the Universal Peace Covenant which was penned in 1996-7 by two dozen teachers.

The effect is both timeless and contemporary. This is not passive peace. Nor is it the polarizing peace activism of recent years. The Invitation seeks to define the ideas and the practices that produce peace. It mixes science with philosophy in a way that encourages personal and social change. "When Linus Pauling - the sole recipient to date of Nobel prizes in two categories (chemistry and peace) - says that we are privileged to live in this extraordinary age, we realize in 2004 we are beginning to live the great future of peace, justice, morality and human well-being that he sees," Condron says.

Bringing to life these men and women from around the world has changed the lives of those who portray them. Those changes are documented by Condron in the book Peacemaking: 9 Lessons for Changing Yourself, your Relationships, and your World.

Throughout history, man has responded to aggression with more aggression. In the 1960's Dr. Martin Luther King followed in the footsteps of Mohandas K. Gandhi to use nonviolence to respond to aggression with love. In his Nobel prize acceptance speech King said, "Gandhi was probably the first person in history to lift the love ethic of Jesus above mere interaction between individuals to a powerful and effective social force."

"Dr. King was a powerful speaker," says computer expert John Harrison who portrays King who was awarded the prize in 1964. "From portraying him in The Invitation, I gained the confidence to bring out and use more of my own personal power. I felt his urgency to do his part to heal racial inequities because he knew his time was so short. Our time on this planet is short, so like Dr. King, I am striving to make the most of it while I am here."

Betty Williams, the 1976 winner, was an office worker in Northern Ireland at the time she shared the prize for founding Peace People. In her speech she acknowledges that the world is divided ideologically, theologically, yet she says, "the whole human family can be united by compassion." Like King, she realizes that compassion is more important than intellect in calling forth the love that the work of peace needs.

"Before playing Betty Williams I thought peace was a nice idea," landscaper Laurie Biswell says of the 1976 prize winner, who was an office worker from Northern Ireland at the time. "From quoting Betty's words in conjunction with the Universal Peace Covenant I have a better understanding of how to cause peace to become a reality. Now I believe that I can make a difference just as these Nobel laureates have."

Each person who witnesses The Invitation leaves their mark in the first floor of the Peace Dome. There an eight foot diameter design by Chicago artist Jay McCormick is manifesting one glass tile at a time. Following each performance guests are invited to place a tile in the Peace Dome.

The nine by eighteen foot relief map of the world on the east side of the Peace Dome is called the Healing Wall. Eventually it will be composed of native stones from all over the world.

When asked if the Peace Dome and the presentation are political statements, Condron quotes one of the Dalai Lama's speeches in response. "Peace, in the sense of the absence of war, is of little value to someone who is dying of hunger or cold. It will not remove the pain of torture inflicted on a prisoner of conscience. It does not comfort those who have lost their loved ones in floods caused by senseless deforestation in a neighboring country. Peace can only last where human rights are respected, where the people are fed, and where individuals and nations are free."

"The Dalai Lama, who lost his country and his culture when the Chinese invaded Tibet in 1959, teaches that responsibility does not only lie with the leaders of our countries or those appointed or elected to do a particular job," Condron says. "It lies with each one of us individually. Those who experience The Invitation have a heightened awareness of what all of the laureates know – peace starts with each one of us." •

TWO BREATHING EXERCISES

Exercise One
Breathing In

Set a timer for 10 minutes, or have a friend notify you when 10 minutes have passed. For the entire 10 minutes you will give your full attention to your breathing. Do not try to alter your breath in any way, just breathe naturally. Stay with the flow, experiencing the act of breathing, observing the movement.

After this exercise note your thoughts. What was your first thought when you learned your time was up? Did you stay with the breath the entire time? Did the breath remain the same or did it change? Did the time seem short or long? How do you feel now? Physically? Emotionally? Mentally?

Be as detailed as possible in your account, particularly if this is the first time you have tried something like this. You will reference this many times in the weeks and years ahead.

Each day for the next week repeat this same exercise, journaling afterwards. Then you will be ready for Exercise Two.

One of the intuitive reports is called a Dharma Profile. Dharma comes from the Sanskrit word *dhr* meaning to sustain, to nourish. Dharma can be seen as the soul urge working in divine order of universe. It is one's duty. One's action that pleases the lord. Dharma is what leads a soul to union with God. The Dharma Profile describes the soul's reason for being here.

One woman's Dharma Profile (972002BGC3) identifies her dharma as "inspiration." It is described as *"the ability to utilize the thoughts in such a way as to be able to discern what needs to be done."* Motivating others is a driving force within her. Ironically, she had fallen into a pattern of interaction that most would not see as inspirational at all. It is described in this way:

> We see that many of the experiences that have been producing this have been in regard to confrontative situations. We see that some of these have been worrying situations or conflict of that nature. We see that there have also been conflicts within, between this one and others on a more interpersonal vein through lifetimes, and we see that it is through this where there has been disagreement that this one has begun to expand the vision to realize that the call to action is one which is obvious when there is some kind of conflict to resolve. We see that this one has practiced this form of inspiration for a long period of time and we see that it is within the present that this one has afforded the Self an opportunity for a different way of looking at it, a different way of experiencing it. In the present time this one is investigating and drawing to the self the spiritual aspects of inspiration and the ability to be able to provide a kind of motivation for the Self and for others in this regard.

Suggestions given to help this woman image productive uses of inspiration begin with a new definition:

> Inspiration is the ability to draw inward as well as to stimulate in an external fashion. It is the **breathing in** that enables there to be the transformation and we see that this process of breathing in has been unconscious for this one in many of the learning experiences...there is a need for this to reach its fruition, for it to become conscious in all levels of this one's existence.

How we receive energy shapes our experience with the breath of God and influences our relationships with others.

Exercise Two

Breathing Out

Now you will give your full attention to your breathing for ten minutes. This time you want a clock in the room so you can be aware of the passing of time. Again, do not try to alter your breath in any way, just breathe naturally. This time you will mentally note the number of seconds you inhale, then the number of seconds you exhale. This will probably change in the span of 10 minutes. Just note the time inhaling, time exhaling.

When the 10 minutes is over, note your observations. Were you inhalations or exhalations longer, the same length? Did your breathing slow with the passing of time or speed? What do you attribute changes to? Is breathing getting easier? How do you feel after the 10 minutes?

Do this exercise once every day for a week.

Breathing out is the way we express ourselves through mind into the physical. This is most apparent in our speech. Start studying yourself and the people around you. Look for the energy levels of those who are open and loving, witty and talkative, quiet and inward. What do you see?

Who are the people you know who can light up a room, hold a crowd in their hands, mobilize others to action? Watch how these people use breath, and learn!

Breathing Life into Something

When I teach anything that takes physical strength, endurance, stamina, agility, effort, I always teach rhythmic breathing with the activity. I noticed a long time ago that when I bucked hay, tossed bales of hay up on a flatbed truck and breathed rhythmically I would energize myself and get stronger as the day progressed. When I ran long distances in track or cross country I would breath rhythmically with my pace and become faster and call upon extra energy at the finish line. Any kind of manual labor always becomes easier when I focus on breathing with it.

When I lift something upward I inhale. When I set something down or toss it I exhale with some kind of push like a huh, huh. I see shot putters do this in the olympics where there is an explosion of breath as they release the shot put during their toss.

Many students at the College of Metaphysics have experienced the strengthening and exhilaration that comes from using the breath during activity. Whether we are shov-

elling manure, pounding fence posts, bucking hay, carrying water buckets to trees, the rhythmic breathing helps.

It is not just a physical skill. Following the mental breath unites the whole mind. I remember several intuitive breathing sessions where after doing connective breathing for an hour I experienced the healing energy of God (that is what I called it at that time), God power. It came from the breath coursing through my whole being. I received healing, visions, images of my mind and connections with humanity. The experiences are usually energetic like seeing the energy grids around our campus or healing energy being sent to everyone on campus, or between another star system and earth. These experiences cause me to believe that the breath not only links my soul to my physical body, but that it links the energy of God, of the infinite universe to each I Am.

I have a new meaning to the thought of breathing life into something. It is giving a complete and whole energy and receiving an infinite abundance of energy from the Creator. – Tad Messenger

Exercise Three

Breathing

This third week, you will once again breathe for about 10 minutes. Do not set a timer or have someone tell you when the time has past. You will use your own inner sense of time.

Lie on your back and place your left hand on your midrift, over your solar plexus. As you inhale your diaphragm expands and your abdomen pushes out. As you exhale your diaphragm contracts and your abdomen recedes. As you inhale lift your right hand up, elbow and upper arm remaining on the floor or bed. As you exhale lower your right hand down.

As you breathe, allow your body to sink into the floor. When you think 10 minutes have passed stop and relax.

Make note of your thoughts and feelings and the actual time that transpired. You are now learning how to use your breath for mental, emotional, and physical relaxation. This is a good exercise to do before going to sleep. It will promote rest and clear dreams.

Advanced Energy Work

Boiling Water with my Mind

In the third cycle of lessons, there is a lesson which suggested holding a cup of water in your hand and directing mental energy to speed up the prana (energy) to cause the water to boil. I did this every day. At first there were no results, then one day I decided, "This is my mind. It is for me to discover how it works. I am going to see how this works."

This shift in my attitude changed the results. Instead of doubting whether it would work or wondering if it would work, now I was learning how it worked. I practiced and practiced and one day I saw little bubbles rising to the surface of the cup. I did it again to make sure that I was really doing it! Moving my mind helped me to move the energy. – Dr. Laurel Clark

"The last function of reason
is to recognize that there are
an infinity of things which surpass it."
– Pascal, 1670

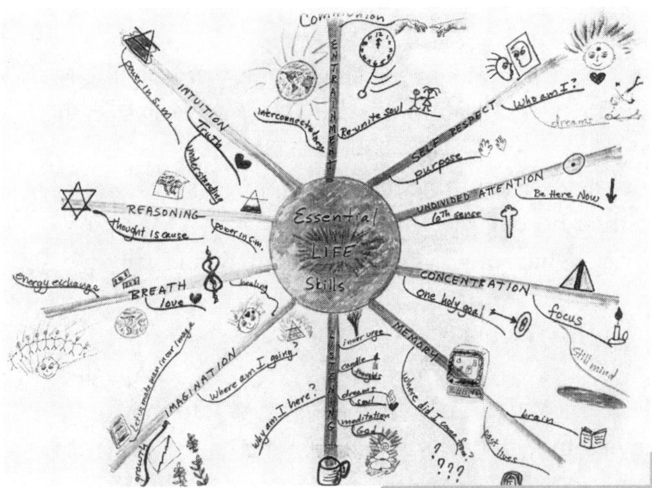

"The power of
a thing or an
act is in the
meaning and
the under-
standing."
– Black Elk, 1930

Reasoning

A Universal Language of Mind Story

The Cave

"Let me illustrate in a figure how far our nature is enlightened or unenlightened," Socrates begins. "Behold, human beings living in an underground den which has a mouth open towards the light. They have been here from their childhood. Their legs and necks are chained so that they cannot move. They can only see before them, being prevented by the chains from turning their heads. Above and behind them a fire blazes at a distance. Between the fire and the prisoners there is a raised way with a low wall like the screen which marionette players have in front of them, over which they show the puppets.

"Imagine. Can you see men passing along the wall carrying all sorts of vessels? Statues and figures of animals made of wood and stone and various materials?" Socrates asks. "Some of the men are talking, others are silent."

"You have shown me a strange image," Glaucon, his student, replies. "They are strange prisoners."

"Like ourselves," Socrates replies, pausing. "They see only their own shadows, or the shadows of one another, which the fire throws on the opposite wall of the cave."

"Yes, how could they see anything but the shadows if they were never allowed to move their heads?"

"And of the objects which are being carried, they would only see the shadows?"

"Yes," Glaucon replies, mentally seeing the images his teacher paints.

"If they were able to converse with one another, would they not suppose that they were naming what was actually before them?" Socrates asks.

Glaucon nods in reply.

"Suppose further that the prison had an echo which came from the other side. Would they not presume when one of the passersby spoke that the voice which they heard came from the passing shadow?"

"No question," replies Glaucon.

"To them," Socrates says, "the truth would be literally nothing but the shadows of the images."

"This is true," Glaucon affirms.

"Now in your mind's eye see what will naturally follow if the prisoners are released, and their errors in judgement brought to light. At first, when any of them is liberated and compelled suddenly to stand up and turn his neck round and walk and look towards the light, he will suffer sharp pains. The glare will distress him, and he will be unable to see the realities which, in his former state, he had seen as shadows. Then conceive someone saying to him, that what he saw before was an illusion, but that now, when he is approaching nearer to being and his eye is turned towards more real existence, he has a clearer vision. What will be his reply? You may further imagine that his instructor is pointing to the objects as they pass and requiring him to name them. Will he not be perplexed? Will he not fancy that the shadows which he formerly saw are truer than the objects which are now shown to him?"

"This would be certain."

"If he is compelled to look straight at the light, will he not have a pain in his eyes which will make him turn away to take in the objects of vision which he can see, and which he will conceive to be in reality clearer than the things which are now being shown to him?"

"True," the student agrees.

"Now suppose the man is reluctantly dragged up a steep and rugged ascent. He is held fast until he is forced into the presence of the sun. Is he not likely to be pained and irritated? When he approaches the light his eyes will be dazzled, and he will not be able to see anything at all of what are now called realities."

"He will require to grow accustomed to the sight of the upper world. At first he will see the shadows best, next the reflections of men and other objects in the water, and then the objects themselves. Only then will he gaze upon the light of the moon and the stars and the glittering heaven. At first, do you suppose, he will see the sky and the stars by night better than the sun or the light of the sun by day?"

"Certainly."

"Finally, he will be able to see the sun," Socrates continues, "not mere reflections of the sun in the water, but he will see the sun in its own proper place, and not in another. He will contemplate the sun as he is."

"Yes."

"He will then proceed to argue that this is what gives the season and the years, and is the guardian of all that is in the visible world, and in a certain way the cause of all things which he and his fellows have been accustomed to behold."

"Clearly," Glaucon says, "the man will first see the sun and then reason about it."

"When he remembers his old habitation, the wisdom of the den and his fellow-prisoners," Socrates proposes, "do you not suppose that he would reflect on the change, and pity them?

"Certainly, he would."

"And if they were in the habit of conferring honors among themselves on those who were quickest to observe the passing shadows and to remark which of them went before, and which followed after, and which were together; and who were therefore best able to draw conclusions as to the future, do you think that he would care for such honors and glories, or envy the possessors of them? Would he not say with Homer, 'Better to be the poor servant of a poor master, and to endure anything, rather than think as they do and live after their manner?'"

"Yes," Glaucon replies, "I think that he would rather suffer anything than entertain these false notions and live in this miserable manner."

"Imagine once more," Socrates continues, "such a one coming suddenly out of the sun to be replaced in his old situation; would he not be certain to have his eyes full of darkness?"

"To be sure."

"If there were a contest, and he had to compete in measuring the shadows with the prisoners who had never moved out of the den, while his sight was still weak, and before his eyes had become steady (and the time which would be needed to acquire this new habit of sight might be very considerable) would he not be ridiculous? Men would say of him that up he went and down he came without his eyes; and that it was better not even to think of ascending! If any one tried to loose another and lead him up to the light, let them only catch the offender, and they would put him to death!"

"This is the way with most men," Glaucon replies.

"You may now perceive, dear Glaucon, this allegory. The prison-house is the world of sight. The light of the fire is the sun. You will understand, if you interpret the journey upwards to be the ascent of the soul into the intellectual world according to my poor belief, which, at your desire, I have expressed whether rightly or wrongly God knows. Whether true or false, my opinion is that in the world of knowledge the idea of good appears last of all. It is seen only with an effort and, when seen, is also inferred to be the universal author of all things beautiful and right, parent of light and of the lord of light in this visible world, and the immediate source of reason and truth in the intellectual. This is the power upon which he who would act rationally, either in public or private life must have his eye fixed." •

In the "Allegory of the Cave", Plato uses his teacher, Socrates, and a student as the primary characters. He symbolically depicts the predicament in which mankind finds itself, and he proposes a way of salvation.

"The Allegory" reflects most of Plato's major philosophical assumptions. Plato believed that the world revealed by our senses is not the real world rather a pale imitation. The real world he asserted can only be apprehended intellectually. Plato's exerience told him that knowledge cannot be transferred from teacher to student. His belief that education consists in directing student's minds toward what is real and important and allowing them to apprehend it for themselves is clear in the interchange between Socrates and Glaucon.

Plato had faith that the universe ultimately is good. His conviction was that enlightened individuals have an obligation to the rest of society, and that a good society must be one in which the truly wise (the Philosopher-King) are the rulers.

Plato was, himself, the son of a wealthy, noble family who planned on a political career until the arrest and execution of Socrates changed the course of his life. He abandoned his political career and turned to philosophy, opening the Academy, a school dedicated to the search for wisdom. The Academy was the first Western university.

Plato's university expected people to become reasoners, to know the Self, to examine the thoughts of Self in the context of a much greater whole. Only through reasoning can we hope to come out of the cave into the light of day, Plato would have said.

Plato taxes the limits of the reader's imagination in this tale. He challenges us to follow his images, to reach similar conclusions. Through his dialogue he asks that we open our minds to consider the nature of our own comforts, our own compulsions, our own limitations that hold us down and away from the light.

The Republic, from which "The Allegory" is taken, is regarded as a utopian blueprint. It is dedicated toward a discussion of the education required of a Philosopher-King. And those are most worthy adjectives for describing one who wields the skill of reasoning.•

Reasoning is

"...capable of problem solving, but even more so of envisioning new and different ways to live life or to accomplish or to create physical atmospheres, and it is through the pursuit of this, without hesitation that this one will begin to realize the dharma fully." (91399BGC4)

When coupled with the will, reasoning produces a mentally, emotionally, and physically successful individual. (SOM Lesson 5A)

When reasoning is activated, understanding is forthcoming. (SOM Lesson 14)

Most people do not think of artists as great reasoners. Adjectives paired with artist are more likely to be words like starving, liberal, advant-garde, inspired, unpredictable and depressed. The cause for this is deeper than cliches and prejudice. Insight into this is described in one woman's Creative Mind report.

A talented artist from Europe, Saf came from a family of artists and was university-trained. From painting to sculpting to landscaping, her talents were varied. Yet it was a Creative Mind Report (1062001BGC2) that gave insight into Saf's artistry and the place reasoning holds in the maturing of it. The first line describes the secret of her creativity.

> This one relies very heavily upon the subconscious mind for creativity.

The subconscious mind is the inner recreative faculty in human consciousness. The storehouse of understanding, subconscious mind adds a brilliance to any thinking endeavor and for creative people it provides the "talent" that can become genius and even mysticism. Saf had experienced emotional highs and lows often shared by other artists. What she didn't realize was the cause for these. In its description of how the person is using the creative mind, her report shed light upon this.

> We see that there are significant ways that this one attempts to bypass or to manifest without benefit of the conscious mind and conscious reasoning. As a result this one does have a tendency to have the physical mind undisciplined and move as it would .... therefore we see that the creativity although it does change, it tends to remain somewhat the same. We see that this one becomes highly excited emotionally with something new and we see that this one does have the capacity for directing the mind and the creativity when this one wants to. This is however an act of separation (for) we see that when this one does seek this action that seems to work so well for her alone, when she opens her mind to other influences there is a breakdown of what she is able to do. This is due to the lack of using the conscious mind and its reasoning power. (1062001BGC2)

After years of struggling as an artist, Saf was able to admit what had eluded her. The barriers to her success in art were of her own making. They had nothing to do with others appreciating her pieces. The obstacle came from her own dependency on emotional excitement and her subsequent failure to reason. The lack of reasoning was also apparent in the level of success she could achieve in her business and family endeavors.

> ...This one's creative mind is often separated, segmented. There is the ability for the subconscious mind to push aside the conscious mind, to operate in ways which are most creative. However they are not necessarily understood by the self or others because the conscious mind is not involved in such a way to interpret the energies that are being expressed. (1062001BGC2)

The pattern Saf had created for the self was to work alone. She enjoyed losing herself in painting a mural or sculpting a bust. Her talents were varied as long as she could create what she wanted. She even championed the freedom to express as she wanted, seeing it as the reason for coming to the United States from a more repressive and dictatorial government. Freedom of artistic expression is available in a climate like the United States however Saf discovered that freedom does not mean financial independence or security.

Others would pay for her talent to bring to life *their* dreams, not hers. She found it difficult to receive images and instruction from another so she could fulfill their desire. This mirrored her own refusal to respect and utilize her conscious mind. Her resistance to using reasoning to satisfy her commissioner was the root of her failure to use her art to support herself financially. Her report described this as *"at the times that the energies are being interpreted by the conscious mind, the conscious mind must be disassociated from awareness of other energies from other intelligence."* For Saf to create the way she was accustomed to she believed she had to shut out other people and their ideas. When she would try to receive what someone else was saying, she experienced *"disorientation, confusion and host of emotional reactions because there has not been the entrainment of the inner and outer self in the creative endeavor with conscious awareness."*

This highlights the importance of the conscious mind in any creative endeavor. The source of this one's limitation was the lack of awareness of her own relationship with creation. Saf's definition of creativity expanded greatly when she asked what she could do to cultivate genius. The response brought insight into the universal action known as reasoning.

> This would be maturing of the reasoning. This would be in stilling of the outer mind in order to be more attentive in what is received not only from the inner self and what this one considers to be her own, but to receive energies from wherever they come. It would be helpful for this one to practice reproducing what already exists with authenticity. The changes in consciousness that this one would need to undergo in order to do this repeatedly, not only in artistic endeavors as would be this one's least line of resistance although this is important, but also in speech, in recitation, in imitation, any form where this one could use as the standard by which she is learning the ability to accurately reproduce something that is not of her own making. This is an essential part of the creative mind that this one has not honed and has not developed. Therefore it is missing in her creative process. Most of the other elements of the creative mind are present and therefore this one needs only focus on this in order to give her what is missing. This then would enable this one to move forward and begin to unite elements of creativity that have before inhibited her. (1062001BGC2)

Here the elements of reasoning are clear. *Stilling of the outer mind* is the employment of the **will**. *Reproducing* brings **memory** into the present moment. For instance, Saf began to copy, to re-create, famous art pieces, line by line, color by color. As she went through the motions she engaged both memory and **imagination** in the present moment. She could begin to *think* like the master painters! The ability to reproduce was becoming hers through harnessing the power in her *conscious* mind.

An Intuitive Health Analysis (12304BGC2) given at the request of a young woman describes another function of reasoning – the capacity for reasoning to elevate homo sapiens beyond instinct into homo spiritus. The report is so rich, it appears here in its entirety.

> This one has very strong ideas for the self. We see that the strength is from this one's desire and we see that this one has a very strong combination of understood experiences that are present within this one's existence. We see that this one needs to learn how to interpret these energies so they might become beneficial and useful to her in accomplishing the ideals that this one holds.
>
> This one has attempted to this point to be able to manifest the ideals from instinct or psychism. We see that by doing so this one has brought to the self many experiences but they have not been understood. We see there needs to be a strengthening of the reasoning ability, particularly of the will, and we see as this is built there can be the ability to hold within this one's line of attention an experience or an element of experience until it is understood. This one has had the tendency to go through experiences and become somewhat cursory where this one merely moves from one thing to another. We see that there is the ability however within this one to think deeply and to be able to draw connections beyond merely the physical experience itself. We see there is some sense of this and there is a belief in it but it has not been matured to a knowing where the consciousness can be viable and flourishing in that regard. We see that this will happen as this one becomes more creative.
>
> We see that this one enjoys creativity in other people but does not particularly see herself as talented in that area. Would suggest to this one in this regard, there is a need for this one to expand the idea of what this one believes creativity is. This one has a talent and a creative ability with people. We see this one needs to honor this and to value it.
>
> This one has the ability to think and to draw together ideas when this one is focused and sustains concentration. Therefore it is the ability to hold the attention at will that will aid this one the most in calling forth abilities within the self. This will also give this one a way to understand the returning of energy for we see that this one tends to use energies and to allow them to disperse. There is a need for this one to understand a

certain line of obligation of debt that is owed to the self for making the most of the experiences that this one chooses.

In the emotional system we see that this one becomes frustrated with the self quite easily. We see there is a high level of self judgement that is polarized and we see that in this there is difficulty in this one being able to see clearly and maintain a sense of equanimity. This will be built as this one's will is strengthened and this one can sustain and hold the attention at will. This is necessary for being able to observe the movement of the emotions within becoming involved in them.

We see that this one has a certain ability to do this with other people, an objective sense. But this one does not know how to do it in a subjective sense. We see in order for this to occur, this one must be able to sustain undivided attention for a prolonged period of time. This will free this one to be able to then see the movement of the emotions as it occurs within her for this one can be quite expressive emotionally and this one can be able to experience, and to a certain degree verbalize, the emotions that this one is experiencing. This is a valuable skill and when paired with the command of the attention will give this one an ability to perceive and to act upon that which is making itself known in the physical world. This is a kind of precognition. It is a kind of clairvoyance. We see that this one has potential in that regard.

This one has learned a pattern of denial where this one can see something coming and does not want it to occur or does not want to own the realization that this one has foreseen it. Therefore there is a pattern of denial that this one will need to admit and to allow to disperse. We see this affects the physical body as do some of the other attitudes stated, particularly in regards to the eliminatory system, the colon. This body could process food more readily and more completely. We see it would aid for this one to take into the body more raw foods, less processed foods, more water would be helpful.

It would be helpful also for this one to learn how to use the body – to appreciate its movement, its motion, its range, and its capacity. Therefore any form of movement that would stretch this one in this direction would be possible. There is a tendency for pressure in the area of the gall bladder and liver. We see that the energy is often stagnant here. Acupressure could be helpful in stimulating energy flows in this area. It would also relieve some of the pressure upon the upper torso, the lungs, the heart.

We see there is a kind of arhythmia or rapid beating of the heart that occurs at times. This is particularly when this one is shutting down the compassion. Would suggest this be taken as a signal for this one to be more heart centered at those times.

We see that this one's tendency toward being unconditional often causes the body to not use the nutrients that are taken in. It is as if the body itself does not commit to flourishing or even surviving. In order for this to change there will need to be a commitment made within the mind for the learning and a commitment towards responsibility for the self - mentally, emotionally, and physically. Would suggest this one practice grace in the movement of the body. Would suggest this one practice sustained moving within perimeters, within predesignated ways.

We see there is some buildup of cholesterol in the bloodstream. This is primarily due to the tension in the liver at the present time. There is a need for this one to move energy, to understand how to harmonize with it and to move with in. Anyway in which this could be done would be helpful as well. This is all. (12304BGC2)

Collectively humanity is reaching a point of critical mass, a tipping point in consciousness. In the last century reasoning was largely employed in the service of military arms, the war games of two world wars. In the latter part of the 1900's, reasoning was employed in making technology widely available. Now as we enter the third millennium, we must learn to wield this conscious power as a creator. This will require the integration of the Essential Life Skills into a single mental action called Reasoning.

When reasoning is present understanding follows. The depth and clarity of thought provides greater illumination in the event at hand. Previously polarizing situations can be neutralized. Heart lessons – acceptance, allowing, forgiving, thanksgiving and the like –

can be admitted and made a part of self. In this way reasoning promotes intuition.

The connection between reasoning and intuition is reflected in the answer to a question this woman asked about becoming a better leader. The report suggested she *"begin to develop the specifics of the vision of the ideal that this one does hold in the mind and to bring forward and to use the mind in ways that will reveal to her the potential based upon the understandings that this one possesses. It is important that this one mature the consciousness from the instinct and psychism to reasoning and intuition."* In many ways this is the destiny for us all.

Remember the woman whose Healer's Portrait identified her influential quality as curiosity? That report went on to describe many of the Essential Life Skills and how they could be better used to fulfill the woman's destiny.

> We see that there have been many experiences where this one had failed to be curious, had failed to use reasoning and imagination, and had experienced the consequences which often were devastating. Through these this one learned to value the ability to move forward, the ability to see what is missing, the ability to add to, the ability to move forward. We see that all of these different qualities have come together in the form of curiosity and in the form of being able to have the power of receptivity. We see that there is a very strong urge within this one in this vein, and we see that it is a power that is magnetic and it is healing at the same time. (39026BGC)

When she asks, "What is it that gets in my way of being a healing presence?" the answer is dual: doubt and dishonesty. When the woman asks for ways to recognize the dishonesty more easily and readily this is the reply:

> This is when this one falls prey to her own tales or her own lies or the lies of others that this one has made her own. The limitations of belief, the limitations of the physical world, and any thought that is associated with these becomes the means by which this one denies her innate understanding of receptivity and the part that it

plays in wholeness.

What we choose to receive from our environment shapes and molds the opportunities. Being at the right place at the right time is a factor of birth circumstances and how we respond to them. The world is filled with stories of unfortunate births and horrific childhoods transcended by admirable leaders in all fields of endeavors. Reasoning is the power that produces such character. We must act upon what we receive.

> It is most important for this one to set an ideal for the Self. There is incredible potential within this one that can be brought to fruition through the conscious and willful use of the creativity that exists within the curiosity. This needs to be channeled. It needs to be directed, therefore, this one needs to create a solid and profound image that this one is willing to move toward. Work on this has already begun but there must be the elimination of the dishonesty so that there can be the elimination of the doubt. (3902BGC6)

This excerpt is outstanding for it highlights one of the two stumbling blocks for every individual desiring change – doubt. (The other is fear.) Doubt loses its grip on our memory as we realize its source. Through disciplining the conscious mind we cultivate an honest conscious ego. No longer at the mercy of inferior or superior notions, the mind is free to be still. When the mind is still past doubts (memory) and future fears (imagined) are released. The mind is free to use its great power.•

REASONING

is the combined use of memory, attention, and imagination to fulfill the duty and purpose of the conscious mind through building understandings.

Reasoning
What is It?

The sink in the college kitchen had lived a full life. It had helped prepare over 20,000 meals and cleaned 5600 milk pails. With caulking becoming a monthly chore it was time to let go of the old sink-counter arrangement and move toward the equipment needed to feed more than 100 on a regular basis.

Technology had evolved in 20 years to one piece counter/ sink durable ensembles perfect for our constant 24/7 use. This sink would never know caulk.

We contacted the local building supply store which had recently opened in the nearby town. The salespeople were friendly and helpful, eager to build long lasting relationships. The kitchen department manager listened to our needs and reviewed the detailed diagram one of the teachers had made. He planned a "T" oak cabinet with a corian counter and sink to fill them. To make sure the new unit would fit into the space (and to visit the Peace Dome), he came out on his day off.

Some lack of communication led to the first postponement. It turned out that the counter was being built by one company and the furniture cabinet by another. The building suppliers were the middlemen acting as a manager or planner organizing the "event". We didn't know this until three days before the counter was to arrive.

The counter people called at the end of the month giving us the earliest date they could have the sink unit ready. It was a disappointing month away but we were willing to adjust our activities to accommodate the soonest opening. A Thursday was decided upon. As the time neared we received no word from anyone about when the cabinets would arrive. This was a necessary part of the sequence of events since the counter had to have something to sit upon.

On Sunday we began planning the movement of energy necessary for the installation. Our current sink and cabinet needed to be removed and new pipes run. Our daily routines would be disrupted during this time which affected the preparation and clean up of meals.

We streamlined the operation, even adding a new sink on a porch, and began the operation the next day.

We realized we needed to know more about the cabinets in order to place the pipes in the correct place. A couple of men who were going into the store to buy the plumbing equipment said they would check it out. They returned with distressing news. It seems the cabinet was set to be delivered on Thursday also. This could work if the cabinet came early morning and counter in the afternoon. In order for this to work it would need to be more than theory.

Our manager friend wasn't at work on Monday, so we had to wait until Tuesday for a response. Turned out the cabinet was arriving at their store on Wednesday - sometime - and would be delivered until Thursday - sometime. He contacted the counter people who said if it wasn't Thursday, the soonest they would come was another two weeks.

Well, here we were. Twenty people on campus eating three meals a day with 75 people expected the following weekend and no kitchen sink. It seemed like a problem.

It was resolved by setting a new installation date, that with the managers coaxing would be in one week. This would mean we would have a sink before the big weekend. We would adjust.

This time the cabinet was set to arrive on Thursday and the counter on Friday. We expected to be up and running by at least Saturday morning.

Thursday the cabinet installers arrived in the morning. I was helping our son with math tests when Daniel came to ask if I could get away.

I sensed it wasn't good, "Bad news?"

"Some. Not too bad," Daniel replied. "You need to hear it."

When we walked into the kitchen, two men, an older and a younger, were measuring and looking a good blend of busy-concerned-bored. I listened to their stories. "You'll need to put spacers so your doors will open." "The pipes need to be moved or you'll have to cut holes in three cabinets instead of two." "They may need to redo the countertop." Then quickly adding, "You shouldn't have to pay for it." It wasn't about the money, if the company had erred, the company would be accountable in all areas. It was about time.

How much time was this relatively simple exchange going to take?

"Who measured this?" the guys were starting to look for someone to blame. "Is there a template?" A call to their bosses said their company had tried to get a blueprint all week. I wonder how they could know how to build a counter without one.

Then the extreme, "These will need to be redone. They won't fit." I'm looking at the cabinet unit in place in the kitchen and wondering why. "You'll need to have new cabinets made and probably a new countertop." This is the kind of radical statements disguised as a solution that start many marital and world wars.

All of a sudden I smile. I've been practicing these life skills I talk about here - undivided attention to listen, the still mind of concentration, and the receptive imagination. What I see is the blind monks and the elephant. Are you familiar with the parable? Three blind monks are in the marketplace one day and they hear a trumpeting sound. They follow the nearby sound and come upon the animal. Their amazement reflects in their sounds of awe and discovery.

"I didn't realize an elephant is like a tree," said the monk whose arms were wrapped around the elephant's front leg.

"No," replied his brother, "it is like a rug, wide and flat – and hard!" This monk was standing alongside the animal, feeling his massive bulk.

How ridiculous thought the third monk. "An elephant is long like a thick rope. Most flexible! Are you blind?" And of course they were, not merely physically blind but mentally blind. Each had a piece of the puzzle, a part of the whole, but because they would not listen to one another they were all self-delusional, thinking they had the answer and the others were wrong. In reality they were all right.

The situation in the college kitchen was this parable brought to life! How amazing. The cabinet workers had their piece, the counter people had theirs, and the building suppliers there. We had the image of the "elephant" and the manager was the only one - because he had made the final designs - who had the whole picture. Until he arrived, the left hand did not know what the right hand was doing.

What occurred to me in this experience is that the great lesson in specialization is the need to communicate. With communication more people can be a part of a creation, in this case the three different companies and those they contracted out to install their custom-built products. When communication is slack or altogether missing, the creation dissolves into chaos with many vying for king with no subjects to be found.

Separation is enriching and advancing when the whole is in mind. Reasoning is what separates, identifies, admits, and connects. There were many tenets of reasoning that were being used and broken in the kitchen this day.

Communication was the cure. Once plans were faxed to us, the cabinet guys could tell what needed to be done, what was intended. "It would have been better to have a 54" cabinet here instead of a 48." When they can tell we aren't going for this new recreation option, an alternative comes up. "The one you have can work," now he's starting to reason with the resources at hand, "if we move it out a few inches and cover the open space with a spacer board." This is a use of memory and will, then he adds imagination, "That space will actually provide a place for the pipes." We have a reasonable conclusion.

Once the "blind monk" began communicating, the whole could be seen and we had our solution. The only thing it cost any of us was time.

Reasoning enables us to see a whole picture – in mind. It frees us to becoming mental creators like the Creator who gave us existence.

Reasoning requires whole brain activity. The Essential Life Skills empower you to use the existing mind potential.

Vision Quest is an excellent example of reasoning. *Vision Quest* is the codename we gave to the painting of the college barn. The story of how this two story, 22,000 square foot canvas was painted by 80 volunteers over eight weeks is told by those who lived it in an hour documentary-type film. It exemplifies all the skills in every way – its conception, its creation, its implementation, its impact on those who see it. Reasoning is the skill that put that mental image on the barn.

Since 1975, classes at the School of Metaphysics have opened with a mental projection of personal and common ideals, goals, and purposes. What is imaged is the activity that will manifest these ideas. The projection moves through three phases, the third being a lofty goal of building a college, a university of the future for intuitive, Spiritual Man. The image of the campus has remained the same for three decades.

"Now in this collective pool of energy, mentally see the College of Metaphysics. Envision the large pyramid-shaped building in the center of the campus that will serve as the common meeting place on campus. Surrounding the pyramid, see domes in clusters of three which will house students and their teacher. See people of all backgrounds, races, religions, cultures studying Universal Law at this place, learning how to use their full potential....."

Thousands of minds have added energy and substance to this image. Each one has contributed to the dream and in doing so expanded their own awareness of creation. This is the process known as visualization. Visualization is the art of mental imaging and the science of manifestation. This begins in the conscious mind, for what sets visualization into motion is one's power to reason.

I teach people visualization. In over 30 years of teaching I have learned that some third eyes are open and some are closed. Some people "see it" and some do not. Through those years artists who "see it" have tried to illustrate the dream on paper so others can see it too. It wasn't until an exceptional artist came into the School that the idea of placing the opening projection on the barn was conceived.

The idea didn't come right away. Chris' talent is noteworthy. Formally trained as a graphic artist, he's made a living from painting pictures on people's bodies, from tattooing. I had to still my conscious mind when I met Chris. He was quite imposing. Over six feet, dredlocks two feet long, with tattoos on his neck, arms, hands, chest, and I didn't know where else. His intense stare could be disarming, and experience told me, intentionally so. Meeting Chris was a great stimulus for some personal brainwashing of old ideas from movies and parents and the like that harshly judged people with tattoos.

In time, I learned of Chris' capacity to envision when he and his teacher brought a 4' by 4' scale model of a dome that could serve as a building for SOMs in cities. The prototype told me Chris knew how to do something with his ideas. He had the ability to reason required for any creation.

A year later Chris came for full time study at the College of Metaphysics. Wanting to give him ways to exercise his talent that would benefit others, I asked him to illustrate the Paz story in a myth we had written at a Peacemakers gathering during the time the Peace Dome was under construction. When my husband saw the beautiful colors Chris used, he asked Chris to create a cover for the book he was writing on ***The Tao Te Ching Interpreted and Explained***. Chris' thought forms adorn that striking book cover today.

When I saw what Chris had created I was astonished. Appreciation of his skill filled my mind. I also saw that every bit of space was filled. As a book publisher, those things matter for an eye catching book cover needs both pictures and words. With Chris' drawing he had left no space for words.

I learned something valuable about Chris that day. His art demonstrated that the subconscious inner self is pressing forward to make itself known. Since the inner mind communicates in pictures, I knew Chris' inner urge is strong. His talent allows others to see what is in his mind to the degree he can illustrate it with lines and colors. He does with images what I strive to do with words. As he described it later, the urge is so strong that before studying at SOM it expressed itself only through the many and varied artistic tattoos on his and others' bodies. What I learned, and the process through which I learned it, *is* reasoning.

Chris' Tao painting told me he is learning about space. His beauty created a dilemma for me for in designing a book cover. He has created a complete 9" x 7" painting that did not invite tinkering. It filled the entire front side of the book jacket. Adding the title and author name would require creativity, skill, and diplomacy.

Chris and I talked about space, the use of white in art, the purpose of silence in form and color, the things not seen. With still mind, he could receive the images as I spoke, and I learned that Chris' inner urge is stronger than his ego as an artist. Chris wanted to learn also.

From that time, I began looking for ways to help him build rapport with that inner urge. Chris demonstrated several qualities in this period. His determination showed as he volunteered and followed through on what he said he would do. Dedication to an ideal was demonstrated each morning as he led the reading of the Universal Peace Covenant in the Peace Dome at 5:30 a.m. With a dharma described as steadfastness, Chris' actions are permeated with willfulness, a necessary element for reasoning.

One day I asked Chris if he'd ever painted a mural. That's when I learned he'd gone to school to study graphic design. It had been several months since the dedication of the Peace Dome and we needed a schoolwide goal to act upon in the present. These were the qualifications in my mind:

The project needed:
- to manifest the ideal and purpose of the School of Metaphysics
- to include anyone who wanted to be a part of it
- to empower every person involved to learn something(s) new
- to be accomplished in a short amount of time, six months
- flexibility in its execution
- to cost little with big impact

Memory images from murals on the sides of buildings and even barns came forward to merge with the present reality of Chris' talent for graphically illustrating ideas then project to the two meeting on the sides of the College barn. If this mental action was an equation it would look like this: Memory + Will + Imagination = Reasoning.

The beauty of *Vision Quest* is this part of the story was just the beginning,– the seed idea. In order for this seed to grow and mature, a series of mental actions, sequences of reasoning would need to take place. First, was talking with the college chancellor to secure the go ahead. Initial resistance birthed a new idea (imagination) in my mind. We could paint (memory and will) the campout shed, a much smaller building, as a prototype for others to see. After a few days I was given the go ahead.

Next came working with Chris. Initially he was onboard, excited. He could "see" it. The shed project took eight people less than two weeks working on it a little almost every day. Chris began to feel that time was being squeezed in for the project and his enthusiasm began to wane. He had help but not as much as he had imagined. Yet when he had the opportunity to ask for help he was reluctant. These attitudes revealed what he needed to learn.

He began avoiding talking about the barn project. The elusiveness of one who does not want something to happen was apparent. Each time we spoke of the shed, I counseled on the beauty of working with others. I taught about the principles of mind beyond the art. I brought to Chris' attention how people who did not believe they could paint were getting involved, painting leaves, flowers, bushes where only a white metal wall had been. This is the magic of creation. I knew Chris experiences it and I knew he had what it takes to provide the vehicle for others to experience it. That was my purpose in this endeavor. Ideal + Purpose + Activity = Success is another reasoning equation that works anytime, anywhere.

It would require several people to help Chris see the light. He describes the turning point of his inertia in the *Vision Quest* film, "I had a revelation this morning. I realized the worst case scenario that I'd imagined, what I feared could happen was that no one would want to help me, that little or no effort would be put toward it. It would just be me working on the barn and it would take a long time. I wouldn't learn much from it or be able to create something beautiful on the land.

"That worst case scenario was basically the same as if I didn't do anything! I'd be by myself. Dr. Daniel Condron, my teacher, helped me see that. I received the whole image of myself, there was lots of crying, lots of receiving, and it's within me now." From that point Chris was fully committed to himself, the project, and to others.

From the sketches to the full color representation to the outline to the three dimensional manifestation of the idea, the elements of reasoning present in *Vision Quest* are universal. Even transferring the image from a 16 x 20 inch piece of paper onto a 30-foot structure could only happen through the application of reasoning. The first day I helped paint I noted the vertical lines and rivets on the metal building. They were evenly spaced. What a great natural grid line

for Chris to follow! I immediately understood how he had completed the outlines so quickly. His process was to simply transfer the lines on his drawing onto the magnified surface of the barn wall. This was a math challenge, which is why reasoning and math are often linked.

Another math challenge was the relationships of people to the project. There was no way Chris or I or students living at the college could accomplish this goal alone. We needed help. "Never underestimate the power of a small group of committed individuals to change the course of history," said Margaret Mead. "It is the only thing that ever has." A student recently taught me this quote which we both appreciate, largely because it describes the endeavor we are committed to in the present time. Painting the barn was a focal point for this kind of energy. Accomplishing the goal would require relationship.

People were easily inspired when they saw the shed. From a distance it seemed to blend in with the trees and woods behind it. Only as you came closer did you realize what you saw was someone's dream.

Chris began drawing the outlines on the barn in mid-August. Magic marker and spray paint were the tools to create what I described to him as a paint by number canvas. I felt secure that he would understand the reference and begin seeing it as his connection with those who were about to change their beliefs about themselves as artists. For the next eight weekends people came from 12 states to volunteer their services in laying green, blue, and copper colored paint where Chris instructed. According to his desire, he painted very little.

The reward came every day. Inspiration swept through people cleansing doubt or disbelief. The reality of dreaming was becoming a reality as the creative mind was stirred into action. The thrill of creation was imbedded in every brushstroke and the end result reflects it.

"At the end," Chris says, "was definitely a self-reflective time. I'd gaze out from the roof of the barn and see the Peace Dome, the ridge where the Octagon will be, and even further into the land where the pyramid will be constructed. I could see people coming and going. I also could see I was experiencing the other side of a dream come true and it was a surprise! I can't think how many times I've been that surprised by my own potential and the potential of others. That's what I get out of bed for every day because I want to be surprised!

"When plans unfold in the mental, emotional, and physical experiences, the experiences are complete and I have grown so much from it. It is awe inspiring. It must be like what it is to place a flag on the moon and look back at the Earth and say, 'Today man reached a greater potential than he had before'."

Living life well is a reflection of our ability to reason. With reasoning, we can receive the benefits from the past and make them useful in the present moment to produce a future we look forward to living. It is the great lesson of all humanity today.

Many confuse opinion with truth, rationalizing with reasoning. How do you tell the difference? In the conscious blend of the art and the science of reasoning, understandings are made and intuition is produced.

Reasoning answers "why am I here?" As you reason, you ask "Why?" There is a reason. Beyond the judgements of good and bad, right and wrong, there is a reason for each experience in your life. And you want to find out what that reason is. You become so entrained in the mind that you become a channel for infinite energy and in that you can go forever. All residual inklings of wanting to go unconscious leave you.

Simply stated, reasoning is the ability to be conscious in the waking, Conscious Mind. Intuition is the ability to remain conscious in Subconscious Mind.•

Where Science and Spirituality Meet

Reasoning is a culmination of several essential life skills. Reasoning combines the directed use of memory, supporting imagination, with the undivided attention of using the whole mind. Reasoning would not work if we simply used memory, imagination and attention. Attention does exist in the body itself. Animals exhibit the power of attention. However, undivided attention requires the use of the will in keeping the whole mind present, not just the body's senses. Therefore, reasoning is a mind skill, not a brain skill. It includes and demands the presence of the thinker. Reasoning is the result of past, present and future all converging into a single point, the now, with a thinker present to cause there to be motion somehow.

Reasoning requires breath. it depends on the thinker being fully present, in command of the mind, the ego, and the body all at once. Conscious breathing is what brings the thinker fully into the present and physical so the thinker can guide a situation to a desired outcome.

Evolutionarily, we are in the later stages of developing reasoning. We as a human race have been developing our capacity to be fully present in the body, to know its workings and abilities through sport and science, as well as know our self as through introspection, psychology and science. Science keeps revealing indirectly that we are more than our physical bodies, and psychology keeps wondering what we actually are. Introspection, through meditation, reveals our true nature as light beings. Bit by bit science and spirituality are converging on the same conclusions, that we are spirit inside a body. The more these two systems converge, the more present the thinker is in the body, and the more purposeful the thinker can be. This is the development of responsibility as a thinker, which is the later stage of Reasoning Man as a sort of species. –Paul Madar

Reasoning to Intuition

One thing leads to another

I'm just beginning to get how having a developed, disciplined conscious mind and reasoning ability allows for intuition. The moments where I've had clear intuitive perceptions have been when click, click, I put two and two together and had the reception of Truth in a situation. I did this a lot as a holistic therapist and body worker. Clients would come in with complaints. Because I have some physiology background I was able to work with and look into the body to identify more of what was happening inside. Once this was known and confirmed with muscle response testing we were able to identify the actual cause of their disease often by using the book Permanent Healing and often later through health analysis. I'm learning to appreciate the value of being familiar with the seventh level in order to align with the subconscious mind. – Ivy Norris

ELS#8

A Short Class on Reasoning

Dr. B: You can teach people to understand the difference between needs and wants through teaching the power of reasoning. Most of the wants in an individual's mind are a product of beliefs that are based on somebody else's thoughts, not yours. They're based upon what other people have told you for years that you should want, that you need in order to have a good life, to be happy.

Briana (a 12 year old I was tutoring) and I are reading a book called The Life and Death of Arithmetic. It's a series of essays and one of the essays is about advertising. It describes four kinds of "stupid buying." One of these is emotional buying. According to the author, emotional buying is "this will make me sexier. It will make me more handsome. It will make me more respectable. It will make other people think better of me." Emotional buying is based on how you've you've bought into advertising. The author illustrates his point of how advertising directs the buyer's wants by linking ideas like: improve your personality and sex, give you esteem and sex, everyone of the desireables had *"and sex"* attached to it because that is the emotional appeal of advertising.

Look at any magazine. What do you see? Men and women in embraces and various displays of masculinity and femininity. The message is you buy this product and you have this. They don't even show you the car. They show a bird flying off. It represents freedom. In other words, they're using the language of mind, and people are clueless. Most don't stop to think about what's happening to them. Their subconscious minds are being controlled by other people and they don't even know it. They buy it, hook, line, and sinker. It's what our economy is based on and that's what this whole chapter of the Arithmetic book is about.

You don't "get rid" of your wants. You **understand** them on a new level. You learn to reinterpret the energies and that process is creativity.

Dr. L: That's why dream interpretation is very important in this step. As someone learns the language of mind they can interpret energies more accurately. People begin to take notice of how images are used, the purpose they fulfill, both in their own communication and in receiving communication.

Dr. B: Yes, night dreaming and daydreaming are related. Night dreaming requires a still conscious mind to receive the inner, subconscious mind's message. Otherwise the dream echo is fades and is lost. Daydreaming occurs when one is awake, in the conscious mind. It can appear as visions or desires and is most often a passive state of mind watching the thoughts of others. That's why we say people are "spacing out" because if asked they won't be able to tell you what they were thinking in the last five minutes.

SF: So that's why visualization is like controlled daydreaming. There's more attention given to what your mind, your thoughts are doing. You are where your attention is.

Dr. B: Yes, whether in the past, back when you were in high school, or the future when you retire. Most people spend very little time where anything is accomplished, which is the present.

SF: So is the exercise of visualizing a flower an exercise in imagination?

Dr. B: Visualization is very important. Being able to create that flower in your mind is an act of concentration, aggressive concentration, not receptive. Receptive concentration is the candle exercise. Aggressive concentration is visualization. It's essential because you' want to wield your thoughts. When you can you become aware of, and then free from, the pairs of opposites that entrap human consciousness. It requires creativity to do this, and creativity is an act of reasoning. The components of reasoning are...?

JM: Memory, imagination and attention.

Dr. B: Or will. When all three are present reasoning can occur. First, we have to harness that imagination. What happens to imagination in the hands of an undisciplined conscious mind?

Dr. L: Fear is produced. And doubt.

Dr. B: When the first five skills are applied, the conscious mind is disciplined. Then the imagination becomes a tool for soul growth. You begin to transcend your own ego. Creating your wants, your desires, becomes less important. What takes its place?

SF: Wanting to give what you have to other people.

Dr. B: You want to create something less and less. You want to give what you already have because the first five Essential Life Skills cause the mind to begin to become entrained. This synchronization starts to reunite the soul. It doesn't lead you away from soul, out into the material world. It leads you inside. Life skills still the outer mind enough that the inside, the Light can shine and from that inside stuff comes everything that you want. Those first five steps, using them, gives you awareness, awareness of who you are, where you came from, where you are going, why you are here. Breath gives you experience, and Reasoning gives you understanding of that experience.....•

This first email is written about starting new classes. I include it here because with the application of reasoning you will quickly see the principles it outlines and the Essential Life Skills it employs can apply to starting anything new – a new project, a new career, even a new relationship.

Dear Dr. Barbara,
Inspiring someone is awakening a viewpoint that realizes that something that seemed impossible can actually be done. - Harry Palmer

Indy's two cents
Two of the three classes I have taught had 10 or more students the first night. Here is what I have done to produce this. (Note my Dharma is Initiative: "We see this one to have a very aggressive energy..." Kelly's email is a good one on receptivity)

I think of the last week before a class starts as a race. And I don't stop running until after class night.

1. Every day visualize the class full of students, the joy, peace and wisdom. AND visualize yourself as a beacon of light and that every person you meet is someone who needs and wants to be in the school. Reading the Transcendent Oracle will help.

2. Every day take activity (make phone calls, put out fliers, set up lectures, interpret a dream for someone, give a flier to the guy standing behind you in the bank, and especially CLEANING YOUR SCHOOL is creating a receptive space) While you are taking activity hold in mind the vision of what you want to create and have the intention of why you are doing it. Are you washing dishes to wash dishes or are you washing dishes to create a space to receive students, where is your attention?

EVERY TIME we clean and rearrange the Indy school I get calls.

3. Who you are being is VERY IMPORTANT. Not too long ago I was teaching a student to go flier-ing. People would walk by and say "No thanks" because of his attitude of thinking he was bothering people. I did a few and he was amazed at the different responses. I said, "Imagine this is a solid brick of gold, you are giving them the most valuable gift in the World! I told him to straighten his posture, smile

more, be more aggressive, expect them to LOVE what you are saying."

While you are doing this use your MIND! A couple of attractive girls jogged by and the student I was with tried to give them a flier. "Sorry got no where to put it" was the response as they sped by. I sent them love and light and held them in my mind for a minute. Less than five minutes later they came back, "OK, what do you have?"

4. Many of the emails I have read talk about starting classes like it is impossible or at least very hard and mystical. YOU KNOW MORE THAN YOU THINK YOU DO! If you have had lesson three you have immense power and if you have lesson 9 you have received exercises that are the fundamentals for every exercise you will learn in the school. My desire is for people in the school (myself included) to see their inner value. And when you don't know how to do something instead of thinking of yourself as weak or incompetent, think of yourself as a baker who doesn't know recipe, or mechanic who works on domestic cars and has yet to learn about BMW. Or better still, a child learning a new game (beginner's mind). Can I play? What are the rules...that was neat how did you do it...good try, but it is more like this. Learning can be FUN and pleasurable when we stop believing we are the result and thinking we are dumb for not knowing.

Love Chance

Dear Chance,

Your $.02 is more like that brick of gold! Your voice needs to be heard by your peers more often for it is another voice of REASON. Unlocking reasoning is part of the purpose the School of Metaphysics serves in the present time. So much of humanity's existence is programmed (see Lucy's email out today), in essence a handful of minds determining the thought forms that will be broadcast in very physical ways (media, all kinds) to reach physically-thinking people who allow themselves to be controlled by their bodies. As Dr. Daniel says, "These kinds of people think the same thoughts over and over." You only think the same thoughts when you fail to reason. Reasoning elevates every thought. Reasoning employed produces intuition – knowing.

Most people attracted to SOM study are unique. They have always thought differently than the norm. This needs to continue in the study, not become further cause for rebellion, denial, or conflict. Anything becomes hard when the thinking is negative.

Reminding ourselves, our students, and each other that there is a better way to think, a better way to act, a better way to live is the beauty of the School of Metaphysics. SOM is a place to grow in spirit and in LIGHT. I know this education is a part of every person's destiny so I keep my mind open. And as you are discovering....it works!

Thank you for your experiences and write again soon!

O Dr. Barbara

Email 2

Hi,

I have been and still am really working on becoming a scientist in thought. This is not natural for me at all and it is a constant candle flame during the day. I need some suggestions on how to maintain a scientist kind of thinking. Dr. Sheila has told me to look for the effect of the exercises in my day. I also learn a lot from others who pay attention to what they do naturally. This kind of person looks to see how what he does with energy or breathe, etc. effects his day and mind. Is there anything else? This is one of my ideals for myself because I want to combine heart and mind.

Thanks,

Jen

Hi Jen!

Thanks for this great mind stretcher! We can all go lots of places with this and I'll bet when we all put our minds to it we'll have a great little book! So let's start it.......

Science! Ah, yes. Male energy, separate and identify, classify, organize, art built on principles. Let's start with what the word means. From the Latin "scientia" meaning knowledge, from "scio" to know. How do you like that?

So science in its purest form would be knowledge that responds to the desire to know. Knowledge in the true sense of the word, not the common day vernacular of brain info. Real knowledge then feeds the soul.

The disciplines we teach are scientific because they are the means by which knowing occurs. When you have a personal experience with concentration you know the power of the mind. When you have a personal experience with breathing you know the power of prana, chi, ki, etc. When you have a personal experience with astral projection you know that you are a soul. When you have a personal experience with past lifetimes you know the physical is temporary.

No one need tell you that these principles and theories work, you know from experience. The beauty of what we teach is the universality. Metaphysics is the study of Universal Laws and Truths, what connects all of creation, all life. It's a most exciting science because it addresses first cause, and we know that first cause is THOUGHT.

Now for a few more ideas. Hezekiah has a textbook that explains science on a fourth grade level. I love its simplicity. There are **four steps to being a scientist**. *Here they are:*

1. **Look carefully.**
2. **Observe and think clearly.**
3. **Hypothesize (make sensible guesses)**
4. **Test (with experience)**

Sound familiar? Like anything you do.....everyday? When the world is your laboratory, everything and everyone becomes part of your learning. You are the scientist and your life is the experiment. Science describes the way we use our conscious minds to experience and gain understanding. This requires reasoning which is why science has received credit for the past 1500 years for man's "advances."

As students of metaphysics, we must set our sights beyond the physical world, beyond physical causes and effects, physical experience. The true meaning of science is to know which opens the door to intuition. That is a most exciting endeavor to think that science can lead us to God as can art. I have been working them together for quite some time and they open doors of creative potential every time.

So use the steps above and you'll understand the mechanics in what those you admire do. It's all in the applying the benefits of the exercises. And that changes the consciousness. Just keep in mind the most powerful tool is a still mind, because a still mind can see God.

I love you,
Dr. Barbara

A REASONING EXERCISE

Thought Maps (Treasure Maps, Mind Maps, storyboards) are excellent tools for organizing your thoughts. Organizing your thoughts requires reasoning. Thought Maps include the cooperation of words and images. The conscious mind uses words for communication. Subconscious mind uses pictures. Describing thoughts using both is an act of reasoning which calls into motion the laws governing creation on your behalf.

Here are 4 rules to follow to produce an effective Thought Map:

1. Use a central image. Define your topic. *The Thought Map on the next page was created to illustrate our common ideal to send THE SILVER CORD around the world.*

2. Branch off from this image with pictures that further define your thoughts. *Ours show eight distinct avenues we plan to use.*

3. Simple words give conscious clarity. *The avenues are named: Education, internet, media, mail, contact, Society for Intuitive Research (SIR), SOM centers, and film festivals.*

4. The use of lines, symbols and color illustrate the relativity and connectedness of different areas. *THE SILVER CORD map uses these to move the idea forward and out, ie.from "media" comes cable networks, public television, newspapers, magazines, radio.*

SILVER CORD THOUGHT MAP

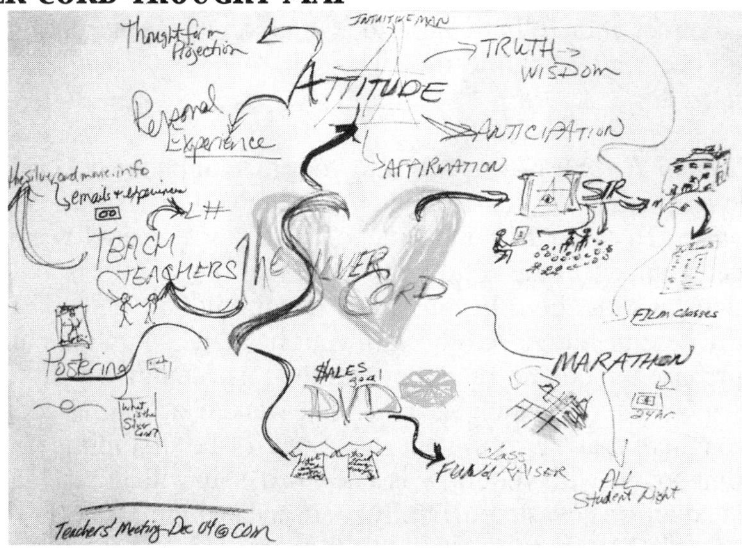

Eight Steps for Practicing Visualization

The means by which we realize our desires is to experience in the imagination what we would experience in the flesh when we live our ideal and achieve our goal. This imaginary conscious mind-experience of the end mobilizes the will. Purpose provides the fuel for our motivation to give. The subconscious mind, with its broader viewpoint, then constructs the means necessary to realize the accepted end.

The focused and concentrated mind finds it natural to assume a state which is beyond sensory experience. You can direct your mind to encounter an event before it occurs. Just follow these steps. Begin by giving yourself a half hour or so of quiet, private time.

Number One: Take a moment to list who and what you are most grateful for in your life. Keep writing until you have more than 100 "I am grateful fors" listed.

Number Two: Read your list aloud every day this week.

Number Three: At the end of the week, again set aside a half hour for you. Think of what you want to add to your life. This is your most heartfelt desire at this time in your life. Write down on a piece of paper, describing in detail what you want.

Number Four: Now, sit comfortably in a chair and think of that state of mind just as you are waking up in the morning. This is a state of reverie. Once you are calm and centered, close your eyes and direct your full attention to a situation or event you believe will occur *after* your desire is realized.

Number Five: Put yourself into your mental picture. Don't observe, participate! Performing your role stimulates your imagination. To cause the mind to act on your desire, mentally experience yourself in the action until it has all the vividness and distinctness of reality. If your event is a promotion at work, mentally hold the larger paycheck in your hand, take it to the bank or purchase a much needed item that the raise can give you. Give focus to your attention so it will not wander off into associated thoughts far away from your intention. If the first thing you are going to buy with your raise is a new bed, stay with that. Don't be visualizing a new stereo, family room and swimming pool. When your mind wanders, return it to the chosen imaged event.

In your mind all of this is happening in the now, not at some future time. The imaged future event is now a reality in a dimensionally larger world that goes beyond your conscious mind. The difference between feeling yourself in action here and now, and seeing yourself acting as on a movie screen, is the difference between success and failure.

Number Six: Permeate your mind with the feeling that your desire is granted. A state similar to drowsiness facilitates change because it reflects the integration of inner and outer minds. Both are working on your behalf now. Be advised: Do not be pushed to the state of sleep though. For if you lose consciousness altogether you are no longer able to control the movements of your attention. A moderate degree of reverie is all you need to direct your thoughts.

Number Seven:
When you are fully present in your imaged outcome impress the desired image with thanksgiving. You might mentally say, "I appreciate this ability to reap what I sow" or "I am thankful for the opportunity to fulfill my desire." Experience the fullness of thanksgiving. Allow it to dominate the mind.

Number Eight:
Repeat your visualization daily, updating your images as signs of manifestation begin making themselves known.•

Reasoning & Dreams

Today when I was checking dreamschool email, I responded to a woman who had written an email to Dr. Barbara concerning her son and her situation with him as well as a dream that she had recently that was troubling her. Dr. Barbara was leaving town for several days so she asked me to respond to this woman. The email trail from before when they corresponded was to be found in the "Kids" folder. I read all the emails back and forth. I gave my full attention to this woman's story and the wisdom that Dr. Barbara chose each time she responded to her. I wondered why she chose to respond the way she did each time as I tried to think like her. Afterward, I reread the woman's email in light of what I now knew, which was a lot.

This woman has an Indigo whom she doesn't understand. She feels like she has tried everything and is running out of options. Fear and doubt have caused her mind to close down. She is afraid of change and avoids it. What she is on the verge of realizing is that her experiences will continue and with greater and grater magnitude until she surrenders to changing.

The dream she wanted help with was that she was very weighted down. She could barely move. In her hands she held keys and a lighter, both of which she kept dropping and having to go to great lengths to pick up.

What I explained to her is that she needed to take action. She needed to find a way to think outside the box, to consider options that she had not thought of before. I suggested that she make a list of 10 new options, choose one and make it happen.

I also offered her a story that I use any time I am needing to think outside of the box. It came from an email that I heard once that has always stuck with me. The email was about a question asked on a job application. There were 100 applicants. The question goes as follows:

You drive up to a bus stop and it is raining. At the bus stop you see an old woman who is about to die, a good friend who once saved your life, and the man/woman of your dreams. You have room for one other person in your car. What do you do?

The first time I heard this I decided that I would take care of the woman who was about to die. The email said that out of all the applicants, one of them gave the following answer:

I would give my car keys to my friend so he could take the woman to the hospital and I would stay at the bus stop with the man/woman of my dreams.

When I heard this, I was so impressed. I thought this example might help this woman.

After I was done composing and sending this pretty lengthy email to her, I walked down the stairs appreciating how good it felt to have helped someone. I thought about how it is that I am able to do what I do, how it is that I have the capacity to help people. I realized in that moment that a lot of it had to do with my capacity to receive and to remember. I have learned how to be the way that I am from watching my teachers, those in my environment who know more than me.

This is reasoning, drawing upon what you remember in order to apply it to new experiences in the present moment.

–Stacy Ann Ferguson

"The intuitive mind is a sacred gift and the rational mind is a faithful servant. We have created a society that honors the servant and has forgotten the gift."

–Albert Einstein

Intuition

A Universal Language of Mind story

From the Land Down Under

Bamapama, the crazy man, lived in Dreamtime where anything is possible. Where he lived the sun stayed in one place all day long, never resting. Far underground was this place and it was always very hot.

One day Bamapama decided he would go up to the surface of the earth to hunt. Once out in the open, a kangaroo pounced by. Bamapama began his chase only to find the kangaroo could cover great distances very quickly. Bamapama was not one to give up so he stayed with the marsupial as the sun sank further and further in the sky.

At last the kangaroo stopped running. Bamapama came so close he knew he could spear the animal. As he pulled his throwing arm back, the sun fell completely below the horizon. Bamapama had never known darkness. Where he lived it was always light. He was scared and began to cry until he fell asleep.

The night passed and when Bamapama awoke the sun had returned. He was happy to find the daylight again. A thoughtful man, Bamapama observed, "Here they sleep at night and rise with the sun. This is a good way to live."

Upon his return underground, his people asked Bamapama where he had been. Bamapama told them the story beginning with the kangaroo into the night and the return of day. "It's a different world," he told them. "Come with me. You can see too. You can sleep at night and rise with the sun. It's a good way."

All the people followed Bamapama to the surface of the earth. Darkness came, the people were frightened, and like Bamapama, they, too, started climbing trees. "Don't be scared!" Bamapama counseled and so the people came out of the trees and slept.

When the sun returned, the people stretched under its warmth. "This is a good way to live," they said. "It is cooler here even with the sun overhead. If we get too cold we can get wood from the trees and make a fire. This is a good place to stay."

And so it happened that Bamapama and his people stayed never returning to the underground.

–An Aboriginal Story

I love the juxtapositioning of this story with Plato's cave allegory. How different in approach, how similar in intent. The desire for Light, the need to understand ourselves and our place in the world, is universal. We want to know that our lives have counted for something. Human progress depends upon it.

While Plato's fable stimulates reasoning, this Aboriginal story illustrates the power of intuition. Socrates leads Glaucon to new truths through the power of imagination applied to experience. This is the nature of reasoning. Bamapama shows his people how to accept and live new truths. This is intuition, the direct grasp of truth.

The ease with which Bamapama overcomes his own fear, updates his experience from constant light to light and darkness, and then shares the understanding of his experience with others illustrates the steps that produce intuition.

Once understandings are stored as permanent memory, we find ourselves possessing the kind of acceptance and initiative Bamapama displays. Where there is acceptance, there is no fight. Where there is initiative, there is change. Where these live together the peace that surpasses understanding can be yours.•

I N T U I T I V E R E S E A R C H

Intuition is

"...This is a very developed and sharpened intuitive sense capable of experiencing more in a metaphysical sense than what the physical experience itself would allow. Therefore it is easy to move beyond the limitations of the physical when this is entrained with the inner mind and with this dharma." (982001BGC4)

An aware conscious mind that is master of the body uses reasoning to produce intuition. (SOM Lesson 5)

Intuition Analysis is a new prosearch area of investigation. "Prosearch" is a term coined by Dr. Daniel Condron, senior Intuitive Conductor and Chancellor of the College of Metaphysics, which describes the forward-thinking and affirmative activity we conduct. We are not so much re-searching the past as we are pro-searching the relevance of the present to the past and to the future.

Over thirty years this work has enabled Daniel and me to aid thousands of people. In the early days we were partnered with others as we prosearched time travel and alternate realities. In the mid-80's we came together, traveling the Midwest to teach and give Intuitive Reports. By the 1990's we had learned enough to responsibly offer truthful, wholistic, and useful intuitive knowledge in progressive realms. This period is when many of the reports excerpted here began to take form. The Intuition Analysis is one of these.

The Intuition Analysis is given from the innermost part of Subconscious Mind. We refer to this as the mental level of consciousness. Here is where all ideas created in your waking conscious mind begin their journey toward manifestation. Daniel and I chose this perspective for the depth and clarity it affords and because it gives a complete picture of the intuitive cluster – in this case the individual's intuitive ability itself – being examined. In intuitive prosearch, analyses describe mental DNA whereas past life profiles from the Akashic Records relate mental heredity factors.

Prototypes of the Intuition Analysis are being refined. As you will see with the four excerpts that follow, the Intuition Analysis holds a great deal of promise in what it offers the individual who is the subject of the report and for others who desire to understand the inner workings of Mind.

The Intuition Analysis begins with a specific command to relate those factors necessary for the individual to better respond to his or her own intuitive faculties. Many people do not acknowledge their intuitive abilities. Thus the vast potential existing within their subconscious minds remains largely untapped throughout the life. This is how the report for a woman who takes her intuition for granted begins:

> This one has a very strong image of the self and how this one sees the self as being intuitive. There is a very

definite pattern of thinking that this one has adopted and has reinforced within the self that does cause this one to not only accept intuition but also to often heed it. This has been very useful to this one. We see that it has caused this one to be able to make decisions that in many cases were more rounded and more complete and more accurate than without it. Therefore there is a kind of respect and a kind of acceptance that this one has of intuition in working in her own life.

What escapes this one is the universal application of it and as much as this one believes this is her own special faculty and not one necessarily that can be learned or taught or developed. Therefore there is a considerable amount of area that this one could explore and expand upon that would aid this one greatly. This would neccesitate this one being willing to become uncomfortable which this one does not enjoy and this has been the reason why this one has not developed more in areas for quite some time, because this one has reached a level of comfort that she does not want to upset.

There is a need for this one to recognize that the degree to which this one has refused to continue moving, to continue the motion of consciousness is the degree to which this one has caused the energies to become depleted, has caused there to be an arresting of the growth of awareness, a compromise or a settling for, as this one might identify it out in the physical mind. What has occurred however is the structuring of consciousness in such a way that it has led to a false sense of security and peace. Therefore there are many instances because this one's inner drive is so strong where there will be reactions in this one. The reactions are there as stimulators for this one to once again cause movement and growth, there is a need for this one to recognize them as such rather than to recognize them as a distraction away from this one's own learning and growth. They indeed exist for this one's learning and growth. The resistance to them is the degree to which this one is attached to things being as they have always been.

There is a need for this one to begin to embrace movement and change. To fall in love with learning, for learning does promote change and it does cause there to be the movement toward aligning the self with superconscious mind. **In order for the intuition to flourish, as is capable within this one, this one will need to admit that the inertia that is experienced, what this one would see as being happy with what she has, actually comes not from an inner happiness but an outer fear that she might lose what she has if she investigates it or changes it or questions it.** Would suggest that this one consider that what this one possesses in consciousness and awareness cannot be lost nor can it be taken from her, therefore the fears that this one sometimes allows to control the self in this regard are not based upon truth. Intuition is truth, therefore the way that the thoughts are constructed hold this one away from the truth rather than moving this one toward it. Would suggest that this be considered. This is all. **(71200BGC5)**

You will offer suggestions on how to apply the intuitive faculties in the life for soul growth and spiritual development.

This one has certain patterns of thinking that have been established that do clue this one in or help this one to identify that the intuition is working for the self. Would suggest it would be very helpful for this one to retrace, to remember how this came about, how this was learned. In this process there will be much illumination for this one in being able to understand the point of cause or origin for that which this one now has found the comfort in. There is much that this one does have operating in terms of the subconscious mind, the subconscious mind is very viable within this one and is most ready to respond to the commands and desires of the conscious mind.

> There is a need for this one to respect this more greatly rather than to use it in habitual fashion to begin to become imaginative and explore and to go into areas that are not known and therefore might be uncomfortable or fearful to her. There is a need for this one to begin to explore the capacity to change the self, to recognize the self as cause and to, from that point, be able to transform the self and the life in whatever way this one can imagine. There is a great desire for this within this one but there is just as much if not more a hesitation and fear of what it might mean to have this kind of total responsibility. Would suggest that this one see it in that vein and begin to recognize it as this one's destiny, as this one's purpose for existence, as this one's capacity to align with the Creator, as this one's ability to move toward understanding the self as spirit, for this is in reality what it is. In this light this one would not hold this from the self. In the present construction of thinking, this one finds it acceptable to do so. This is what needs to be explored and developed in order for this one to be able to expand the consciousness concerning the intuitive faculties, the movement of energies, the interpretation of energies that are beyond the physical, this one has a great capacity to do so but this one will need to make the choices that will bring it to fruition. This is all. **(71200BGC5)**

We exist at an amazing time in the history of humanity. Before this time, extrasensory perception was the realm of singular individuals in a society. Shamans, priests, and wizards were born or chosen, not developed. Now we are capable of seeing the relationship between reasoning and intuition. As we do, our core beliefs begin to change. So do our fears. This fear is addressed in another report.

> There is some fear present in regards to (developing intuition). This would be what would need to be altered in order for there to be an appreciation of this one's experience of intuition. Some of this fear, in fact most of it, has come from external sources. It is information that this one has absorbed from

other people primarily in regards to the interpretation of her experiences and their own. We see that from this, this one has built a fear of being able to experience that is debilitating energy upon this one's desire and willingness to develop her own intuition.

There is a basic belief that this one holds on to that this one is intuitive. There is however not the bringing into the conscious awareness the reality of this, and therefore it is not being actively moved into a state of knowing where there would be the capacity to interact the capacity for communication between the conscious and subconscious minds for there to be a kind of awareness of energy flow as it does exist within this one. Therefore this one remains unconscious and it is within this frame that the fears fester and do predominate. Therefore in order for there to be a change in this there would need to be the willingness upon this one's part to make what has been unconscious conscious. Therefore this one will need to be willing to examine the beliefs, to examine where they have come from, to examine those which included fear and which were in fact fear beliefs and to begin to assess each one and to change them into what this one would desire to be. **(7700BGC4)**

As a young child this woman displayed a high degree of extrasensory perception that was unappreciated primarily because it threatened those around her. She knew telepathically of her parents' marital woes. They repeatedly denied these, even as the girl aged, and the infidelities became known. In the beginning she was told she was "imagining things." In this way she learned to identify mind to mind communication as imagination rather than intuition. For years, she functioned under this misconception, confusing a waking, conscious mind function with an intuitive, subconscious one. Her ability for telepathy was unconscious, often becoming a source of confusion in her young adult years. The report gave suggestions for changing this.

> There is within this one the concept that the intuition can be most beneficial and helpful. We see that there is an openness to this kind of thinking. This is the idea that needs to be developed in order for this one to become more cognizant, more conscious of how the intuition is working within the Self. The maturing of this one's Self will come by the transformation of the information which has been previously stored and is currently held. There needs to be more information received so that there can be the kind of comparison and the kind of change and the kind of maturing that has been described. It is through these kind of mental processes that this one will have the capacity to be able to explore the intuition purposefully with confidence, with expectation with hope and with ease. This is all.

Some time after this report, the woman began having spontaneous Kundalini experiences. Sometimes these showed themselves as shivers up the spine, sometimes as the ability to affect physical matter. On one occasion, while preparing a meal with me, a heavy glass tumbler shattered in her hand sending slivers and shards in every direction. The look on the young woman's face said everything. Plainly written on her face was the fear instilled in her from her childhood. My response was to take the occurrence in stride, reassuring her in thought and action that what had just happened was extraordinary and explainable.

Teaching this woman how to develop this telekinetic power is the key to replacing those fears with confidence and authority. This is in alignment with the suggestions given to her for developing her intuitive abilities for her soul growth and spiritual progression.

> It would help greatly for this one to begin to become more versatile in her capacity to think and verbalize what intuition is. It would be helpful for this one to begin to expand the mind along the lines of how the fully functional intuition can aid anyone to progress in their own spiritual and soul de-

velopment. How it can be the capacity to help people make the changes they desire to make that will be permanent rather than temporary. How it can assist in this one or anyone else in being able to have a more expanded world view to be able to recognize the connections between all people and the similarities between all people so that there can be a development of the consciousness both in a personal and a universal vein. That there can be more sensitivity to the needs and desires of Self and others and how they blend and mold. That there can be ultimately a greater understanding of harmony with the Universal Laws that govern creation. In this there is the bringing forth of innate intelligence the infinite intelligence the perfect intelligence which does exist within each life form within our known universe.

As this one begins to explore and develop these kinds of concepts of what intuition is, and she comes away from the previously held ones which were in some part filled with fear or trepidation, then there would be an unlocking within her self of the capacity to unify the reasoning capacity with the power of the subconscious mind which is intuition. This then would lead to the unification of the energies of the inner and outer Self which would promote a spiritual growth and soul advancement. This is all.

A teacher, this one asked how intuition might aid her in her profession. She was encouraged to learn that teaching would help her find new images of intuition.

....this is where the new lines of this one's incredible capacity for love will become very apparent to her and it is this capacity for love that will then override much of the fear, in fact replace it, and will then become the motivating factor for this one to be able to utilize the intuition in ways that this one has yet to imagine.

The need to allow intuition to become part of the collective consciousness is being emphasized again and again in the Intuition Analyses. As a species we are conditioned to identify ourselves as physical beings. Salaries, the medium of value exchange currently used, are a good examples of this. Entertainers are paid more than educators, athletes more than peacemakers, lawyers more than clergy. We value having fun more than learning, competition more than resolution, physical law more than universal law. Changing this requires putting our minds to the task of evaluating and defining our ideas of Self as an intuitive, spiritual being.

> There is a need for this one to define the meaning of intuition. There is a need for this one to begin to cause there to be an application of this one's considerable mental energy in that direction. This one has a great command of the reasoning capacity in that this one can see cause and effect relationships. He can develop and see patterns of energy movement which create thinking and the duality nature of thoughts and activities. There is a need for this one to expand the thinking to include the intuitive faculties and the capacity for a greater grasp of what is universally true.
>
> This has always been of interest to this one and there have been many strides made within his own awareness that have also been of benefit to others in that regard. There is much more that this one can ascertain as there would be an expansion of this one's thinking in regards to cause and effect relationships particularly. There is a tendency for this one to see this in a linear physical manner and it would be helpful for this one to see it in a more vertical multidimensional fashion. For it would not only open this one's vision, but it would also create the potential for this one being able to understand cause beyond the mundane physical world.
>
> The urge to do so is present within this one. The major difficulty in doing so is in what this one believes and finds acceptable. Therefore it would necessitate an examination of this one's beliefs concerning the power of the mind, the limitless of it

and its capacity to be universally connected. By beginning to recognize how this one is connected with others beyond merely physical interaction or conscious activity, there would be the movement in that direction of expansion. This would be in becoming much more sensitive to the power of thought and the faculty of influence through thought. Being willing to discern within his own existence in life how this occurs and being present when it occurs would be the opening factor. It would be a temptation for this one to physicalize it and this will need to be faced by this one and admitted so that this one can move beyond that threshold. For we see that intuition although it can be expressed in the physical world it is not of it. This is all. **(7800BGC1)**

A sociologist and therapist, this man was quite brilliant in his ability to study systems from different origins and catalogue their similarities. In professional papers he had published several connections between philosophical, psychological, medical, and metaphysical theories. The report suggested this refined use of reasoning could be called into action regarding his own theories, ideas,thoughts, and with great success.

This would first be as has been stated in the reorganization of the beliefs. The examination of previously held beliefs which no longer apply within his own existence and his own experience. In effect this is the capacity for this one to update this one's ability to understand consciousness and to understand its relationship to the world. This would be in the capacity to examine the use of the imagination and to begin to recognize the imaginative faculty which this one uses very well in the process of reasoning is related to but is separate from the intuitive faculty of clairvoyance. This would be a place to begin because the imagination is so active within this one and often this one does pull upon intuitive energies in an unconscious fashion.

> To readjust the beliefs that this one could become clairvoyant and could have the command of the thinking where this one would be able to discern that this is the capacity being utilized would be a beginning point for this one. Clairvoyance is something that this one does use often particularly in his dealings with others when he is attempting to help them. Yet this one does not recognize its power because this one does not recognize its origin as this one would begin to separate the physical workings of the consciousness from the subconscious functions there would be a greater degree of understanding and therefore control of his skills. This is all.

Clairvoyance is one expression of intuition. The French word literally translates to English as "clear seeing". Subconscious mind, not being limited by the physical body and senses, has the capacity to "see" the past, the present and the future. Clairvoyance describes this action of the mind.

Another intuitive ability is known as psychometry. This ability and how to use it was described in another man's Intuition Analysis in answer to one of his questions.

> The strongest intuitive expression within this one is through the intuitive sense of what would be the counterpart of touching or feeling. The inner sense of psychometry is very strong in this one. There is a great capacity for this one to use touch, therefore to experience vibrations and to interpret them. It would be helpful for this one to place more attention on stilling the mind, as has been stated, and then to allow the images to come to this one, rather than for this one to try to make images be there.

> We see that through the utilization of the etheric body in the use of touch there would be the capacity to discern thoughts before they manifest and this is part of the intuitive skill. Would suggest that this one become much more sensitive to what is happening within this one when this one touches someone or something, to be more sensitive to the types

> of environments that are more comfortable or uncomfortable, the types of materials that are more pleasant or unpleasant. The types of clothing that are one or the other, the actual touching of people and whether it is pleasant or unpleasant, inviting or repulsing. It is in those moments that this one will begin to give more credence and therefore more attention to the operating of the intuition through that faculty. This then would be the beginning of further development of greater discernment in using psychometry. This is all. **(7800BGC3)**

The future of this type of intuitive investigation invites change in how we see ourselves, individually and collectively. It makes metaphysical exploration immediately applicable in our daily experience. The subject of the next report is a 45-year-old female who has meditated for 25 years and displays exceptional clairvoyant skill as a spiritual teacher and counselor. The investment she has made in Self knowledge and Self awareness is reflected in the information conveyed.

> This one gives much consideration and thought to this. It is a part of this one's manner of thinking and pattern of thinking to include this awareness in the mind, for this one is quite active in that regard. (6292000BGC1)

Most people have not been encouraged or taught how to identify their intuition. This area of skill remains vague and often misconstrued, sometimes shrouded in mystery or superstition. This woman has devoted her life to investigating intuition through reasoning. Her approach is scientific, thus moving the beliefs forward into the knowing that comes from personal experience.

> There is a very strong belief in intuition and there is a strong dedication to proving its existence in this one's life. This one is quite alert and attentive to interpreting energies in the realm of intuition. There is some difficulty that arises in doing so when there is emotional attachment to either the idea or the

> person with whom this might be engaged. It does cause there to be some difficulty in this one's clarity of perception because this one has very definite ideas of what this one wants and how this one would want situations to exist. This then becomes a kind of detriment to this one's capacity to align the minds and to find them fully functional as a unit, in as much as this one becomes engrossed in the structures she creates rather than in the movement of energies present. Intuition most readily expresses itself through energies and therefore it does seek to utilize structures to express itself. (6292000BGC1)

The connection between intuition and mysticism is making itself known here in the references to attachment. For thousands of years human beings have recognized the perils of desire. Every religion counsels against it. In Christianity the counsel is to seek first the kingdom of Heaven then "all else" will be given to you. The Hindu teachings go into great detail concerning action and nonaction. Expectation of reward from action is seen as a cause for rebirth. For the Buddhist, desire is seen as the root of all suffering, echoing the woman's desire for the fruit of the tree in the Garden of Eden which is the source of all misery for three major religions. The Greek parable of Pandora's box teaches this same lesson. Attachment is seen as the cause of pain and here we learn why – it leads to engrossment in the structures created. It's like buying a bigger house and never keeping it clean or eating without thinking so you don't even remember tasting the food.

In this report we learn the connection between intuition and energy.

> This one is quite aware of this in regards to the human body for this one has invested considerable time examining that avenue.

A minister, this woman had invested considerable time in understanding the relationship of thought to the physical body. Her work in ministering to others had brought many experiences of distance healing and hands-on healing. Her father had died from cancer when she was a teenager and her husband in his early 40's from complications of a childhood disease. The latter had precipitated a broad range of learning from Eastern to Western healing modalities. She had come to understand the theory of many structures and the ways the mind exists or is altered by them. Now as she experienced perimenopause her own body was becoming a laboratory for understanding subtle energies and the Kundalini.

> This one is less familiar with it in terms of the construction of thought patterns or of ideas, belief structures and things of this nature. This is the area that could be improved that would enhance this one's understanding and recognition as well as utilization of intuition. It would require some re-appropriation of beliefs. It would require a greater command of stilling the mind and a greater embracing of spontaneity.
>
> There is a need for this one to place greater value upon the recognition of intuition working in her thinking. The recognition and communication of them does strengthen this one's command of them, understanding of them and realization of them as well. The degree to which this is not done is the degree to which this one does frustrate her own efforts in being able to understand the intuitive faculty for she allows it to remain inner within herself, rather than causing it to come forward and to become part of the awareness. This is all.

The "re-appropriation of beliefs" stirred this woman's curiosity, and when she asked for more information the insight she received is helpful to anyone desiring to understand and free the self from attachment and limited thinking.

> .....(the change) is more in regard to structures that she has accepted into her thinking for the structures have become limiting to her. They have caused her to be less attentive and less spontaneous in regards to the movement of the mind. Therefore these beliefs will need to be re-evaluated, re-assessed for flexibility.

> One of the most outstanding (beliefs) is the anticipated way that others will receive what this one has to say, particularly in regards to the need not to embarrass other people. This structure of belief is stronger than this one's desire for the truth and willingness to pursue the truth, respond to the truth and act upon it.

This was at first surprising to this woman, but as she began to consider the ideas presented she became aware of new layers of conditions she placed upon her giving. She began recognizing when she would have thoughts about another's actions and would hold back from expressing them. Her reluctance was sometimes due to anxiety over their response. Hearing this report gave her the food for thought she had been seeking.

The suggestions for applying the intuitive faculties in the life for soul growth and spiritual development given to this woman were both a validation of what she had produced to the present and a clarification of the next step to advance her soul progression. They elucidate the movement from intuition to the entraining of conscious and subconscious minds.

> In many ways (applying intuition) is being done. The greatest accelerator of this would be in embracing the spontaneity of the willingness to allow energy to move through her more openly and in that, to be able to harmonize the minds in a very natural flow of energy, rather than one that is contrived or is manipulated in some way. It is the centering into the self with ease and comfort and confidence that will aid this one greatly in being able to enjoy the ebb and flow of the movement of energy. This will be of the greatest asset to her soul growth.
>
> (Centering Self) would be in taking the capacity to still the mind to a deeper level, to be able to see the self as being a vessel for energy to move through rather than for a place for it to collect or to be routed in some way. It would be helpful for this one to speak the thoughts, even in talking to the self would be highly beneficial for this one as a means to con-

nect the thoughts with the outer expression of them, in essence to connect the inner and outer minds. This is all. (62920001BGC)

Intuition
What is It?

Over 4000 years ago a man sat meditating by the Lo River in China. His name was Fu Hsi. As he contemplated the nature of the life and humanity, a tortoise emerged. In a flash of inspiration, Fu Hsi realized the entire Universe reflected in the markings on the shell. In his mind's eye he perceived solid and broken lines arranged in threes.

Eight centuries later King Wen (1150 BC) combined eight trigrams with each of the others to produce 64 hexagrams. Each of these hexagrams had a textual interpretation added to it, first by the Duke of Chou and later by Confucius, forming the Chinese classic book the I Ching. I Ching means book of changes and has been a revered book of insight and divination in China for 3000 years.

An intuitive breathing session illuminated my current subconscious fascination with this system. What made itself known in a Wesak vision in 1993 was being revealed to my conscious mind in stages. It was as if I had to bring to myself certain experiences before the next revelation would come. Many aspects of my life – teaching adults, the birth of our child, counseling, the development of Taraka Yoga, the physical release of my mother – moved my consciousness forward, waking me more and more to the work I find myself doing in the present. That work includes an evolutionary arrangement of the trigrams that facilitate energy to stimulate genetic change.

The most recent revelation of its application came in a lucid dream following a weekend devoted to raising awareness and stimulating interest in constructing a SOM world headquarters building on campus. The weekend was rich in all ways. Mentally, for the classes in mental techKNOWlogy created by the college teachers and students. Emotionally, for the excitement and satisfaction of erecting the 30 foot octagon maypole. Physically, for the beautification of campus accomplished by willing hands and an amazing cheesecake auction that raised almost $8000 for the building fund. Spiritually, the fellowship and camaraderie of our common ideal lifted our spirits and mobilized our goal.

In this climate came my dream experience. Through prosearching trigrams in the inner levels of consciousness, a new system of trigram patterns had emerged. Moving in a spiral form reminiscent of the fibonacci series, this arrangement frees consciousness from the wheel of death and rebirth, the matrix of contemporary times, the enslaving of thought. Over time, the connection between this form and the DNA code of the species is being revealed.

Anyone familiar with Feng Shui, King Wen's arrangement, understands how elemental forces of water, fire, air, metal, and wood can be used to keep the cycle going in a home or building. These will most probably find a place in the world headquarters building as well. This did not tell us how to create the building so the energy would be encouraged to move in multidimensional ways we desired. It would have to be more than an eight-sided structure. And it was clear the building would need to be more than a circle surrounded by an octagon. There would need to be an impetus for the energies to elevate, to lift into the spiral.

The question on my mind when I laid down to sleep was "How do we create a building structure to reflect this new arrangement?"

When I became conscious in the inner level dream state my answer was there, in the form of a fourth dimensional image. By merging the sphere and octahedron three-dimensional forms the energy will move in such a way as to effect the desired end. Beginning with the sphere, the wholeness of the egg – the seed – will create the necessary movement. The half above being heaven, the half below being earth, will capture the essence of as above, so below. This will be the core of the structure and its integrity will move energy to the center by centripetal force.

Once the dome is inflated, eight wings will draw in receiving I Ching energies which comprises the whole of physical existence. The value of stability will be experienced in this space. Connected by hallways, energy can move from any point toward the center of the space. The urge will be toward wholeness. The form was indeed moving toward being an Octadome!

The inner level, intuitive image revealed what was needed

was for the second floor of the Octagon wings to be rotated 22.5° from alignment with the first floor. This would encourage the energies to lift similar to how flaps on airplane wings perform the same function or arms outstretched and lifted to the heaven elevate consciousness.

This building will be an experience. Entering it will not do something to you. It can do something for you. The entry space will beckon consciousness to focus, center, rise toward wholeness. Its creation is a testimony to the influence of intuition in our lives.

The most common experience of intuition is dreams.

The proliferation in worldwide dream research during the 1900's is as much a response to man's inner, evolutionary need for Self revelation as to his outer curiosity about an experience he shares with everyone else on the planet yet knows painfully little about. At the School of Metaphysics researchers have explored the role dreaming plays in altering and in reflecting changes in mankind's consciousness. Drawing upon the dream experiences of young and old, rich and poor, formally educated or self-taught, devout or irreligious, the world has become a schoolroom teaching us the difference between fact and fantasy, truth and myth.

As it turns out dreams are more than experiences of the day senselessly replayed; psychic garbage to be dumped. They are also more than veiled memos to yourself from yourself. SOM research indicates dreams are an evolutionary gauge for humanity. Dreams give insight into our past and portend our future both as individuals and as a race of people. The wide range of metaphysical knowledge – be it informative, precognitive, or revelatory – available in dreamstates, indicates an escalation of subconscious activity seen before only in the rare individual: the visionary, the scientist, the philosopher, the artist, the statesman. Now, however, the quickening seems to be occurring more often, and to more people.

The ability to dream is not uniquely human, evidence of brain activity that points to dreaming occurs in studies with animals and even plants. The ability to remember dreams and describe the memory is uniquely human and what occurs while our outer consciousness is sleeping reveals fertile potential. In fact, history illustrates that remembering dreams advances humanity, as well as the individual.

The creative genius is mindful of dreams, seeking to incorporate nocturnal images into his or her waking work. The list is indeed impressive – from Danish physicist Niels Bohr who conceived the model of an atom from a dream, to composer George Frederic Handel who heard the last movements of The Messiah during a dream, from Elias Howe who received in a dream the image of the kind of needle design required for a lock-stitch sewing machine to Mohammed to whom the Koran was revealed in dreams. All of our lives have been enriched because these people cooperated with the workings of their inner minds.

Researchers believe the increased subconscious activity prevalent in the outstandingly creative will increasingly be experienced by all of us. Dreaming reveals the inner mind's intuitive range in several remarkable ways.

1] Flashes of brilliance and genius

Intuition is the direct grasp of truth. While the outer, waking conscious mind must discern truth through reasoning and direct experience, intuition frees man to draw upon timeless truths that are universally applicable. These are transcendental truths. They exist independent of physical differences, regardless of age, race, nationality, culture, while being relevant to all whether ourselves, our neighbors next door, or the strangers half a world away. Coleridge's *Kubla Khan* or Shelley's Frankenstein; or, The Modern Prometheus, both arising from their author's dreams, have outlived their creators because they embody universal truths that apply to anyone, any time, any where.

Rene Descartes, 17th century mathematician and philosopher, also realized transcendental truths because he was attentive to the workings of his inner mind. He experienced illumined perspectives from dreams that led to his theory of dualism: man's physical body functions in a manner similar to that of other animals while his mind operates on a metaphysical basis under the influence of the soul. Descartes' discovery of Analytical Geometry was the result of a dream which revealed that all sciences could be combined through mathematics. Such insights will become more common place as mankind enters the next century.

2] Problem solving

Different parts of mind have unique functions to perform. When all are working, cooperatively, they are like an orchestra or like the revolving of the planets around the sun. Human consciousness is a cohesive effort that is at once individual and collective. The coming together produces what would be impossible for any one part to accomplish alone. Thus what the waking, conscious mind spends days and even years pursuing is brought to fruition within seconds by the subconscious mind in the form of a dream.

Consider Dmitri Mendeleyev. A Russian chemist during the mid-1800's, Mendeleyev was trying to create a means to categorize the chemical elements based upon their atomic weights. "I saw in a dream a table where all the elements fell into place as required," he reported. "Awakening, I immediately wrote it down on a piece of paper. Only in one place did a correction later seem necessary." As a result of this dream, the Periodic Table of Elements was created.

Many times an answer appears as it did for Mendeleyev in a dream. In the coming years, people will reach beyond physical knowledge to cure the malaise in the world. They will turn more and more to the inner fount of creativity and guidance for solutions. Whether gained through lucid dreams or waking visions, the results of this self-reliance will be a responsive, positive consciousness that generates a productive society.

3] Prophecy

About two weeks before his assassination, Abraham Lincoln dreamed he heard sobbing. Leaving his bed he sought the source. Arriving in the East Room of the White House, he saw a coffin lying on a platform. When asked who was dead, the soldiers guarding the body said, "The President. He was killed by an assassin." When the dream came to pass only days later, the president was laid in state in the East Room guarded by soldiers.

Prophecy is an intuitive ability arising from clairvoyance, the capacity for “clear seeing”. It is part of the innate nature of subconscious mind that we are able to see lines of probability. Some people fear this, preferring to not know the probable outcome. Most of us ignore clairvoyant perceptions and so find ourselves in the same kind of difficulties, over and over and over, maybe different people, maybe a different setting, but the same themes recur in our experiences. As long as we ignore we cannot learn, and increasingly we will find our denial brings nightmares that will not be ignored.

We must stop rejecting our own supernatural development, and embrace the transition into intuitiveness. WWII American General George S. Patton is an example of someone who respected his intuitive foresight. He believed in his psychic faculties, often calling his secretary to dictate battle plans that had appeared in his dreams. One involved a successful surprise attack on German troops just as they readied an offensive on Christmas Day during the Battle of the Bulge. When we accept our ability to clearly see, the choices we make in life produce a very different outcome, changing the lines of probability. Prophecy is man’s next step in understanding the full meaning and impact of freedom.

4] Peace of Mind

Peace of Mind is the most prized state known to man. Yet money cannot buy it. It is not acquired by birth or by association. Someone else cannot give it to you. Inner peace must be cultivated by every individual through his own desire and effort. Establishing a rapport with the subconscious mind is a first step toward inner peace. Being attentive to your dreams indicates your desire for that rapport.

Salvador Dali's fascination with dreams began upon reading Sigmund Freud’s <u>Interpretation of Dreams</u> which he said was one of the discoveries of his life. He tried to preserve his dream imagery on canvas calling his work "hand-painted dream photographs." A surrealist, Dali's goal was the resolution of two states, dream and reality, into an absolute reality. The most famous surreal painting, flexible watches melting over a barren branch, is Persistence of Memory painted by Salvador Dali.

In many cultures the bringer of dreams, the subconscious mind, is known as the soul. Your subconscious mind is capable of permanent memory, recall beyond the present life experience. Your subconscious mind is not a physical part of you; it is not capable of peace depriving, misery-making attachment. The soul offers objective guidance based upon the direct grasp of truth. A knowledgeable and workable relationship with your own inner self, or subconscious mind, transforms your awareness of what is real. Dreaming enables us to experience other realities where we exist and live independently of the physical world's limitations. Learn to exist in both worlds and peace of mind is yours.

5] Accelerating soul progression

Charlotte Bronte, author of Jane Eyre, told a friend she used dreams to help her describe sensations she had no way of understanding in reality. If she needed to know what it would feel like to take opium, she would fall asleep "wondering what it was like, or how it would be." When she would awake, she would describe her dream experiences, incorporating them into her novels.

The subconscious mind utilizes a universal language for communication that transverses territorial boundaries, cultures, religious beliefs, even the limits of personal experience. These are all of the physical world; dreams are of the spiritual realm. Research shows dreams are potentially Self-revelatory messages sent by your subconscious mind while your waking mind is at rest. They bring freedom; the blind see, the lame walk, the pauper is a king. In dreams you can be anyone and anything. It is mind expanding to realize that the physical world is only one realm for experience. As is true with the waking choices you make each day, how you respond to this freedom determines whether your consciousness is enriched from the experience or untouched by it.

Recognizing dreams as the means for inner mind communication enables you to relate on deeper levels. This kind of Self knowledge is what everyone is seeking. Courting this knowledge accelerates your soul progression thereby enhancing humanity's evolution.

6] Fulfilling spiritual destiny

People describe destiny in different words: a calling, God's will, fate, a sense of mission, or even lucky coincidence. Whatever the description, adhering to the spiritual destiny your soul reveals to you brings the peace of mind each of us seek. Many have found their destinies revealed in the form of a dream. Such accounts are recorded in holy scriptures of every culture. Accounts of destiny and fulfillment abound throughout the Bible, from Jacob's dream of a stairway to heaven to the angel Gabriel appearing to Joseph to announce the coming of the birth of Jesus to John's dream which is the entire Book of Revelation. Much of the Koran, the sacred book for the Muslim, was revealed to Muhammed in dreams. Gautama's (who became the Buddha) mother, Queen Maya, dreamed of her immaculately conceived offspring before his birth, as did Mary the mother of Jesus and Jain master teacher Mahavira's mother.

Seeking meaning in dreams is the result of enhanced awareness, a self-consciousness that precedes destiny's other-consciousness. Those who seek relevance in dreams usually find it, and many have changed history because of it. Before the American Civil War, Harriet Tubman successfully made nineteen trips leading hundreds of other slaves to freedom claiming dreams helped her find safe routes. The nonviolent mass strikes of 1919 were a turning point in India's efforts to achieve self-determination.

After weeks of meditation, Mohandas Gandhi dreamed the people of India could suspend their usual business activities for twenty-four hours, devoting that time to fasting and prayer. His dream served as the inspiration for the strikes which helped free his people from British colonial rule.

Tubman and Gandhi both found the meaning of their lives enriched and their destinies fulfilled because they listened to their dreams. Listening to your dreams gives you security; they are your soul's feedback concerning how you are conducting your life and what you can do to make your life better.

Most people do not count themselves among those who are historically noteworthy, but research shows we should for what these dreamers experienced sheds light on the future for all of us. Research indicates that people who are creative, or who are religious, remember their dreams more than others. This reflects the expansiveness of their consciousness, their willingness to think in innovative ways. Dreamers whose ideas change the way we live are influential thinkers because they are using more of their potential than their contemporaries. They are evolutionary pioneers. In addition to brain power, they draw upon the inner resources of subconscious mind for inspiration, problem solving, and creativity. The clearest indication of the ascent of subconscious activity is a proclivity toward intuition. Awake or asleep, intuition is a porthole for ageless wisdom. It is a mental satellite sending and receiving thought, an internal equivalent to the Internet's information superhighway connecting all subconscious minds. Become aware of the many facets of your dreams, and you accelerate your own evolution and soul progression.

Dream awareness produces a consciousness that is very open and receptive as well as curious and quizzical, not skeptical in shutting things out but open-minded in terms of discovery. This awareness makes you much more inclined to be attentive to any experience whether awake with your eyes open or in the closed-eyed reverie of a meditative dream state. You pay more attention to what those experiences are and you look for the meaning in them. You actively seek the truth experiences bring. And to this end it is well that we remember the advice of Friedrick A. von Kekule.

A chemistry professor from Belgium, von Kekule had been attempting for some time to solve the structural riddle of the benzene molecule. He fell asleep in a chair and began to dream of atoms flitting before his eyes, forming various structures and patterns. Eventually some long rows of atoms formed and began to twist in a snake-like fashion. Suddenly one of the snakes seized hold of its own tail and began to whirl in a circle.

Kekule awoke "as if by a flash of lightning." He constructed a model of a closed ring with an atom of carbon and hydrogen at each point of the hexagon. This discovery revolutionized chemistry.

When Kekule described his dream-discovered insight to a scientific convention in 1890, he concluded his presentation by urging the audience, "Let us learn to dream, gentlemen, and then we may perhaps find the truth."

To help precipitate your own intuitive connection, here are a few dreams of the dreams we have received and our feedback.

INTERPRETING OBE's

Hello,

*I've recently purchased your books *The Dreamers Dictionary* and *Intrepreting Dreams for Self Discovery*, and have found them extremely helpful and have enjoyed learning to interpret my dreams.*

However, I have a question about interpreting OBE's and/ or astral projections. I've been able to have conscious OBE's for the past 2 years and have always taken them literally. I assume a real-time OBE would be taken literally, but what about astral projections? I haven't been able to find anything on your website or in your books about interpreting conscious OBE's where I am projecting into the astral plane. Is it your school's philosophy to use the same symbology for projections as you do for dreams?

Thank you for your time and thank you in advance for your reply.

With Love & Light,
SM/female

Response

Thanks so much for your questions. It is always gratifying when people find what we have learned to be useful in their lives.

There is a book in the works that is actually linked to many of the dreams that we have received from all over the world and interpreted right here at dreamschool that will address your question and many others. The phenomenon of dreaming is the means by which human man becomes aware of the infinite potential of his own intelligence. It's kind of like the picture books we might read to a small child. We understand that the scope of reading, of communicating thought, is very expansive. We introduce the child to this wonderful world in steps which he or she can receive, digest, and understand. You might look at dreams as the picture books the subconscious mind gives to you.

Since you are becoming aware of the abilities in subconscious mind, it's like you have grown from childhood into adolescence. Adolescence we understand as a time of experimentation, a kind of "let's try this and see what happens." There is significant research based upon personal experiences that have been verified in a number of ways that inner level experiences (like your projections and OBE's) are as real and significant as sensory experiences in the physical waking world. This area of exploring human potential is what the School of Metaphysics pursues.

What we have found thus far is that even with actual inner level experience (OBE's, visitations, telepathy, projections, precognition, retrocognition, and a host of other intuitive abilities) what the conscious mind receives as a dream is still in the Universal Language of Mind and can be interpreted for its message value to the dreamer. Therefore, even in the case of your projection dreams these would be talking about your developing ability to function and move in the inner levels of mind.Δ

TIME MACHINE

Hello, I just wanted to tell you about my dream.

Two nights ago I dreamed I was going back in the past using a time machine that looked like a treadmill exercise machine. I was traveling trough a parallel dimension that took me into the past where I saw some relatives and people that are not physically in this world any longer. They were talking to me and they asked me to help them go back in time so that they could talk to their relatives already "dead"

I know from the dream that it it possible to achieve it if you apply a universal magnetism law that will let you tune into

the right frequency that will help you transform your present energy form into a different one making it possible to travel to another dimension.

Please advise.

Thank you,AB/male

Response

Time travel is a reality in our universe. We do it every day. When you get in your car to travel 60 miles in 1/10th of the time it would take you to walk that distance, this is a form of time travel. When you pick up the phone to talk to someone on the other side of the world as if they were sitting in the same room with you, that is a form of time travel. When you remember the people and activities of the best day of your life, recalling it in such detail that you remember conversations, aromas, and feelings, that is a form of time travel . When you can imagine where you might be 50 years from now, the kinds of clothes you might wear, how your surroundings might look, how the planet might be, that is a form of time travel.

All of these examples alter how we measure and value time. Some speed up time. Some eliminate the distance of time. Some throw us out of sync with the present. All are functions of consciousness. Twenty years ago we in the School of Metaphysics might have been heard to describe cars as a lazy man's teleportation. In the same light, telephones were a lazy man's telepathy. This was in an effort ot illustrate that as man's thinking progresses he does create technologies to fulfill his desires for expanded consciousness. In other words people have been using consciousness for mind to mind communication for centuries before the telephone was even thought of. Unfortunately humanity's consciousness does not always keep pace with the advancement of technology.

Your dream reminds us of the many accounts of how creative and inventive people like Einstein and Picasso have found the dream state very useful. As far as creating a time machine that would advance the world technologically, I would suggest you go back to the source which was your dream. It is very possible to use your dreams to draw upon subconscious intuitive wisdom. Everyone does this but few respond to it vision and determination. You might very well be one of these exceptional people. Your dream says that you are.

PROPHETIC DREAMS

Dreamed about space debris, came true,Feb.25,2003,
Dreamed about art, semitrucks,lightpoles. came true.Mar.11,2003
dreamed about a missile launch, launch was unsuccessful, came true.
Have a list of dreams going back 3 years.
E/male

Response

Prophetic dreams are evidence of one of the abilities of subconscious mind -- precognition. Precognition is the intuitive ability to perceive lines of probabilities of future occurrence. Beyond the educated guesses and calculated bets of the conscious, waking mind, this psychic ability can be refined and understood. People often have precognitive dreams as a means for the subconscious mind to get its message across to a very active, and often inattentive or forgetful conscious mind. This would not appear to be true in your case since your dreams seem fairly frequent and regular over a long period of time.

You haven't really asked any questions, yet we can offer this suggestion. Precognitive dreams are also message dreams about the state of your awareness so learning how to interpret your dreams would give you a skill that might help you understand why these dreams are coming to you. Second, beginning to become conscious about your choice to respond or not respond to what you perceive would be in order. Precognitive dreams give us foreknowledge based upon the reality that if all factors continue along the same lines as at the time of the dream then "this" (what happens in the dream) will occur. Should anyone involved change their mind, the outcome will change accordingly. For instance if you dream your best friend marries your sister on Saturday and their wedding is set for this weekend, this could be seen as a prophetic dream. If your best friend gets cold feet and doesn't show up for the wedding, your dream would no longer be seen as prophetic because the outcome changed. Foreknowledge, as is true with any kind of knowledge, gives you an advantage and a responsibility. Go to a deeper place with what is happening in your consciousness.

You might also look for the identifying markers that a dream is precognitive. Learn how to identify them before the actual physical event occurs.

Symbolically speaking, your dream is giving you feed back concerning how you have learned from the past and encourages you to revisit it to deeper understanding. In the physical material world time is measured by experiences. In the inner subconscious world time is measured by understandings. Your dream says that you are learning the difference. Δ

Can dreams be from PAST LIVES?

My husband dreams every night. All of his dreams are so vivid that he feels like the dreams are more real than actual reality.

His dreams are always in earlier times and go back as far as early Scotland, i.e. castles, battles, etc. Almost ALL of these dreams are battle dreams. He feels the heat of battle, the blades as they cut, the feel of the metal. In one he was a knight and had a son and wife and of course looked nothing like he does now.

Is it possible these dreams (which occur every night and have for 20 years or more) are some message from his past lives, if such things exist OR is he picking these dreams up out of the cosmos and they belong to someone else from another time?
MMC

Response

From the information you've supplied, it's entirely possible your husband is drawing upon subconscious memory. The waking mind draws upon the brain to remember what happened yesterday, or ten years ago. Experiences during our life are stored in the physical brain. The understanding we gain from experiences, are stored in what is most often termed the soul. The subconscious mind, being the inner thinker, draws upon the soul for permanent memory. An example of this would be a talent or skill that you've never been taught in this life yet have demonstrated a "natural" affinity for as long as you can consciously remember. This explains how personal memory works. Δ

INTUITION

is perceiving the universal truth, the underlying cause, within an experience.

ELS#9

A Short Class on Intuition

Dr. B: A lot of ideas revisited me this past week. There was as much learning in working on the website this time. When I was looking for pictures that tell stories about who we as a school are and what we do, all the thoughts I have about group consciousness surfaced. Before my eyes was evidence of the group consciousness that has been one of the core configurations of energy in the School of Metaphysics from the very beginning. The manifestation of love in all forms, and regardless of physical form. Acceptance, allowing, forgiveness, sharing, the bittersweet, all ingredients that make up love expressed between, with and among male and female, young and old, rich and poor, different races, backgrounds, nationalities.

I started to see on a whole new layer of understanding the place the School holds in fulfilling the need of humanity to accelerate learning *because* we learn as a group. As we learn as a group, humanity's evolution is accelerated. It's symbiotic, resonant. It's yin/yang and it's intuitive. As that reality turns the wheel, then also it is true that we must learn in a group in order to be accelerated. This is the consciousness part of what we have been talking about vibrationally this morning.

As a scientist, I see this wonderful chi-movement of energy in acts of creation, like the creation of the Peace Dome and One Voice, and I see it equally in detracting acts. When we experience "trouble" within the organism it's when we are working against the turning of the wheel; when we do not want the group interaction, when we are closing off, when we are repelling, when we are saying "I don't want to hear that! I don't want to do that!" The conscious mind is getting so noisy that the whole of the mind, the group that the mind is, can't get through.

Dr. P: It's like the story about the ants pushing the morsel of cake into the anthill. When they work on the same side progress is quickly made. When they all take a side of the cake and push, they just tire each other out and the cake stays where it is.

Dr. B: When someone asks how they can become more intuitive (often they are using the word psychic) I explain the connection between the conscious mind and the subconscious mind and teach about what we're talking about in this class, the Essential Life Skills. Using those skills makes your minds work together, in harmony, as a single unit. A whole, functioning Self. When they want to know why the subconscious mind is distant or seems to work inconsistently, I talk about the most direct access to subconscious mind anyone has.

PM: Their dreams.

Dr. B: Yes, their dreams. For the undisciplined thinker, the only time the subconscious mind can get "a word in edgewise" is when the conscious waking mind is set aside. These subconscious messages we call dreams. When the conscious mind is asleep is when the rest of you gets to weigh in on your experiences and how you're conducting your experiences out here in the physical world. This is what the student works to change all the way through the lessons so you no longer have to go unconscious in order for the other six levels of consciousness to say "This is what we think about what you're doing."

Dr. Dan and I were wrapping presents yesterday and we were talking about something and had one of those Taurus/ Aquarius moments and I said, "I'm just doing great." I heard my words, the tone, the vibration, which I would describe as a bit cynical or sarcastic, and I stilled my mind and said, "Just a second." I adjusted my attitude to let go of the very old - 30-year-old frozen consciousness thought - and to reflect my appreciation in the present moment. I repeated, "I'm just doing great," in a different way.

He smiled and replied, "I like it when you don't do brain." I said "Me, too." Freedom is in the mind, not in the limits of the brain. Your brain is a resonator for the memory of experiences, the most complex computer that only genetics over hundreds of thousands of years could evolve. You are the computer programmer, not the computer. Identify with what the Gita calls the Real Self then there can be a real appreciation of the love of the Creator in people. It's the love, the charisma, that draws people to you and that's what creates what we call groups.

LJ: It's soul connection.

Dr. B: Inside and out. Within Self, and between you and others.

One of the most beautiful progressions in developing intuition - even beyond the steps for astral projection, perceiving the chakras, or the supersenses like telepathy - is how we teach dream exploration. Dream interpretation is a joint endeavor between conscious and subconscious minds. It requires both reasoning and intuition, and when both are present entrainment is the result. Let's explore this a bit.

First, some students already remember dreams easily. Some do not. Yet anytime we sleep we can dream, so when we fail to remember a dream the most common cause is a busy in conscious mind. The potential dreamer is filled with wants, desires, worries, fears, guilts, etc. Lots of conscious thoughts that left on like a radio on static. First step is to help that student learn how to concentrate. Concentration leads to better memory, and what do we say, "I *remembered* a dream last night!"

At first the student remembers dreams and learns to be a scientist, faithfully recording the details. Not embellishing, or leaving out unattractive parts. Honesty is what interpreting dreams is all about. The details are the symbols in the dreams that can be decoded. They are the subconscious mind's means of communicating its thoughts, its perspective. They are vibrations that need to be interpreted for understanding. Learning to interpret dream vibrations is the beginning of the two-way communication between subconscious mind and conscious mind. It is the beginning of the Real Self learning how to use these parts of mind for soul progression and Self awareness.

NG: That's like the basis for intuitive reporting, learning how to interpret vibrations in the mental and emotional system like in Intuitive Health Analyses or to "read" the Akashic Record.

Dr. B: Yes, someone who knows how to intuitively interpret dreams, is able to transfer the skills. For instance, when you can create the still mind, your consciousness is aligned. Then you have acumen, greater awareness of where the information is coming from that you are receiving. Because you know how to identify it. You know how to trace the energies. You know how to interpret them as you receive them. This is intuitive intelligence.

NG: So what about the student who is always talking about visions they see, guides they talk to? People who have the "I see dead people" experiences?

Dr. B: Listen. You can be of great service to someone through listening. They used to call it having a sounding board. Listen, so they can listen to themselves. Show them how. Model it, because in doing so - vibrationally, you help them to learn how to do it themselves. Still your mind so you don't get all wrapped up or distracted by the content of what they are saying. Remain steady in the state of your consciousness. I have seen many sound-minded and good-hearted people get caught up in others experiences and begin to compare themselves unfavorably. They become insecure and lose their sense of self respect because "I never had those experiences! They must be more evolved than me! What do I have to offer them?"

Still your mind. Stay calm, controlling your emotions and imagination. Be a reasoner. See the whole picture. Then think with your mind. Hopefully you will always have students who are better than you are at something. That's a good thing. That says there is hope for the planet. So rejoice in that. Be a reasoner so you can help them reach their potential....•

Dear Dr. Barbara,

It's 1:30 in the morning and I just woke up from **an amazing experience**. Last night in class we got the last lesson of the 2nd cycle on Lucid Dreaming. I've had this lesson before and the first night after I got it then I had a dream where I was more lucid than I had ever been. I was able to accomplish in that dream most of the suggestions the lesson offered for what to do when you become lucid. And it was really cool.

So, after class last night I was talking to Dr. Sheila Benjamin about how I feel like I have tried everything to gain some consistency with exercises and pretty much everything that is productive in my life and nothing I do seems to work. This was on my mind on the drive home and then right before I went to sleep I felt like I was longing for something and had been for a while but couldn't put my finger on it. I was telling this to my spirit guide and I said to myself "I wonder what I am longing for?" And then went to sleep and had a dream.

There was a cat and at first I thought what a cute little kitty and as soon as I thought this I became lucid and said "that's not a cat, that's a habit!" At the same time saying that remembering what Dr. Sheila and I had talked about with consistency and stubbornness. Then Dr. Laurel (Clark) appeared. I knew it really wasn't Dr. Laurel so I said, "you're a superconscious aspect." and she nodded yes. I asked what I should do and she said she would leave that up to me. so I said I would kill it. I tried everything to kill that cat. I threw it down the stairs. I stepped on it and then I had the thought that I should cut off its head and wondered if that would even work and then remembered how I told Dr. Shiela that I had tried everything and nothing seems to work. So I asked Dr. Laurel what to do and she said I had decide. So I looked up, stretched my arms out and said okay, I SURRENDER! Then everything became white light and the cat disintegrated. Then Dr. Laurel said "Let's look in the mirror" and took my arm.

This is where things really got interesting. Just as she took my arm, she was no longer an aspect in my dream but someone else, a real entity in a white robe and there was another in a white robe. They were on each side of me and each had one of my arms. This was no longer a lucid dream. This was a lucid experience in a real live place. Just as tangible, if not more, than the physical. I looked down and the floor was like golden alive light. The entities said, now let's look into the mirror and were turning me around to look. Then I guess I started to freak out a bit and my feet went out from under me. The entities were holding me up and new what was happening. I received the thought to breathe, so I did and then woke up in my physical body in bed.

I thought as soon as I woke up "That is the experience people have when they die." An overwhelming realization that there is a real experience and a real place after death.

My medulla oblongata felt tingly and still does. So, that was the experience. I wanted you to know about it. I've had the idea that experience on the inner levels is as real as the physical and I've had lucid dreams and some experience with the inner level exercises and astral projection, but until now I really had no idea of how real REAL life beyond the body could be.

I hope to talk to you soon. I send you my circle of love. Cassie•

Hi Cassie,
Thanks for sending the dream experience. It can serve many. I will be emailing it to the directors since most of them are studying similar material, and I will use it in the future for dreamschool and Dream of the Month Club members. Use what we talked about on the phone to return to that place again, then hold your attention on the question I gave you. I look forward to hearing more. Perhaps if you are here Thanksgiving or Christmas time we can work out that that intuitive breathing session. You may be more ready now than ever. I send my circle, Dr. Barbara

Hi, Dr. Barbara,
I am glad you sent this e-mail which is inspiring! I have several thoughts. I have been talking with Dave about his dharma, perseverance, and Cassie's, persistence. I wanted to understand the difference because I kept mixing them up. It is intriguing to me that by universal law they ended up in the same city at the same school. This is always such a splendor to me, to see how people's lives interweave in such ways.

Anyway, I finally looked up the words in a dictionary so that I could get an image of perseverance and persistence, since I thought of them as the same. "Per" means through, so perseverance is to keep on moving forward even when there are influences that could interfere or separate (sever) or be obstacles. Persistence means to stand firm, kind of like satyagraha, holding on to truth. The "sistence" is the standing firm.

So, since I had been thinking about persistence, this dream/lucid experience made sense. I can see Cassie's willingness to stand firm with her desire and ideal to know reality beyond the physical. I know some of her background and history and the many ways she has tried to do this, and how the disciplines in the School of Metaphysics have given her the way to KNOW TRUTH.

This is remarkable, awe-inspiring, and uplifting. It shows that these mental exercises WORK, even when you think you are not making progress you are. The very fact that you do the exercises every day means you are making progress.

To Cassie, I encourage you to tell your story by giving some lectures. You could be of great help to hospice workers or to people who are dealing with life threatening illnesses like cancer. Isn't there a big cancer research center on Business Loop 70 in Columbia? You could help the nurses and doctors to help their patients by telling them this story. How many people could benefit from feeling the authority that comes from you because you know this and didn't have to have a near death experience for it to happen. That is very rare.

I am proud of your accomplishments and your growth and
I send my circle of love,
Dr. Laurel

Life Skills Math
Intuitional Computation

Intuition is the first of the Life Skills that I have experienced that I did not have to consciously work all the other life skills to cause it. To cause intuition, the primary ingredient is a still mind. Now, if you look at what goes into being able to still the mind, you find all the mind skills. That may be why some people call it psychic instead of intuitive, because they don't directly see how they caused it to happen with their consciousness. The consciousness that causes intuition comes from stilling the mind to that intersection point of undivided attention and steadying the breathing and holding the still mind with concentration.

My first Past Life Profile, on lesson 7, let me know that I had a lot of natural intuitive ability and I needed to learn how to still my mind of distractions to allow it to come forth, for me to sense it and trust it more. That was the significance, so that was the karma. Since then I have realized how important a disclosure that was at that time. The report gave me the essence of what I need to focus on this lifetime to unlock my true potential, or at least to have a fulfilling life. Focus helps me tremendously in bringing forth my intuition.

When I am not focused, I become fearful, angry, mean, tired, arrogant, and disconnected. And that can happen any time I forget to image my day or the next day or even forget to image an activity beforehand. That's where it first starts to slip. I forget to use my mind skills. Then I start playing catch up with physical senses and physical learning, which gets me by, but I don't grow very much from my experiences. There can be weeks where I couldn't tell you what I learned because of the lack of visualization employed at the outset of experiences.

My use of visualization has a direct impact on how good my intuition becomes. Intuition stands on the shoulders of Reasoning. Reasoning, in turn, stands on the foundation of the controlled use of images—memory images, present moment image interpretation, and the formation of new imagined images. Using images from past, present and future connects time into a continuum in the thinking, which in turn releases the thinking from separate, temporal identity. Reasoning in effect launches one from physical, temporal life into non-temporal life. Likewise, spatial separateness is decreased in reasoning also. Reasoning connects a problem with its solution. It connects a cause with its effect. In that way, events and circumstances in the life are connected over time and space, and spatial and temporal existence is merged with the non-temporal and non-spatial existence. Conscious and subconscious existence is unified, creating a fluid use of intuitive ability. ∞
Paul Madar

One of the best ways to free your mind is to get outside your brain box. One of the easiest and most fun ways to get out of your brain box is to draw. Here are two practices that will open your mind to the infinite possibilities *in you!*

Leonardo da Vinci suggested the artist "begin with a detail and only move from one detail to another when you have fixed the first firmly in your memory and become well acquainted with it." He thought the mind of the painter should be like a mirror. He called this way of looking *"knowing how to see"* and this exercise incorporates all the Essential Life Skills you have learned!

DO NOT TURN THIS PAGE UPSIDE DOWN until you read the following exercises.

Exercise One

As you learned by performing this exercise with Essential Life Skill #2, upside down drawing stimulates mental attention. It activates the mind to go beyond patterns and habits. To access the inner, subconscious mind and its intuitive faculty, we must be familiar with Self in this land of free thinking.

In a moment you are going to draw everything you see in ***figure 1*** (next page) in the space provided at right. Keep in mind: Do not turn this page or your drawing upside down until you are finished. Copy everything you see, then you can turn the page and your drawing around to see what you have drawn.

Ex 1 Prototype figure

Your Representation

Exercise Two

Draw this image with your nondominant hand, the one you do not use to write with. Pay attention to your thoughts and feelings as you make the lines. What happens to your awareness and perception? Where do your eyes go, how does your hand move?

Ex. 2 Prototype figure

These exercises stimulate Self awareness. They use both the left and right brains, thus employing more of your brain power. Activity in more areas of the brain *simultaneously* is an indication that you are using your Mind. You are moving from physical thinking with the body and senses to the mental thinking of the soul.

With mental thinking more options are seen. When you are "in mind" you can linger in possibilities. If, after completing these exercises you want to do them again, this is an indication that you are receiving an inner urge to know your Self in new, deeper, and more meaningful ways. This is the open door to intuition.

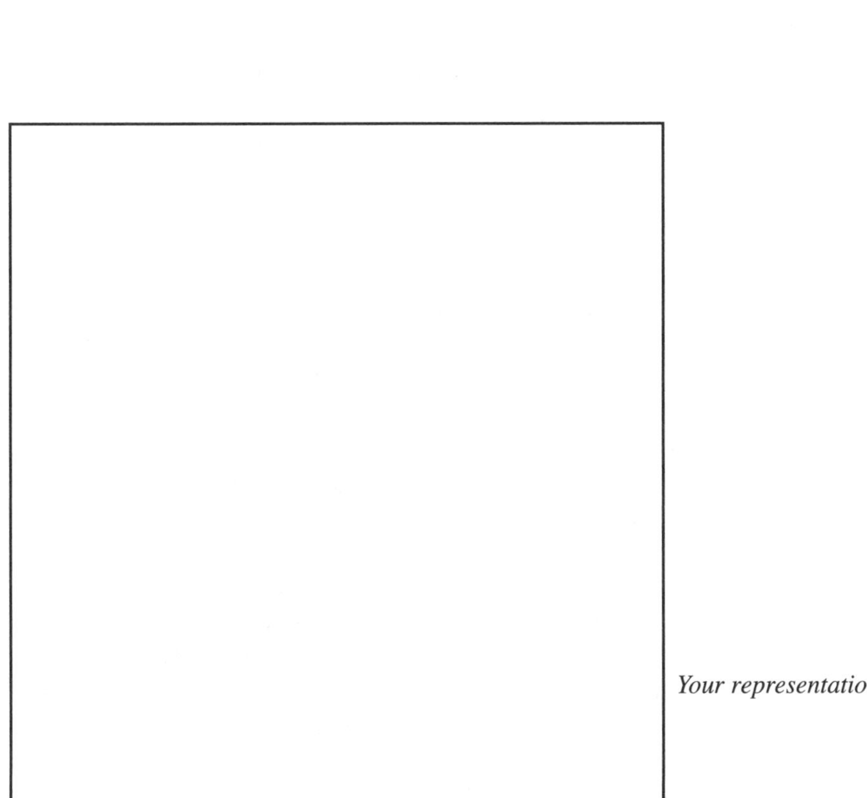

Your representation

So, how intuitive are you?

You're probably wondering how you might measure up on a typical intuitive assessment scale. Here's a quiz to evaluate yourself.

An I(ntuition) Q(uotient) Test

(Respond with frequently....sometimes....never.....not sure)

Part One

1. Do you find yourself sensing a friend or loved one's feelings from time to time without any benefit of verbal communication?
2. When you are concentrating intently on a given thought or idea, do other people seem to know what you are thinking?
3. Have you ever sensed the thoughts of a stranger or acquaintance moments before he or she relates the idea in words?
4. Do friend and relatives sometimes act upon your unspoken wishes or desires moments after these thoughts have come into your conscious mind?

Part Two

1. Have you ever received mental flashes of people you know are miles away engaging in a certain task or activity, and discovered your impression of what they were doing at that given moment proved accurate?
2. Do occasional psychic images of distant places, people, or events which are occurring in the present time register in your conscious mind?
3. When friends complain that some personal belonging has been lost or stolen, do you seem to instinctively know where the missing object will be found?
4. Do you hear voices or vague whispers when alone and in a stable frame of mind, or just prior to falling asleep?
5. Have you ever seen an apparition (ghost) or mentally sensed the presence of such phenomenon in your home or other surroundings?

Part Three

1. In daily living, do you seem to know what is about to happen in your immediate environment?
2. Do you have valid prophetic dreams?
3. Can you regard lucky hunches or warning premonitions you may have experienced in the past as being accurate?
4. Have you ever perceived a vivid mental flash or impression of some important future event which has actually occurred?

Part Four

1. Do your minor bruises and injuries seem to heal in record time?
2. Does it appear that you have an unusually talented green thumb for growing house plants?
3. Have you ever influenced the motion or shape of physical objects solely by the process of thought?

Part Five

1. Are you able to recall vivid impressions or recollections of having lived in a previous lifetime?
2. Upon meeting a new acquaintance, can you accurately sense what kind of childhood he or she has undergone, or tune in on important memories in their distant past?
3. Do you possess an uncanny knowledge of certain historical events or cultural eras that cannot be logically explained?

Part Six

1. If you have children, do they seem to know your thoughts without receiving any tangible clues?
2. Are your child's dreams or cryptic sayings prophetic?
3. Can the youngster perceive apparitions (ghosts) in your home or immediate surroundings?
4. Does the child possess a familiarity with events in the distant past which he could have no logical way of knowing?
5. Have you noticed any other unusual, specific psychic abilities or extrasensory powers in your child?

These questions evaluate how awake you are to the inner workings of your mind.

Frequent answers show a high aptitude for developing the psi. Your mind is strong and already making its presence known in your everyday life. Disciplined study will enable you to teach others how to do what comes naturally to you.

Sometimes answers indicate the areas where you are conscious of your mind's power. People often demonstrate talent in certain areas - telepathy or healing, for instance. When awareness comes or goes the intuitive understanding is being viewed as a "gift" from an unknown origin. Identify its source and you increase the frequency.

Never answers indicate the areas where change will be easiest to recognize. They are the first goals to set in waking your consciousness to the power of your own mind and that of others.

Not sure responses show a desire to be open to the inner workings of the mind. Mental activity is occurring, what you are unsure of is how to identify it. The work here is separating what you believe from what you know from your own experience. Reviewing your beliefs can be insightful here.

Each group of questions resonates specific intutive abilities. Just as we have five distinct ways to identify experience in the physical world – we call them senses – we have corresponding ways to identify understandings in the mental world. Your responses today have opened doors into that world.

Instant Manifestation!

Whenever you find yourself getting too boxy, when ideas are stymied, you're stuck. Try the following to open your mind. It's one of the quickest ways to move from physical thinking to mental thinking.

Turn this book, or any other reading material upside down and read a page. You will be surprised what repeated practice brings in clarity of thought.•

"It has been preached in every country, taught everywhere, but only believed in by a few, because until we get the experience ourselves, we cannot believe in it."

– Vivekananda, 1893

Entrainment

A Universal Language of Mind story

King of the Wise Hearts

When Solomon became king of all Israel, the Lord promised him anything he desired. "Please give me a wise heart so I may rule your people," was his only request.

The Lord was pleased by this answer and promised to give Solomon what he asked for and so much more. Solomon would enjoy all the material pleasures of the world and his people would prosper.

Through the years Solomon's reputation spread. He was known as the wisest of the wise, understanding the nature of all things be they plant, animal, or human. His judgement was revered among all.

One day two women were brought to the King. They quarrelled over a baby. Patiently, Solomon listened to their stories.

"We live together in the same house," said the first woman. "A few weeks ago we both gave birth. Mine was born first and hers a few days after. She accidentally rolled over on her baby in the night smothering it to death. Then, while I was asleep, she got up at midnight. She took my baby and put her dead baby in place of mine. When I awoke I found the baby in my bed was dead. When I looked at the baby in the light I saw it was not mine. She stole my baby!"

"No, your baby is the one who died," the second woman exclaimed. "Mine is the one that lives!"

Solomon thought for some time. Finally, without any other word, he called to his guardsman, "Let me see your sword!" Everyone waited to see what the King would say next.

The guardsman gave his sword to the King. "Since you both claim the same story, and only one can be true, there is no way to discern who is telling the truth. So we will cut the baby in two so each mother may have the child she professes to love."

The real mother cried out, "No! Do not kill the child. Give the baby to her."

The other woman replied, "Go ahead. Let it be neither mine or hers."

At this Solomon lowered the sword. He came forward to pick up the child and handed it to the woman who wanted the child to live for she was the babe's true mother.

The tale of his judgement spread throughout the lands, and people marveled at how the wisdom of God was in the heart and mind of the king.

I remember hearing this story as a child. I was abhorred as I heard the King's command to divide the child. Even at five years of age, I knew the child would be hurt and probably die. I didn't understand how a king could do such a thing. I had heart, with little reasoning. I had yet to learn from experience that the true mother would rather see her child alive than maimed. The King was indeed wise from the blend of reasoning and intuition.

Entrainment yields a wise heart. Within each of us is a storehouse of understandings. Some call this the soul, or te, or yaweh. Most people only know this reality from effect. Those possessing a high level of soul understanding are talented. They are virtuous. They are kind. It is super-natural, not of this world for the refined abilities have not been learned in the present life. Such thinkers do not have to think with their heads.

Entrainment also yields a compassionate head. The intelligence within us extends beyond the brain into the levels of consciousness, the recesses of the mind. Still. Thoughtful. Contemplative. Those with a strong mind are trustworthy. They are decisive. They are knowers. They do not have to feel with their hearts.

The person whose mind is entrained experiences the open mind and the open heart, simultaneously. He is awake in his dreaming thus freed from illusions. He is an interpreter of dreams, a living example of Spirit. What is a risk to some, is resolve for a Solomon. What requires courage for others, is the wise one's duty, what she must do.

When the mind is entrained, when the inner and outer work together as one, the way you see the world changes. What was a stimulus for desire, no longer tempts. What at one time brought tears, now is cause for joy. Entrainment teaches us to see with what the Tibetans call the wisdom eye, what the esoterists call the third eye, what scientists call the observer. With Entrainment the experience of reality forever changes.•

I N T U I T I V E R E S E A R C H

Entrainment is...

"...as if there is such a power arising from within the self of wanting to express the affection and love that it is immediately given without any reservation on this one's part. All of the limitations that would otherwise be present are gone." (10999BGC6)

"When this one forgets about the self and puts all of the attention, all of the consciousness upon what is before him, these are the times when the greatest harmony between inner and outer are experienced." (10999BGC5)

Entrainment is a blend of aggressive and receptive actions working in conjunction with one another. It is symbolized in the Taoist symbol of yin and yang. The true symbol includes the light and the dark, in equal portions, swirling like a drop of water, each fitting comfortably into the other to form a whole, a circle. Within the largest area of light is a single drop of darkness. Within the largest area of dark is a single drop of light. Thus at all times receptivity exists in aggressiveness, and aggressiveness in receptivity. This is how wholeness is created.

Entrainment in the consciousness of the individual is built through the aggressive and receptive factors of concentration. The capacity to withdraw our attention from all stimuli save that which we desire to hold in mind. This is a receptive action of the mind centered upon an aggressive desire. Through aggressively focusing our attention upon a single idea, person, or thing we can receive that idea, person or thing. This developed sense of concentration in Raja yoga is known as Dhyana, the ability to transcend the physical senses, thus discerning deeper meaning. When the object of concentration is the Creator and the minds entrained as One, the individual can reach samadhi, the highest expression of thought. In samadhi, ecstasy can be experienced.

A woman whose life had seemed an emotional roller coaster of highs and lows learned the reason why equanimity escaped her through a Meditation Portrait (10999BGC4). This kind of Intuitive Report asks for the *"state of harmony existing between the inner subconscious mind and outer conscious mind."* This is asking for the potential and reality of the individual's entrainment.

> It is very easy for this one to have a state of harmony when she is in a receptive position where she is merely receiving stimuli from the environment. It becomes a challenge for her when she wants to take action or become aggressive in some way and harmony seems to not be as strong or to dissipate all together.

She had found this to be true in her marriage. As long as she went along with whatever her husband desired, harmony reigned in the home. As the years went by she found that becoming more proactive, more decisive, did not always meet with favor from her children as well as her husband. Her choices sometimes disrupted the routine they prized. So she would shrink back, just allowing things to evolve as others chose. She had begun to think she was sacrificing her own goals in the name of family member's needs until she heard the following:

> There is a great joy this one experiences when she is merely enjoying life, when she is allowing life to unfold and to happen to her. We see there is a kind of security that this one derives from this point of view and we see that these are the moments when this one is in the greatest connection inwardly: when this one has no worry, no concerns, no active brain activity but merely the intuitive sense of presence. (10999BGC4)

This woman had been relying on her intuition all along! This is why she was drawn to this frame of mind, why she kept returning to it. The external "hassles" existed to stimulate her to retreat into herself, to go beyond the busyness of the information in the brain and reach toward inner harmony. The outer disharmony could now be an indicator of what she was doing within herself.

The balance between conscious and subconscious minds would be achieved not through ceasing being receptive, rather through learning how to bring forward her power of receptivity in her thoughts and actions.

> It would be helpful for this one to cultivate this and realize this is part of her to become much more cognizant of its presence and to allow the self to settle in to this consciousness, so when this one wants to speak or act this consciousness is what motivates it. There is almost a divorcing that occurs in this one between the natural experience of wholeness that she is capable of experiencing and the times when this one needs to act whether it is through thought, word, or physical movement. In order for this divorcing to be altered, this one will need to become more cognizant of the harmony that exists and integrate it into her thinking so that it can be present during times of aggressiveness. (10999BGC4)

This information required reflection upon her part. The report encouraged her to examine some of her ideas about aggressiveness, suggesting that it is *"merely the capacity for energy to move."* Once she could admit that she saw aggressive females as unattractive, her mind opened to what she had experienced as a child with her mother and father. Her mother had been a stay at home mom, caring for the kids and father. She didn't even know her mom had needs or desires that weren't fulfilled until long after she had left home. Like her mother, she could *"become very passive in harmony (that) she allows it to stagnate."* The report suggested that she *"begin seeing the need for harmony as the way of giving life. For this is aggressiveness at its zenith."*

The need for both aggressive and receptive actions for entrainment of the minds is beautifully described when this woman asks how she can recognize passivity.

> The passivity begins at the point where receptivity ends. This is a time when this one is enjoying what is occurring around her, which is the receptivity. Then for whatever reason there is an alteration in consciousness. There is a change in the attitude where this one no longer is receiving. This one is beginning to become busy in her thoughts whether it is through wanting interaction to discontinue, wanting to leave, making judgements upon her self or others concerning what is occurring, and there is a need for some kind of aggressive action to be taken. When the aggressive action is not taken, then this one becomes passive. (10999BGC4)

What an enlightening description of how the yin and the yang seek to work together. Always the aggressive and receptive principles are acting upon, through, and within consciousness. It is the creative thought of the thinker which either dances with these Universal forces of creation or abandons them. This woman would follow along in life's tango and then suddenly decide to waltz, leaving her partner behind. She is stymied. She wants to waltz, and if her partner is unwilling to respond (to be receptive) she waltzes alone or gives up the dance entirely. Either way there is a lack of balance that will lead to wholeness, and she is unsatisfied.

The remedy for creating wholeness in this one's thinking is found in the development of the will. *"The will must be cultivated. It must be strengthened. It must be wielded and understood for true progress to be made. There is no other substitute."* The will is the ability to point the mind in a direction and sustain momentum. Think of the will to live. Many have returned from serious diseases owing to the action of will combined with a strong seed thought.

Before we leave this woman's report, I want to share the suggestions given for attuning the conscious and subconscious mind to the superconscious mind, for they are useful to anyone who wants to use more of their mind.

> It would be of great benefit for this one to contemplate the nature of worthiness. There are many ideas associated with this within this one that are not in alignment that are not illuminated by this one. Therefore becoming worthy of the superconscious existence would be a point of development and growth for this one, a point of sacrifice and union, a stimulus for transformation in what this one thinks about, how this one thinks, and therefore how this one moves in the world. (10999BGC4)

Another woman received guidance during that same Spiritual Focus Weekend which illuminated the benefits of entrainment in relationships with others. This shed light for many in attendance. This woman's Meditation Report addressed an important distinction she needed to make concerning harmony between herself and others, and internal harmony. The answer came in response to the following question.

> **How does the harmony that this one has for another being relate to the harmony within, between the inner and outer minds?**
>
> It is when this one has achieved the harmony within the self, an alignment of energies, a flow of energies, that then the affinity for another is experienced. It is in the relating with other individuals that this one can become more cognizant or aware of the inner state within her own being. It is important for this one to accept that it is the

> inner harmony that exists first, and it continues to exist following the interaction outwardly with another. The harmony is not dependent upon other people, nor is it exclusive to them. It is merely the means by which it is more readily known to this one, the state of inner being. (10999BGC1)

As this woman began to realize the love she felt with others originated within herself, her choices changed. She became stronger emotionally, less likely to be thrown off course by a careless remark or inadvertent snub. This was in accordance with a suggestion for turning her expectations inward. The report described the tendency for this woman to get caught up in others and their situations or problems. Each time this occurred the attention was taken away from superconscious mind.

> ....there is a separation that occurs because of this. In order for this to change there would need to be the willingness on this one's part to still the outer mind and become comfortable with the inner mind. There is some discomfort that this one experiences in that state. This one would experience a deeper fulfillment by purposefully and consciously entering into this state, even when it is uncomfortable, until this one can move past the discomfort and begin to experience a sense of home. (10999BGC1)

The woman was encouraged to purposefully maintain this state even in the face of discomfort. Once she would move past the discomfort she would experience *"a sense of home."* Like Dorothy in *The Wizard of Oz*, she needs to learn there is no place like home! The age old saying, "home is where the heart is" takes on new meaning in light of this Intuitive Report.

Becoming caught up in the physicalness of life is a common experience. As children, we are encouraged to live outside the present moment. "What do you want to be when you grow up?" is a question each person hears thousands of times during childhood. Again and again we are impressed with the need to choose a career, to fashion a life from physical choices of money, position, partnering, family. Each of these hold value in potential learning for the soul, yet how the soul can grow in understanding is not taught, physical skills are. These are reinforced at school, and later in work environments. Our lives become increasingly physical until we make spiritual choices. Another woman was given the following image for becoming more aware of inner worlds of consciousness.

> There is great potential within this one as she would endeavor to learn to direct the attention inward. We see that much of this one's attention is captivated by outward conditions in the life, rather than there being an inner sense of connectedness within the self that is independent of anyone or anything around the self. It would be of benefit for this one to begin to envision the inner world as a garden that this one must tend, that this one has the privilege of existing within and of taking care of determining what exists there, what thrives there, what blooms there, what lives there, and to create it with the love that this one does have within the Self. Through this kind of inner endeavor, there will be a broadening of the awareness and a quickening of the energies that will aid this one to have a deeper sense of connectedness with her whole Self. (10999BGC6)

Visualization is one of the cornerstones for entraining the minds as One. What we choose to image and how well we create the mental pictures that comprise that image determines the resonance of the outer waking mind and the inner dreaming mind. The inner mind uses a universal language for its communication. This language is one of pictures. Both the conscious mind and the subconscious mind can "speak" in this language. Pictures are the language of entrainment. Beyond words, images convey thought mind to mind. The details given here afford this woman the perfect image for her to expand her conscious thinking to receive the expansive nature of her subconscious soul.

Here is one of the best suggestions for directing the attention beyond physical limitations that I've heard in an Intuitive Report.

> It would assist this one greatly to begin to contemplate that which is not seen to bring forward into the awareness ideas that this one does hold of God, of spirituality, of those things which are transcendent. To begin to live

> there more in the thinking, to begin to value those thoughts and realities as much as this one would value something that is tangible, that is within her physical world. It is this shift in consciousness that will open this one's mind to a greater sense of unity within the Self and then will cause this one's mind to move forward toward the contemplation of her purpose for existence and her desire to commune with the Source of her being. It is through deciding to interact with others in the ways in which this one interacts with those whom this one is most open with that will further this one's capacity to live meditatively. (101400BGC3)

For many people entrainment experiences are unconscious. Perfect moments and feel-good times come and go seemingly by magic at the whim of some unknown force. This was the case with a self-employed mechanic who longed to be a massage therapist. The report noted that aligning of the minds occurs most often for this one when he interacts with another. It went on to point out that this happens when he is trying to help someone.

> When this one forgets about the self and puts all of the attention, all of the consciousness upon what is before him, these are the times when the greatest harmony between the inner and outer are experienced. It is when this one begins to think about what is occurring that this one becomes distracted away from the harmony. (10999BGC5)

This testament to the power of concentration describes how the busy conscious mind can draw us away from the power of entrainment moments. How often have you talked, sung, danced, expressed yourself in some way quite naturally and fluently until you began consciously thinking about what you were doing? The moment you directed your attention to a purely conscious thought - "Is this really me talking in front of a group of people?", "I can't believe I'm singing like this!", "Wow! This is a lot easier than I thought" – you let go of your subconscious connection. Fear, doubt, or indecision take over and you are suddenly at a loss for words, squeaking on those high notes, and have two left feet. Perhaps it's not this bad, but you get the picture.

A suggestion for conscious concentration as a means to control the wandering of the mind is given, as is the following insight on Self as cause.

> It is when this one has been of assistance with someone else that this (distraction) is most clear to him and it is because of the harmony within the mind, not because of the response from the other. It would be of benefit for this one to separate these two, to realize that it is not whether what this one has offered has been received well or not that does determine the sense of inner peace and harmony within himself. By becoming free of the attachment to others' response to him there will be a much greater degree of freedom experienced in the inner harmony and this one's ability to understand it. (10999BGC5)

Entrainment can be described as the coordination of the mind and the heart. An open mind enables us to move beyond preconceived ideas. An open heart enables us to give and receive love completely. Both are addressed in the following excerpt.

> This would be in the willingness to go beyond what this one initially perceives. This one has a tendency to link the giving with people, places or things. Would suggest that this one begin to see this as a starting point rather than an ending point. In other words this one has been prone and comfortable with giving to people, and this one needs to begin to expand this away from the delight or joy that it gives the other people to being able to see what the action of giving itself gives to her. When this becomes the focus then this one will have a new understanding of the harmony within the Self and will begin to draw upon superconscious energies in ways that were not possible before. Much of this one's time and attention and devotion and loyalty and love has been conditional, inasmuch as it has been premeditated and has been based upon this one's desire to be worthy. When this one begins to accept her own worthiness and gives from that and receives back from it, there will be a kind of ascension in this one's understanding of love that is much more comprehensive, universal and superconscious. (1013200BGC1)

In English there is only one word for love. The Greeks separated love into three forms. Eros which is sensual, sexual, romantic and erotic love. Agape meaning self-giving love, empathy, acceptance, and charity. Agape is love that endures even when it is not returned. Philia which is brotherly and sisterly love, friendship and companionship. Acknowleding Self through these three filters of love opens the mind to give and receive with fuller understanding. This becomes the practice of divine love.

Experiencing love in all its forms is the purpose of life for human beings. To experience love that is free of attachment is to realize the nature of giving and receiving, to understand compassion. Compassion is a natural outpouring for one whose minds are entrained.

Remember the mechanic? One of the most visionary and practical suggestions for entrainment came in his Intuitive Report. When asked for suggestions on aligning the conscious and subconscious minds for higher states of awareness, the reply underscored the importance of having those we respect and admire in our lives.

> It would be most helpful to this one to begin to emulate the great master that this one has an affinity for or a knowledge of. In essence, to become more like that individual, more loving, more eager to assist. To actively begin seeking ways that he can help others, for it is in this kind of interaction on a daily basis that there will be a greater sense of harmony within him. It will also aid as it builds daily to begin to receive and draw upon energies that are beyond the outer portions of the mind. The emulation will give this one something to reach for with his imagination which is very important in this one's development of consciousness. There have been ways where this one has stymied the imagination and has fallen into habitual patterns of thinking that are eroding the harmony that does exist within this one. These can be replaced through a directed use of imagination. (10999BGC5)

The formation of ideals exercises our innate ability to be like our Creator. Our mental Creator created in Her likeness and His image. Being created so, we are thinkers who have the same attributes. We can create with our thoughts. Too many are taught to fear instead of dream. This breeds patterns of cynicism, alienation, and depression as we age. These can be overcome by the resurrecting of consciousness towards ideals worth living. By reinforcing our values each day, we lift our awareness drawing the mind's attention inward toward the Real Self.

A report (101400BGC4) for a nurse highlights this conflict in self and how this one uses the profession to resolve it.

> There is a tendency for the inner and outer selves to move in opposite directions. They find the greatest cooperation when there is an apparent need that this one is able to fulfill. This is the strongest drive within this one that causes a sense of harmony between the inner and outer self. When this one can perceive that there is a need that someone else has that this one can naturally fulfill, this calls into action that which is necessary for this one to experience harmony, and it is at those times when this one experiences life in a full sense.
>
> This one has tended to wait for external conditions to present themselves in order for this to become activated within the self. The degree to which this one is attached to that is the degree to which this one can experience inharmony at times when there is not the obvious need present around her. (101400BGC4)

In other words this woman can create a problem where there is none. She has a tendency toward passivity, waiting until someone or something outside the self moves her. This is the root of her disharmony, the reason for breaking the entrainment of the minds. Mental perception will heal this habit.

> This one has an aversion to chaos, therefore this one has put the self in somewhat limited conditions for stimulating this need within her. Therefore, there would be a benefit derived from this one becoming more visionary within the outer mind. This one has a very strong will and it is prone to stubbornness when the intelligence and creativity and vision is lacking. This one finds it much easier to

> come by harmony through compulsiveness than to come to it through choice. In order for there to be the kind of harmony that this one imagines, this one must be willing to coordinate the imagination and the will. This in itself will cause the inner and outer minds to move in cooperation with one another as the opposing directions move, they will move in a cyclical fashion so that there is connectedness and there is a fulfilling of the needs of both. There is a tendency for this one to rely very heavily upon the outer self and to in essence discount the value of the inner self. Then there are times when this one tends to rely totally upon the inner self and to discount the outer. This is the action of the moving in opposite directions. This one will need to bring the two together in order for there to be harmonious action and an experience of harmony.

By unifying the vision and the will, this one can image the highest ideal and beliefs that she can in the present moment. It requires the will for the consciousness to remain in that place. A suggestion to bring the attention to this ideal, over and over again, no matter how many times she finds herself distracted during her day will coordinate imagination and will. An image of this coordination is given.

> It would behoove this one to perceive it in an imagery form such as the movement of a waterwheel that needs to constantly replenish itself in order for it to be in cooperation with the natural laws – for it to cycle, for it to continue and for it to move in a synchronous manner.

When the woman asked for suggestions for attuning conscious and subconscious minds to the superconscious mind, the reply eloquently describes the evolution of Self Respect through all the Essential Life Skills to Entrainment. For those who want to live a higher quality of life than broken promises, dissolving marriages, bankruptcies, and ADD, the response is food for thought for us all.

> That which would assist immediately in the alignment of the minds would be the action of unifying the intelligence and the will. There is a form of understanding in the outer mind that this one has of this that would be most readily

referred to as commitment. We see that it is essential for this one's well being and this one's sense of wholeness for this one to elevate the definition, the beliefs that this one holds concerning commitment, for it is in the flourishing of commitment that this one will find the wellspring of alignment that will enable this one to experience a greater sense of wholeness and completeness within the self. This one has tried to find substitutes for this and knows that they do not exist. Therefore, it is a point of honesty in this one acknowledging this and taking the course of thinking that will cause the transition. This is all. (101400BGC4)

Entrainment What is it?

The first ONE VOICE dedicated the Peace Dome located on the campus of the College of Metaphysics as a universal site for peace on October 11, 2003. People on every continent, including Antarctica, joined in reading the *Universal Peace Covenant* simultaneously!

A few months later we initiated a tradition of reading the covenant at the turning of the New Year. Since 1996 the School of Metaphysics has sponsored a Universal Hour of Peace encouraging leaders in government, business, service, and religion to devote 11:30 pm December 31st to 12:30 am January 1st to peaceful thought and action. A growing number of presidents, governors, and mayors around the world have proclaimed these times of peace. At the Peace Dome we hold vigils for the 24 hours it takes the new year to arrive in every part of our world.

ONE VOICE is an incredible time of dedication, love, vision, prayer and meditation. As we read the covenant with each new time zone we unite our consciousness with those around the planet. When there is joy we add purpose to festivities. When there is suffering we offer healing. We are forever changed from how we spend these hours. The harmonizing of our minds first within Self, then with each other, then out into the world is a life-changing experience.

We know what it means to be the change you want to see in the world.

The best way to describe entrainment is to offer you an experience with it. Here in a few pages are excerpts from the ONE VOICE diary of 2005. Read, visualize, and pray with us.

The Universal Peace Covenant

Peace is the breath of our spirit.

It wells up from within the depths of our being – to refresh, to heal, to inspire.

Peace is our birthright. Its eternal presence exists within us as a memory of where we have come from and as a vision of where we yearn to go.

Our world is in the midst of change. For millennia, we have contemplated, reasoned, and practiced the idea of peace. Yet the capacity to sustain peace eludes us. To transcend the limits of our own thinking we must acknowledge that peace is more than the cessation of conflict. For peace to move across the face of the earth we must realize, as the great philosophers and leaders before us, that all people desire peace. We hereby acknowledge this truth that is universal. Now humanity must desire those things that make for peace.

We affirm that peace is an idea whose time has come. We call upon humanity to stand united, responding to the need for peace. We call upon each individual to create and foster a personal vision for peace. We call upon each family to generate and nurture peace within the home. We call upon each nation to encourage and support peace among its citizens. We call upon each leader, be they in the private home, house of worship or place of labor, to be a living example of peace for only in this way can we expect peace to move across the face of the earth.

World Peace begins within ourselves. Arising from the spirit peace seeks expression through the mind, heart, and body of each individual. Government and laws cannot heal the heart. We must transcend whatever separates us. Through giving love and respect, dignity and comfort, we come to know peace. We learn to love our neighbors as we love ourselves bringing peace into the world. We hereby commit ourselves to this noble endeavor.

Peace is first a state of mind. Peace affords the greatest opportunity for growth and learning which leads to personal happiness. Self-direction promotes inner peace and therefore leads to outer peace. We vow to heal ourselves through forgiveness, gratitude, and prayer. We commit to causing each and every day to be a fulfillment of our potential, both human and divine.

Peace is active, the motion of silence, of faith, of accord, of service. It is not made in documents but in the minds and hearts of men and women. Peace is built through communication. The open exchange of ideas is necessary for discovery, for well-being, for growth, for progress whether within one person or among many. We vow to speak with sagacity, listen with equanimity, both free of prejudice, thus we will come to know that peace is liberty in tranquility.

Peace is achieved by those who fulfill their part of a greater plan. Peace and security are attained by those societies where the individuals work closely to serve the common good of the whole. Peaceful coexistence between nations is the reflection of man's inner tranquility magnified. Enlightened service to our fellowman brings peace to the one serving, and to the one receiving. We vow to live in peace by embracing truths that apply to us all.

Living peaceably begins by thinking peacefully. We stand on the threshold of peace-filled understanding. We come together, all of humanity, young and old of all cultures from all nations. We vow to stand together as citizens of the Earth knowing that every question has an answer, every issue a resolution. As we stand, united in common purpose, we hereby commit ourselves in thought and action so we might know the power of peace in our lifetimes. Only in this way can we expect peace to move across the face of the earth.

Peace be with us all ways. May Peace Prevail On Earth.

signed this 8th day of October, 1997, at the College of Metaphysics

Dr. Barbara Condron Dr. Daniel Condron
Dr. Laurel Clark Dr. Pam Blosser
Dr. Sheila Benjamin Dr. Al Rohrer
Paul Blosser Melanie McManus
Linda Yeingst Ernie Padilla Teresa Padilla
Terry Martin Christine Andrews
Sharka Glet Jay McCormick
Greg Hoeflicker Lisa Kinser John Clark
Patrick Andries Damian Nordmann
Mari Hamersley Terryll Nemeth
Paul Madar Oliver Seger Lyle Branson
John Harrison Traci Byington
Shannon Cordes

The *Universal Peace Covenant* is the document we recite as each time zone welcomes the new year. The covenant is the result of over nine months labor by over two dozen people, age18 to 70, from all walks of life and backgrounds, all teachers in the School of Metaphysics. It is the bedrock for our vigil. Each time we recongregate in the upper chamber of the Peace Dome, we recite the covenant bringing to life images of the words we speak and broadcasting them around the world, particularly to the areas experiencing the birth of a new year.

As we come and go, we endeavor to keep a journal of our experiences. Sometimes funny, sometimes pensive, our minds learn to dwell with those whose hearts are breaking from anticipation and joy for the new beginning and from war, famine or natural disasters.

We realize our words are healing words and that changes us. Here are some of the entries from the 2004-05 Peace Dome vigil. They describe the entraining of the minds within one and among many.

3:30 a.m. Dr. Daniel Condron
I arose in this sweet darkness of early morning and walked in an unusually warm New Year's Eve morning to the peace dome. My still mind received the abundant light of the College of Metaphysics campus. Then I chose to give my attention to the pictures that the words of the peace covenant created. Each of those present at the reading of the peace covenant offered their golden consciousness for the uplifting and peace quickening of the planet earth and its inhabitants.

3:45 a.m.
Ivy Norris
Arising this morning was very easy. It was clear that all of my classmates had the same desire to be in the dome by 4:00 a.m. initiating One Voice across the world. This in itself was heart opening. As we walked outside on this warm winter's morning the moon beamed brightly and was garbed in halo after halo. It is a very special day.

Laurie Biswell

As I prepare myself for the emperience of ONE VOICE I think about the experience that I had last year. I note that that year, the experience changed everything for me. My consciousness was different than when I began. I expect this year will add even more. The year of the Open heart has been such a fast one. It seems as just yesterday we were embarking on our first One Voice. I awoke this morning with awe and excitement. I can relate it to the magical feeling I experienced as a child on Christmas eve awaiting Christmas morning. I had trouble causing myself to sleep. My brain would tell me, "Are you crazy? You are going to stay up for over twenty four hours with only two hours of sleep! You should have gone to bed hours ago." The energy of the moment is too powerful. The morning is so warm. There is a chiming in my ear. This I have come to pay attention to and take note of. I am learning that this is the tone of my vibration. I listen to it as I prepare for the day. I take a shower and soak in the energy of the morning. Afterwards I go down stairs to still my mind and await the hour when I join with others to read the Peace Covenant with Kiritamati, the first place to welcome the new year 2005. I recently learned that Kiritamati is also referred to as the Christmas Island. That is what this day feels like to me. It holds the same magical touch as Christmas eve held for me as a child.

Talina Woods

Today I have become a devotee. Devoted to peace. Devoted to the righteous path. Devoted to friendship, forgiveness, truth and love. Devoted to a still mind. I thank the Holy Mother-Father-Creator for all of existence, especially those with whom I share the precious beauty of this day. Today we all fulfill our dharmas, today we align with our plan, today we set the course for the new year and the rest of our lives. This is more profound than I even have the capacity to understand in this present moment, but I will cherish the awareness that I do have with every fiber of my being.

4:00 a.m.

Stacy Ferguson

When I received the candle that we were passing around as we spoke the Universal Peace Covenant, I thought of the candle as a direct link between myself and the country that we were ushering into this new year. I spoke the words, "Peace is achieved by those who fulfill their part of a greater plan. Peace and security are attained by those societies where the individuals work closely to serve the common good of the whole. Peaceful coexistence between nations is the reflection of man's inner tranquility magnified." As I spoke these words, I felt like an angel or great wise one speaking down from the heavens, giving guidance to a confused and vulnerable people. I want them to have light to move toward. A few days ago, as we were preparing our minds for this upcoming event, I shared at the dinner table that just as I know there really are angels because I have been one when (anonymously giving charity), I like to believe that there are beings who watch over us and guide us. I said that I was going to use this One Voice to be one of those beings for the world.

Damian Nordmann
I am honored to be here now. There is a calm that I experienced and a clarity of being. The group of souls gathered for this first reading of the Universal Peace Covenant sent this calm and peace inwardly and outwardly to the world. Even with several of us with bodily ailments or going to bed late there were eleven of us who came together to initiate this wave of tranquility. I can see and sense the commitment to peace growing stronger in the world. It starts with each individual, with me, with you. Each time one of us chooses peace in any given moment, then peace becomes more real.

Dr. Terry Martin
Peace.
When I walked outside of the Dream Valley House I experienced peace. As I breathed in the fresh night air and received of the stars in the sky, I was somewhat startled by a deer in the yard that ran off. I smiled because it seemed so right.

Ivy
In the Peace dome, as Dr. Barbara talked about the effects of the tidal waves in the East, my mind expanded and connected more deeply with the world and its efforts to repair, to reunite, and to care for one another. I knew we were here supporting with the strength of understanding and the peace of light. It will make a difference. "Blessed be the meek for they shall inherit the earth."

later
Jennifer Childers
I have recited the Universal Peace Covenant four times already this morning. I find this amazing. I get up every morning to read the Peace Covenant at 5:30 because I believe in this document and I believe in the power of thought. Reading the covenant every morning has prepared my consciousness for this moment and day. I feel blessed with what I have and I get to give it to the world all day long.

Damian
These first ebbs of peace are building. I look forward to experience this wave wash through all of us here and the rest of the planet as the day progresses.

Tad, Messenger
What I perceived was an opening like a light coming through a crack. It was a vision looking at our earth from a distance and seeing the energy of peace like light touch, move and open a curved surface over the globe in a curved arc. Later, at the 5am time the arc became thicker and the peace energy moved up into the atmosphere. It was like the sun at dawn.

Stacy
Joy!
The vibration of this area is more joyful than the others. I share in their joy and add mine to theirs.

7am
Tad
Bliss, light tingling throughout my whole body and coming out my crown chakra. I especially tingled as the joy of nine-year-old Hezekiah spread throughout the dome and experienced the coming to my Lord as children. The universe, the world, the Peace Dome ever amazes me. I am still and know my God.

later
Keisha Tafari
Standing on the rooftop of the Gate House, facing the Peace Dome, and reciting the Universal Peace Covenant with Nicholas was a liberating experience. A sense of love for all creation came over me. I knew that I was in the place my soul wanted to be and doing what she wanted to do.

8:30a.m.
Terry
My heart swells with the words World Peace begins within ourselves. As people realize they are cause and devote themselves to creating peace within their thoughts and actions World Peace will truly exist on the planet.

Keisha
How can one connect with and pray for peace for others they've never seen, and yet fail to connect with the one standing next to her? This is what I asked

myself as Nicholas and I hammered siding onto the Gate House. I realized that I did not really feel connected with my teacher and this saddened me. I consciously reached out to connect with him, otherwise, reading the UPC all day was in vain. The circle of love/peace is not complete until you move toward connectedness and peace with the ones in your environment.

10:00a.m.

Ivy

Little one year old Alexandra Grace Madar was an angelic and exuberant addition to the One Voices in the upper chamber of the Peace Dome at this hour. After reading the Peace Covenant she and I went to the healing wall where she and her mom visit regularly, recite the Prayer for Peace and touch all of the continents. Alexandra automatically reached out her hand and touched the continent of Africa.

11:00a.m.

Ivy

We entered the dome, sat down and held hands this time. Emotion and energy again moved through more intensely. It felt as if we were one big, united soul.

Damian

The reading of the Universal Peace Covenant again and again with so many of my brothers and sisters is producing a resonance within me. It started as such a seemingly small vibration early this morning, and each time we give it, it builds within me. It is like the difference between one person trying to lift a very heavy object, then ten people lifting the same object, then 100 people doing the same. It is like the difference between a single person singing and an entire choir singing in unison. It is like one nation under God. It is like summoning a nation within me that I knew not. It is all aspects of Self coming into alignment with the One. I am beginning to understand the potency of One Voice in multi-dimensional ways.

Keisha

The forgotten stone in my pocket: the Rose Quartz I so desperately wanted to share. I show it to Chris and invite him to hold it with me, hand in hand. Aaah, heart connection! The energy is resonating. We decide we must share it. I reach over and grab Damian's hand. Chris holds Laurie's. I am stilling my mind with great aggression, as we read the Universal Peace Covenant, so that my words and the energy are on the same frequency and moving for the benefit of all, in the room, in the world. I look up. A circle of hands. Aaaah, heart

connection for peace. Thank you all for being willing to experiment and share this experience with me, together—for world peace.

11:30a.m.
Talina
Each time I come out to the dome to read the Universal Peace Covenant, my soul seems to become more pure. Last night as I reflected upon my thoughts and actions, my mind clouded by the darkness that comes with the lack of understanding, I prayed. My prayer was that my heart could be clean and open, so that I could give of myself fully on this day of peace. I wanted to be different. I knew I had to choose. Then I thought of the Buddha. The answer to my prayer was on my shelf with a book about the Buddha. It was the very first book I ever owned of a spiritual content beyond Christianity. I picked up the book and began to read. As I read my spirit lifted. With each paragraph I could feel my mind and heart expanding with the peace that only hearing, seeing and knowing truth can bring. All my cares seemed to be carried away. My heart was opening as I resonated with Gautama and his teachings. I thought of Jesus and His message of peace and love. I thought of the relationship I've had with him ever since I can remember. I decided I wanted to develop this kind of relationship with the Buddha of Compassion too. I read until I could no longer hold my eyes open, and before going to sleep I felt my consciousness expand to encompass the whole world. I stated out loud that I wanted to be filled with Buddha consciousness, experiencing and emanating peace throughout the entire day today. This has been my candle flame today. As I fill my thoughts and actions with the Universal Peace Covenant I am coming to know those things that truly make for Peace.

Stacy
It was time to go to the Peace Dome again. Jen said that she was heading out. I told her that I would like to walk out with her. A lovely walk with a good friend. As we reached the door to the upper chamber of the Peace Dome where our sacred recitation would again take place, I exclaimed joyously, "This is fun!" I entered the Dome and sat down. Alexandra was exclaiming and exploring. As always, I was glad to see her. The time approached and more and more gathered. I was glad to see Dr. Barbara. When I left the building she was making a cake, so I wasn't sure if she would be out. A thought of admiration

mixed with appreciation moved through my mind as I realized that she lived her life in such a way that she would time her creation so that she could join us. Seconds away, I thought that no one had yet decided that they were going to ring the bell or light the candle. I told Dr. Christine that she should ring the bell. There was joy in my heart as I looked across at her. In that moment, she was like Alexandra, so sweet, peaceful, sincere, humble and childlike. Love for her filled my heart. She told me with a smile and wide eyes that she was going to light the candle. I was glad. I volunteered to ring the bell. I thought it would be wonderful to be connected to her in this divine act. Ivy told me that Nicholas was going to ring the bell. I giggled as I saw my controlling nature without the usual harsh judgement. I knew that I had just wanted things to happen as they should. At that, I sat back, everything was taken care of. Soon I would recite sacred words of peace with those I love that were gathered. Giving my love and guidance to the countries whose new year had just begun, I experienced the love I was giving within myself.

12:30pm
Stacy
It is a beautiful day here in Windyville. It must be at least 60 degrees with a cool, gentle breeze. As I walked out of the Peace Dome, I saw Nicholas doing his life force exercises in the orchard. I decided that that was a great idea and that I would join him. As I drew energy into my body that after a week of experiencing a severe cold was finally on the mend, I marveled at the fact that here I am on New Years Eve (at least our time — haha!) doing life force in the orchard with a t-shirt, thin pants and no shoes. How beautiful. At that point, I realized that this day is probably my favorite experience yet here at the College of Metaphysics. It is so calm and our energies are pointed in such an elevated direction. Time is different today as we move from one time zone to the next. Today time is not about getting things done or the passage of the sun through the sky, it is about the ushering in of a new year, a new beginning for mankind, wherever on the planet he may be. This is a beautiful day!

1:30pm
Jennifer
The day is moving so softly and quickly. In between the times of making cheese and painting the warehouse I am able to attend the upper chamber of the dome and read the UPC. This is such an amazing experience to be a part of. There is unity between the people that live here. I enjoy everyone's

presence when we read together. It brings me closer to each person. There was a point where I could feel my wall coming up and wanting to keep others out of "my space" to recognize this and respond is a change that I have been working on since I have come to the college. When this wall appeared, or when I became conscious of it, I looked at everyone in my sight and caused myself to see their holistic beauty and appreciate where I was at and what I was doing. I said this before that nothing matters today except giving completely to the world. The identity of "Jen" needed to be put aside and my Spirit needed to come through.

3:00pm
Tad
Bhagdad. It seems when we finished the Universal Peace Covenant there was an air of resonance, an air of stillness that resonated to a higher pitch. I thought of all the turmoil and war in the Middle East and thought of what a moment of peace would bring here. There was a stillness that was similar to the healing power of God. There is a time and a place for world peace and it begins within ourselves as we give and share unconditional love with all of humanity. Peace is a resonant vibration that is attuned to one of the four pulses of the Universe.

5:00 PM
Damian
Everyone needs to have an experience of this magnitude. The consciousness of those here at the College of Metaphysics who are offering this service is elevating and transforming. There is a maturing process that is happening to a greater or lesser degree with each person here. Peace to you all throughout the world. I send you my Circle of Love.

8:00p.m.
Ivy
As we sat at the dinner table this evening in between Peace Covenant readings, I felt more a family with these souls here with me than I've ever experienced. This entrainment has been accelerated all day as we share a common ideal and resonate together time and time again sounding the Universal Peace Covenant throughout the world. We are transcending "whatever separates us."
We are working "closely to serve the common good of the whole" and with it we are creating a family with the whole world.

8:10 p.m.

Nicholas Zajac

I can't lie about it any longer. I need you. I need your love to pass through me. I need this life to show itself through me. I love my family at the College of Metaphysics. I want to say everyone's name out loud, John Harrison, Jaqie Braden, Chris Sheehan, Jen Childers, Ivy Norris, Dr. Barbara Condron, Dr. Daniel Condron, Hezekiah Condron, Dr. Terry Martin, Dr. Christine Madar, Alexandra Madar, Paul Madar, Tad Messenger, Stacy Ferguson, Michael See, Talina Woods, Keisha Tafari, Laurie Biswell. I love my blood family and all the lovers I've known that I have failed to appreciate at all the important times. Thank you everyone for loving and for being who you are. Let this thought stay with me and rise when I'm feeling separate. Let it be permanent within my being. May my mind be a tool of the right use of will and attention. Let my eyes always see the light in my life. May I grow closer to knowing you and your perfect creation, your perfect gift that keeps giving the most valuable morsel of pure sweetness in every moment. Thank you lord, and may this thought spread across the entire world. Amen.

Jaqie Braden

This reading has moved through me on a much deeper level than the others. Each time has worked up to this point. After talking with Nicholas and Chris in the kitchen about friendship also at the table with Dr. Barbara starting a discussion on friendship. The realization of the present moment has really moved through me like a tidal wave. I have so much gratitude for the beautiful souls in my life. The learning I live everyday here at the college has made such an impact on my soul. Seeing the reality of the fact that we here and in the schools are making such an impact on the WORLD. I am finally receiving this into myself, that I am really making a difference in others lives as well as my own. Right now in my life I am learning to have a whole new appreciation for friendships and relationships with others in my life like I never have until now. I think until now I have periodically taken for granted the friendships that I do have. I have been really putting a mirror up in front of my face a lot lately and realizing how I can be very judgmental and unconditional in different ways. I am working on overcoming this ego transformation and old brain pathways. In my past I have been very naive and people have taken advantage of that so I have little trust in people. This is where a whole lot of my walls have come from. Before when I was younger I remember how Happy I used to be always giving to others no matter what and not caring if I ever received anything in return. After all of the experiences I have been through in the past 10 or 15 years I have become very protected, shielded and harsh. It's a very faint memory of mine, yet fortunately I do have a tiny glimpse of how Soft and gentle I used to be. I want to cultivate this part of myself once again. Because now I am realizing how lonely I have MADE myself by shutting myself down and walling myself in to keep out the hurt or pain that someone may cause. I am to the point now that I can see that the only person who can really hurt me, is ME. I want to build divine friendships with everyone I meet. I believe I have the capacity to do so. I now am seeing the value of having loving, caring, honest and sincere people in my life. It has helped me to once again find that part of myself that I thought I had murdered years ago. Yet it lives on inside of my soul. I am finding it again now and bringing it back into the light of day, it's so beautiful. Thank you anyone and everyone who is a part of my life. I love you just because you are. Thank you for loving me just because I am. Peace be with you always.

9:00 PM
Damian
We watched the film "Journey of a Student" then came out to the Peace Dome to read the Peace Covenant. There are two lines from the Universal Peace Covenant that say, "Through giving love and respect, dignity and comfort, we come to know peace. We learn to love our neighbors as we love ourselves bringing peace into the world." These lines are strong in me as well as some lines from a School of Metaphysics lesson which say, "Your best interest is my main concern. I am ready to do anything in my power to aid you." This is the essence of peace that so many people need right now. Keeping another person's best interest in mind is a skill, an art, a science, and most importantly a state of consciousness. The ability to expand the truth of this reality, the desire and choice to keep another person's best interest as the highest priority, is most definitely the key to being a master teacher. I think of every time I have drawn many students to me, and each time I have drawn to me highly evolved souls, it has been when I have been immersed in this STATE of mind. It eliminates all fear, all doubt, all hesitation, all holding back. It allows love to pour forth and a peace to settle upon me. I desire this peace for all people. Amen.

9:05pm
Nicholas
... It doesn't shout at me or try to get my attention. it just is. It's always being, and when I finally decide to say to this all penetrating love, "Hey love, it's good to see you, we haven't talked in a while but I saw you from across the room and that smile you've got on your face and your glossy eyed gaze that

seems to penetrate my soul has got my attention." then it says back "What took you so long, I've been all primped and powdered for you and it's taken you this long to say hi?!... well, lets put all this aside and get a room somewhere and live the ever present now, what d'ya say?" I look into her eyes and say "nothing would be sweeter than......reading the peace covenant for the whole world with the greatest friends one could ever ask for."

10:00pm
Stacy
The candle light shining bright from all the candles symbolizing the time zones and continents filled the room. Hezekiah experimented with the lighting as we recited the Peace Covenant. I enjoyed the changes in lighting that he created. I most enjoyed it when he turned the lights completely off. The candle like was enough to fill our circle and beyond. Its glow was warm and beautiful. culmination" to this year of learning about friendship for me. Thank you Laurie for telling me to share the joy.

10:15pm
Keisha
After reading the Universal Peace Covenant, we proceeded to meditate with Dr. D. I tuned in to the vibrational AUM of others and found stillness inside of it. As I struggled to still my mind, I followed my breath—in, out, in, out. I felt myself—at times—moving inward where there was a vastness and a stillness. I was not able to hold on to this experience, as I continued to move back and forth from my physical body to this inner vastness. Although I was not fully consumed by this experience, I know that the universe is in me. I look forward to exploring this universe and building stability and a peace beyond understanding in my inner self.

Stacy
I thought to myself that I was going to have a special experience with myself of expanding my light. Then, I experienced what I can only explain as sinking back into myself. It was like I realized for the first time that I was a three dimensional being. I realized that before I had only been on the surface of me. Now I was inside of me. There was space inside of me for me to be in. This was fascinating. I think this major shift in my reality of myself came from this holy, wonderful, amazing, devotional day of love and service. Thank you so much! This has been one of the best days of my life. What a way to start a new year.

11:00PM

Dr. Daniel Condron

After the reading of the Peace Covenant I prepared to lead those assembled in a peace filled world meditation. My consciousness flowed into the consciousness of those present as the vibratory AUM we sounded filled the peace dome. This vibration was so harmonious that the glass peace bowl in the center of the room vibrated in harmony with our chanting of AUM. Everyone present seemed to move into a deepened and heightened state of being and peace filled consciousness. After the meditation some of those present reported major breakthroughs in the depth of their meditation. I find joy and fulfillment in aiding these ones in the quickening of their enlightenment.

Talina

This perfection, this Samadhi, this communion, this peace is real. Each time we read we become more entrained, one heart, one mind, one voice. Tonight I closed my eyes and saw the earth before me surrounded in indigo light. I felt a kind of gratitude coming from the being, the essence of the earth and all her inhabitants as this purification of light, love and peace washes over and encompasses all. We are the healers of the earth, the shamans, the nurturers. The reverence of my experience builds with each hour as Stacy and I, keepers of the light, maintain the burning of the candles throughout the night. As we become of one mind, I am transported back in time to lifetimes of friendship in healing and devotion to sacred service.

12 midnight (Our New Years)

Paul Madar

Read the Universal Peace Covenant with Christine as she was feeding Alexandra. We stayed inside the main building for the turn of the new year. It felt good to be reading the Covenant inside the building, christening it for 2005 in peace. I then came out to the Peace Dome to lay a first tile for the new year. Met the Condrons as they were going back inside. I have felt more kindred with them this last year than ever, mostly because of raising a child here at the headquarters, and learning its joys and challenges. I feel reverent today, like I have spent the day in prayer—and I have. I've thought a lot about the people in Indonesia and how I was sending them the Peace Covenant thoughts, light and love. I thought about my new correspondent student Kelly at the 5:00 pm reading, and wondered where he might be reading the Covenant right now. I had a brief thought earlier today as to whether saying the Covenant really did anything for the cities and countries we were holding in mind. It was brief, and quickly replaced with the thought that as I said the Covenant, I was the one changing the world — from inside me, outward. That makes sense, and it fits exactly with what the Covenant says in eloquent ways. It always does something, because the thought is the cause. That change of thought helped me experience the wave of peace moving throughout the planet, including the outpouring of care from all corners for the people of Indonesia. I felt like I was caring for the soul of the planet, and the spirit of the people by building the thought form of peace.

Keisha
The buzzing and zapping started again at the rear throat chakra by 10:00pm. I think about what I've been doing this time with this energy and realize that I have been very positive and productive with this energy today, all day. The power of our words and the thought of the power to use our words to create causes exhilaration to swell within me. On this day as one Voice we have used great power—not with guns, not with aggressive domination—but with our choice of words. Even more powerful to agree upon the words spoken hour after hour. We have used this time productively for the good of all. We have used the power of mind/thought and speech to create peace for all mankind all over the world. Our words shall echo through eternity. Listen for them throughout 2005.

Jaqie
My New Years resolution for 2005 is to be fully committed to myself in areas where I have been currently lacking. Remembering where I am and remembering why it is that I choose to be here right now. I am setting my recent flighty goals into stone and going to work towards them every day. The light has come on for me. The time is now. My soul urge is too strong now to try to ignore or over look any longer. I am dedicating myself to my learning and am releasing my attachment to being stubborn like the bull that I am. Making my ego even more moldable than I have already up to this point. I am ready to embrace who I really am and I am looking forward to seeing what this year has in store for me and I for it as well. I feel very strongly that major shifts are happening and ready to happen in the earth as well as all of the souls on the planet. We are making things happen people and we need to start realizing the impact that we really do have on the planet, in every interaction with a stranger to the energy

of a conversation you have with the person you are upset with or the thoughts you have about something clear around the world. The time is now that we step up and take responsibility for our influence.

2:00 AM and 3:00 AM
Damian
After reading the Universal Peace Covenant at 2:00 am Dr. Barbara started asking those present questions about the previous year, the new year, and how we will be different. It was great! Everyone got to share who there are becoming and receive clarity from Dr. Barbara. I asked Dr. Barbara what one thing she wanted to see happen throughout the SOM this next year. She said she expects to see a maturity and a moving into adulthood, a willingness to live the truth daily in every moment. She used the example of Chris Sheehan coming to the Peace Dome every day at 5:30 in the morning and reading the Peace Covenant since March of 2004. He disciplined himself to be this light every day no matter what part of campus he was staying on, no matter what the weather, and no matter how he felt. She described it as keeping other's best interest in mind at all times. I am excited to move into this adulthood and help others to do this as well.

4:00 AM
Our trip around the world is complete.
Chris Sheehan
Participating in One Voice this year here at the College of Metaphysics was like living in a precognitive dream. My awareness of the reality of what it means to live globally connected was magnified throughout my consciousness during this 24 hour period of TIME. From the space shared with my fellow lightbearers in the choir of light that is the Peace Dome I experienced a fluid movement of energy as we sent our elevated thoughts around the globe. Precise and intentional, a seamless wave of attention encompassing every continent. I saw how the days, weeks, and months of diligence and dedication I have given by reciting the Peace Covenant every morning in the Peace Dome has created a energetic foundation not only for myself but for anyone who has the honor of experiencing the Peace Dome. As Dr. Barbara said, in the final hours of ONE VOICE, we will need to make sure that the reality of our experience lives on, so that it exists within us every day of the year of Knowing Time. This is the year that I will move my consciousness into adulthood by practicing connectedness, living in the present moment and knowing that I AM HE. I would like to give a special thanks to Laurie Biswell for her magnanimous love of the Peace Covenant and for helping to make ONE VOICE what it is. •

One Force
Winning at Volleyball

When I first heard about entrainment I thought of an experience I had at a volleyball tournament. We were finished for the day. I cleaned up and decided to watch the final match in the highest level, Olympic level of competition. There was a team in the finals from California. Just at first glance I could tell that they would win the match. For the playoffs they had changed their uniforms so they looked fresh and together as a team. When the other team was serving the ball, every player on the California team was poised, all concentrating on the serve. They all knew exactly what their role was and they acted as one player, one force. They were awake, efficient and together. They easily won the match. I will always remember the picture in my mind because it is a picture of all parts acting as a whole. ∞ Tad Messenger

ENTRAINMENT

is dedicating every thought and action;
head and heart;
conscious, subconscious, and
superconscious minds
toward becoming
enlightened.

Add your voice to One Voice

by reading the

Universal Peace Covenant

at midnight December 3lst wherever you are!

Resonance in Music

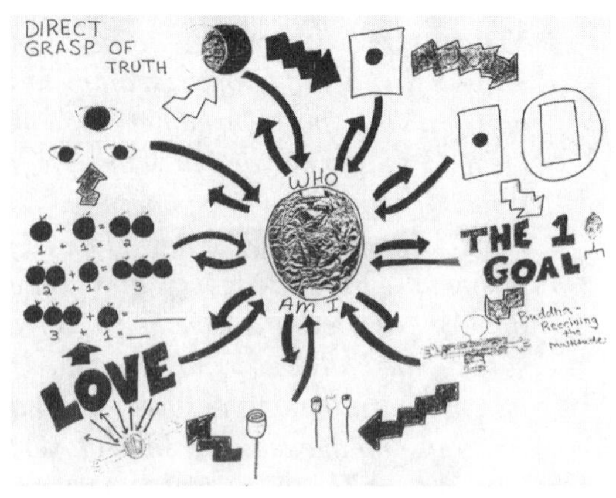

These days I see entrainment as a resonance that is created with previously differing vibrations. Mentally, such as aligning the conscious mind, through disciplining it, with the subconscious mind. Physically, such as singing a song with someone on a tape until the tones match.

Music is becoming more fascinating to me all the time. In looking a little deeper at music as an example I can see more clearly how entrainment is the next step up from the foundation of all the other life skills.

From what I can tell, once reading and playing music has been learned, one can play without thinking. The mind knows what notes to play it can just move and flow with it. It is a good example of understanding structure and how it opens the door to the power of the subconscious mind, intuition.

Resonance, I believe, is sustained intuition. Alignment of the conscious and subconscious mind is held. This is why often when we teach we are able to pour forth wisdom that we had never seen come out of us before. We are entrained, head and heart, conscious and subconscious minds, at these times.

I'm starting to think that grace is related to entrainment. The more entrained I become the more graceful I am. I love especially to see this grace between people. It is a synchronicity, a dance, an open and honest connectedness that creates a space for love to be given and received.

I see this with parents and their children, with the circle of life in nature, with teacher and student. Living here at the College of Metaphysics we comment on the resonance we see between us often. It may come in the person across the table saying exactly what you were going to say in response to a question, or several people wearing the same color of clothing, or moving like a well oiled machine on dish crew. I thought of this today as Jay and I reached to give each other a napkin at the same time and with the extra napkin I, as a part of our one fluid movement, handed it to the person next to me. It was simple, graceful and connected. ∞ *Ivy Norris*

Releasing Thinking

I had an intuitive report that suggested that when entrainment occurred for me, it would be best to still my mind and dwell in it for a while. I am usually too quick to try to understand it, to look at it and start wondering how I got to the entrainment place anyway—and then it's gone. The entrainment happens when I am in a still place of mind and I hold it. Very simple.

Entrainment means to follow along after, which is an appropriate way of describing the process of aligning the conscious and subconscious and attuning them to the superconscious. The whole of the lower mind is following along with the higher mind.

I could tell with the intuitive breathing sessions that I have been receiving that I was experiencing entrainment. There is a peace, a release of thinking that leads into entrainment. When I slow my thinking way down to an extremely slow pace, or even stop thinking altogether, I can entrain myself within the whole mind. In the breathing sessions, I concentrate on breathing so deeply and so fully that the process becomes a culmination of all the Essential Life Skills rolled up into one experience.

I am there because of wanting to know myself—Self Respect. I bring my horizontal attention, the physical stimuli, to one point, as well as unite my inner and outer experience within stillness—Undivided Attention.

I then hold the breathing pattern consistent over time for as long as is needed—Concentration and Breath.

As my mind stills I can listen to the subtle voice that encourages, coaxes and leads me to greater depth—Listening.

Throughout the breathing session I remember why I am here now, what my purpose is—Memory. I use my memory of previous sessions to bring myself to the highest point of consciousness that I had achieved in previous sessions, and then create an image of who I could become if even further enlightened—Imagination.

Reasoning tells me that these sessions are fruitful for me, based on past experience and imagining what they can produce in the future.

My intuition flows while I am so entrained in the stillness, the Silence.

Profound insight and answers to questions I didn't even know I had bubble forth effortlessly. The entrainment fills me full.

Intuitive breathing engages and unifies my whole mind, and it requires practicing the Essential Life Skills to fully reap the benefits. ∞ Paul Madar

ELS#10

A Short Class on Entrainment

Dr. B: It was very interesting at the Atlantean Awakening Weekend because I was sitting where I could see the work of one of the male participants and one of the females. I watched them develop their mind maps® answering the question, "Who am I"? The male just couldn't get anything going and knowing his interest and talent I whispered, "Music". He chose as his central image a note and then he added other notes ending up with four. Then he created a staff and outside of that were all words. Everything was words. Lots of them.

I watched him and I thought, "I wonder how he is going to connect the stem with those words?" He looked at what he'd drawn and realized that the two weren't connected. So he started drawing these little whimsy, curved lines all around, kind of like the tongs on a rake. So that it would kind of connect it. But it didn't really, you could tell it was an after thought. I was so grateful to have the experience of observing the mind in action. I knew I had been present to see how his mind worked!

The female, on the other hand, drew all pictures. She put absolutely no words on her thought diagram. She started with a central image then she created sections of color and had some kind of small image on the outer parts of the paper in each direction. What was really funny was when she stood up to talk to the group about hers, she said, "I did only pictures. I didn't put any words." Then she said something about how there weren't really words to describe her pictures. Then she went on to talk for twenty minutes, and never did see the contradiction in what she had done.

On one level here were illustrations of how a male tends to think: in words, left brain dominant, conscious mind centered. And how a female tends to think: in images, right brain dominant, subconscious mind centered. This is why males have, until now, tended to be the aggressive force in the societies, the ones who create and make the world what it is, while the females have tended to be the receptive force, the conscience and mediators who enable those aggressive forces to work together or apart.

Thought diagrams lift your consciousness beyond the confines of the body, of your sex. You literally rise above the limits of physical thinking. Thought diagrams have structure, order, and clarity. They communicate what is in our minds and reflect back to us what parts of mind are engaged in the topic we are diagraming. Through thought diagrams we come to know our own thoughts.

Every thought diagram is different. Each experience teaches you something, be open to what it gives you. Be willing to see what you are revealing when you create a mind map®. This is learning how to learn. This is how you become awake enough so you can be your own teacher. If you are going to be your own teacher you are going to have to be awake.

Dr. L: The diagrams are a way for me to get centered in who I am. Part of what I have realized is that some of the pictures were clear, but some of my conscious thoughts about the book were kind of half baked, and that is when it get hard, when you haven't really thought through the idea and it's kind of scattered.

Dr. B: Learning how to use more of your mind changes all that. It separates state of mind and content. Fear is the content of an unstable mind. The disciplined mind knows emotion as the means by which ideas become real in the physical world. I believe it was Shakespeare who noted that nothing is either good or bad, only thinking makes it so. The beautiful thing about your mental exercises is that they give you the opportunity to center yourself in your soul, instead of in your physical body and how things look. When the measure of your life is how things look, that's entrapment.

NG: And purpose centers you in how things are.

Dr. B: Explain.

NG: Purpose is the change you will make by accomplishing a goal. When I was first studying I wanted a higher paying job in a better environment. That was the goal. My purpose at first was freedom because I'd have more money and could move into my own place. Once I got the job, I realized other purposes that I hadn't seen before. It was easier to get up to go to work because I enjoyed it. My other job I dreaded half the time so my attitude wasn't the best. I was more confident because others valued the work I did. I felt I was doing something more important with my life because my talents were being used. I hadn't expected those kinds of realizations going into the job.

Dr. B: Entrainment means that your conscious mind is still which is why in your case you could receive your abundant return on your efforts. Entrainment starts when you are respectful. This manifested in your example through the desire to secure different employment. Being willing to examine what you have, Self respect, opened the door to imaging what you could have. Then your conscious mind became still and you brought the past and the present and the future together. Acting upon your desire, you could be completely in the now, in sync, entrained. You were breathing with the universe. When we are in the present, reasoning and intuition can fully function. One of the benefits is to realize higher purposes in life, which is exactly what you did. Your talents, your understandings from subconscious mind, now had a vehicle for expression. It was something you hadn't anticipated, yet it was one of the fruits of your labor. A tenfold return.

I was teaching a group of students mental and physical actions that help create and maintain a centeredness. At the time I was instructing them in a mudra (posture) to balance the energies of the solar plexus. I said, "You can use this anytime, anywhere." I encouraged them to hold the posture and the breathing at the beginning of their day. There was a different posture I taught for the evening. I said, "When you do this every day you cause changes in the way that you think and in the way that you breath. When you are at work you might not be able to go over and sit in the lotus position and do this, however, you could take one breath and find that you are a lot more centered then you were before. So you can cope, you can handle the situation at work differently than is your pattern."

This is the importance and reality of doing daily disciplines, and daily exercises. It begins to filter into your consciousness so it comes into your day. I said, "The ideal is that you don't run off into a corner and "do" these exercises so you can be centered, calm and mentally clear." The idea is that you teach yourself how to use more of your mind and more of your energies *at will*. At will means anytime, anywhere, for any purpose. This is the reality of how we teach metaphysics....•

Hi, Dr. Barbara,

I wanted to take a few moments to write you and give you the update on the **Season of Peace** in Indianapolis. It is my hope that by communicating regularly about what we are doing that other schools will keep it in their mind and realize NOW is the time to act! We are having a ball with this idea.

We started by putting the goal as the number one item on our ten most wanted list! It reads, Every person in the city of Indianapolis receive a copy of the Universal Peace Covenant by December 31st, 2005. We are still playing with the words a bit as we are meaning "receive" to mean they hear it, have it, or see it. We would like all people to actually HAVE it and I have a student who is looking into the possibility of a grant to pay for the printing and mailing costs. He is a student who has access to all the addresses of every person who resides in the city. It is a BIG list and would require BIG money to do. Until we know about that we are looking at a lot of other ways to get this accomplished!

Several of the students work in public and private schools. They are working on getting stories printed in their newsletters with a copy of the peace covenant. Jenny Oler works for Eli Lilly and she is checking on the possibility of getting this into their weekly e-news that goes to everyone who works for Lilly.

That would be huge! :) Kathryn Yost (who is our next teacher) is working on getting this printed in the Indianapolis Star as well as working with me on our plans for one voice/ universal hour of peace. We will be writing letters and contacting as many of the local churches and organizations as possible to let them know about the goal and asking them to print it in their bulletins as well as join us in one voice.

Paula has her sights on proclamations from the governors of Indiana and Ohio! I am going to work on the city (mayor).

Nathan, a new student of Walter's has taken the Peacemaking book to his high school sociology teacher to set up lectures at the school. Nathan is an amazing soul, I cannot wait for you all to meet him at the student weekend. We have several students who have a goal to hand the peace covenant out to a certain number of people per week. For example, Julie (another new student) is working on 25 per week. Walter and I have focused a lot on giving them to people we meet. We tell everyone about the goal. I look forward to receiving our supply order as we are running out of copies fast! :)

I will set my sights more on lectures and community events next. We have a few booths set up soon and I would love to find some holiday events. There are so many concerts and such that I think if we ask the right folks we could be there handing them out. I think the School of Metaphysics needs to be at the doors of the Indianapolis Symphony holiday concerts and the Indianapolis Children's Choir events. I was also thinking that SIR chapters could sponsor events on the campuses as that would be a great way to talk to people on the campus about what we do!

That brings me to this Saturday! As I said, Kathryn is the next teacher in Indianapolis and she is wanting to get her class started before teachers meeting. We were all talking on Monday about ways we could build the class. We decided to go out to a few areas in the city and hand out peace covenants and let people know about the season of peace. It is a great way to talk to people and we will then be able to let people know about the class and the school. I love it because the picture the students have is of giving and that will create a neat experience for them to work with. Paula will be joining us as well so that she can carry this to Cincinnati. What a great way to build a class in a city where we want a school.

I have such a big vision for this. I would love to see a few different things happen.

One idea is to move out from city to state and have the goal of everyone in the state receive the peace covenant.

Another idea was one that Gary Goodhue and I talked about. We were thinking that it would be fun to connect Indianapolis and Fayetteville on a map and then work toward each other city by city until we connected the two. Why not then connect all the schools like a big peace web and then work to fill it in? That would be so much fun! I can see it being a few year project.

I have so many more ideas that I guess I will save for the next update as Leah says it is time to go play! Have a beautiful day! I love you, Amy

Dear Amy,
You made my day extra beautiful with your love and your light! I'm with you in every way I know how and look forward to what the Season of Peace will do to prepare our country and the world for 2012. This is a golden vision that lingers with me in every meditation. It is One Voice living in the stratosphere. It is the hundredth monkey evolving! I look forward to this student weekend when we come together united in common purpose so that

peace may prevail on earth!

Here is one of our recent endeavors here at the College to open the Peace Dome to youth, particularly in this case to homeschoolers. Perhaps this can stimulate more ideas for the Season of Peace. See you soon. O Dr. Barbara

Visit the world's Peace Dome

(just an hour north of Springfield)

Nestled in the countryside only minutes from Bennett Springs State Park is the Peace Dome. Dedicated in October 2003 as a universal site for peace, the two story monolithic dome is 60 feet in diameter and 28 feet at its highest point. Monthly April through October it hosts "The INVITATION" an hour and fifteen minute original live presentation based upon eight Nobel Peace Prize laureates ranging from Albert Schweitzer (1958) to Shirin Abadi (2003). For times and dates contact the College of Metaphysics at 417-345-8411)

On Tuesday, September 20th a homeschooler day will enable children 8 and up to tour the Peace Dome. The tour will begin at 10:30 am with a multimedia presentation including the film "MakingPeace: The Construction of the Peace Dome". This 24 minute film documents how the dome was constructed and is of educational interest for its architecture and as a sociological study. Governmental proclamations from countries, states, and mayors add a historical and political science dimension, as does construction of the Healing Wall, a current effort to unite native stones from every country on the planet. Thus far over 5 dozen stones from Australia to Tibet to Brazil have been collected. Those who participated in the building and dedication will share their stories and answer questions.

Students will read the Universal Peace Covenant, learn a peace song, and participate in a peace circle. They will sign the Peace Scroll and lay a tile in the Peace Mandala, an ongoing mosaic being created in the center of the first floor, before departing. Pack a lunch and plan to stay until around 1:30pm.•

Email 2

"What would you attempt for me if you knew you could not fail?" - Christ

There is a billboard along highway 44 between St. Louis and Windyville that has this written on it. This thought has germinated within my mind during many a contemplative car trip through the beautifully wooded hills of the Missouri countryside.

51 people committed to being students in Cincinnati. The Meijer's Kids Fest occured from 11-5 on Saturday and Sunday for a total of 12 fair hours. That means 4.25 people commited to being students in the School of Metaphysics every hour. We also gave out hundreds of fliers to people interested in attending Dr. Laurel's lecture and book signing for "Interpreting Dreams for Self Discovery" taking place on June 22, created a huge mailing list, and gave out over 1000 pieces of information with the Cincinnati contact information.

All of the teachers and some of the students lived at the Four Points Sheraton and Millineum Hotel during the weekend. Teachers Meeting was held in Room 456 called the "Salmon P. Chase" board room. 13 of us sat around an oval table in red leather executive chairs. The rooms we lived in book out at a rate of $169.00 a night and the conference room that we used all weekend would have cost a couple of thousand dollars to use for the extended time we had it available to us. The total cost of the space we received in the hotel equaled over $4000. We did not receive this space for free. The general manager wanted to receive something of value for the rooms. We agreed to do a training seminar for 40 of the top managers of her hotel in the early part of 2006 as a trade for the space she was grateful to offer to us.

How did all of this happen?

Goal+Purpose+Activity=Success. My initiating thought is wanting to give everyone an experience of huge vision manifesting. I want the people of Cincinnati to have a branch location of the School of Metaphysics. I want Dr. Laurel to have an opportunity to give and create that is big enough to receive the tremendous amount of energy, light, power, love and understanding within her. I want Chris to have the space to direct a School of Metaphysics in my area. I want all of the teachers to have an experience of success so they can know their power as mental creators. I want to give the students in our area an opportunity to see how the opportunities available to them through the School of Metaphysics will enable them to be the kind of light in the world they have always wanted to be. I want to create happenings, events, experiences so that many people have the opportunity to build permanent understandings of creation and the world can become a brighter place. In other words my goal was to aid every individual to become a whole functioning self - to create the space where this would be probable.

My purpose is to accelerate the evolution of humanity by ushering in spiritual intuitive man. The ideas behind this are the same ones that I just told you about. What I realized through this is that I am fulfilled through aiding others. I added to my understandings of commitment and faith among others.

I have had the idea for a long time, and probably talked to some of you about the potential for a group of us to get together and open a new branch of the School of Metaphysics in one weekend. I am in the place of being willing to put my ego on the line. I told Dr. Laurel early on that I would do whatever it takes to make sure we have hotel space donated so we could have teacher's meeting in Cincinnati and the students who would be serving at the booth would have a place to stay.

That is the activity.

I did whatever it took. What it looked like was calling over 30 hotels. I spoke to Lisa Carrere, the general manager of the Millenium hotel we stayed in, the first day I made calls. She told me under no circumstances what so ever would she give away rooms it is against their corporate policy, they were booked out that weekend with a large group of people coming in (the Millenium has a skywalk connecting it with the Cincinnati Convention Center which was hosting a convention of hair sylists who use the product Aveda during the weekend we stayed there).

I kept calling. Some of the places I called laughed at me, some people said we have 3 fairs the first weekend of June every hotel in the city is sold out.

I kept calling. There was no room at any inn. I kept calling. No was not an answer I was willing to accept. I said I would do whatever it takes. Yes lord even if you ask me to accept them laughing at me - even this I will do for you. I kept repeating that thought to myself. Yes lord even if you ask this of me, I will do it for you. I believe this is how to align with Superconscious energies.

Through this experience I began to experience a greater excitement and anticipation - it was thrilling. The first couple of no's were hard on my ego. I began to have a sense that this was a humbleness experience for me. Would I really give whatever it took? Would I really stay centered in the thought of wanting to serve so many people? Or would I give in and succumb to the self-centered, whinning, weak willed, puny, egoic thoughts of I tried my hardest, I did but there was just no space, we waited to long, if only we had sent a letter to corporate months ago we could have a room, if only Dr. Laurel would have known about this sooner. You see the ego is cunning and sly - it will try and make you think that you are less than you really are. It will try to talk you out of going after your big dreams. That is the most egotistical of all - to think, you, a son of god a being of light, - is incapable and weak. After about 20 times of being told no I was determined. There was no more doubt, there was no more fear, there was no more hesitation, there was no more blame, there was no more insecurity. I was left with serving - wanting to serve humanity and my superconscious mind. Yes lord even this I will do for you became more than a plea it became a statement of power, purpose, and duty.

The second time I talked to Lisa Carrere I was different. I explained to her that we were wanting to open a school in Cincinnati. We only need 6 rooms. We are coming because we want to serve the people of Cincinnati. She said, well is there something you can trade for the rooms. I talked to her about trading a seminar for her managers. I explained to her who we are and what we teach. I gave her a picture of how valuable the education provided by the School of Metaphysics is.

I transformed me. I stopped trying to sell or fast talk my way into the rooms. My afirmation worked. I started doing it for my lord. That is what the 30 calls were about. I put my ego on the line. "Banish fear, dispell all doubt. Dying daily fulfill the plan. Follow through Creator Man. Light shines darkness flies. Honesty replaces lies. Crosses lifted. Joy resounds. Great Power of simple love astounds." I had to move past what was inside of me that was in the way of receiving my vision. That is what activity is for.

I made space within my conscious mind to receive what I had imagined. My thoughts about the whole event changed. In the end in talking to Lisa on the phone all my ego was dead. All I had left was the vision of who we are and what we wanted to bring to the people of Cincinnati. She responded when I got to that place within myself and she was able to recieve the full value of the School of Metaphysics because I was no longer in the way. Initially she was only willing to give the School of Metaphysics (you see it wasn't me any more) 6 rooms for Friday Night. I told her thank you and we would keep it in mind but we really needed something for both nights. She asked if she could call me back. When she called back she said she was able to give us the 6 rooms for Friday and Saturday and asked if we would still be willing to do a seminar for her employees. The whole interaction with Lisa is a story in and of itself. It is divine.

I learned something about activity through all of this. What ever is required of me in order to achieve what I want is there to help me clarify my thoughts. All along I had to reaffirm my goals. I had to strengthen my purpose. I had to remind myself that it is my lord who sent me and it is he that has asked these things of me.

The experience that I am left with is an immense amount of gratitude. I felt like I had the opportunity to be an instrument of all of your vision. It maniftested for me in all of the students and teachers in our area along with Dr. Dan and Dr. Barbara - my teachers - and most directly, constantly, devotedly, lovingly, encouragingly, supportively Dr. Laurel the person who has given so much to me. Thank you all for your support, encouragement and willingness to create this. In the end I realize that it was never me and that is why I required all of the activity - it took me a little while to forget myself and realize I was acting on all of your behalf to serve Cincinnati and ultimately God.

O Matthew

Thank you Matthew, for an absolutely perfect story for the Entrainment section of Master Living! It's worth every minute of walking the walk and talking the talk. Thank you for being a stimulus – a force for Good – in our lives. O Dr. Barbara

Mirroring

I was with one-year-old Alexandra at Dream Valley. Her parents were working with some of the students during Christ Consciousness weekend. We were playing a game. She was in 'the zoo' which is a play pen with lots and lots of stuffed animals in it. She loves being there and apparently can be in there for hours and be perfectly happy.

I know she likes to look high and then low, it's kind of a peek a boo type of game. So I would look over the top into 'the zoo' and then look underneath the top through the ribbed netting. She caught on very quickly and as soon as we had looked over the top she would quickly bend over to look underneath.

We moved together for quite some time until something happened in the environment that caught her attention. Then I moved with her as she wanted to get out and run around. I stayed with her as she moved throughout the building, in part because I knew it was helpful to everyone around, but also because I wanted just wanted to be with her.

It's so unusual for me to just be, although these are the times of profound insight. There is an art to being and becoming. It's connected to doing in the physical realm. For most, being is departing from the physical realm.

My experience with Alexandra involved being and doing. I was receptive to her thoughts and actions and moved with her, so I was causing myself to become entrained with her. Alexandra was playing peek a boo with herself in the mirror and I was reminded of old comedy skits when someone is looking into what they think is a mirror only it's really someone else they are looking at who happens to be dressed and appear just as they do. The joke is on the person looking in the mirror because everyone who is watching knows that this is a set up of some kind.

Well, being with Alexandra in the experience is like moving with her, anticipating her thoughts and joining in. I'm thinking now about what it would be like to practice entraining with whatever goes on in the environment. Sometimes I separate myself because I don't want to be entrained with the chaos or the tension that exists in the environment. I think the solution is to remove myself from the environment until it becomes more peaceful.

Perhaps if I moved with the experience of chaos or tension I could become more directive and move it to another place of peace.–Dr. Terry Martin

Taraka Yoga Exercise on Entrainment

To prepare for this exercise you will want time and space. Set aside two hours when you will be uninterrupted. If technology is a problem – cell phones, beepers, tvs and the like – then go to a local park or out in the country where you can sit by a stream in quiet solitude. Choose your time well. For some, early morning hours when most people are resting is a quiet time that allows for contemplation. Others may find the need to set aside an afternoon when all machines will be turned off so no external stimuli steal your attention from the task at hand.

Your task is a labor of love. To exist with head and heart entrained, cooperating and functioning as one, means to be aware of conscious thinking and subconscious thinking. The following exercise will move you in the direction of awareness and responsiveness to your potential as a whole, functioning Self.

You will need pen and lined paper, large drawing paper and markers or crayons, and a tape recorder with a blank tape. A timepiece that can be set to let you know when a specific period of time has passed will be useful. Once your supplies are assembled and your appointed time and place are present, you are ready to begin.

There are nine distinct steps in this Taraka Yoga movement. Focus your attention on the step at hand, completing them in order. Each step produces a mental asana or posture that yields itself to the following movement. You can perform this Yoga as many times as you like. Each time you give Self to it you will experience deeper and more complete states of union.

STEP ONE

Set your timer for 20 minutes.
Begin a stream of consciousness writing on this question:

When am I most aware of head and heart being entrained? Working together?

Stream of consciousness writing is highly effective when accomplished properly. In the beginning it is important to keep writing. Even if your thoughts wander from your topic or seem misplaced, keep writing. Do not lift your pen from the paper. As your thoughts move, write them down. Do not edit them. Each thought arises for a reason that will become clear to you at a later time.

When the timer goes off, stop writing and go on to Step Two.

STEP TWO

List 6 situations where my head and my heart are out of sync

STEP THREE

Draw a picture of a situation where your head rules

STEP FOUR

Set your timer for 10 minutes. Tape record your answer to the following question:

How would the kindest person I know interpret this picture? What would they see in it?

STEP FIVE

Listen to what you have taped, drawing images that convey your attitude now.
When you have completed listening. Look at your drawing and determine one symbol that will serve to remind you to move from your head to your heart. Sketch that symbol.

STEP SIX
Draw a picture of a situation where your heart rules.

STEP SEVEN
Set your timer for 10 minutes. Tape record your answer to the following question:

How would the wisest person I know interpret this picture? What would they see in it?

STEP EIGHT
Listen to what you have taped, drawing images that convey your attitude now.
When you have completed listening. Look at your drawing and determine one symbol that will serve to remind you to move from your heart to your head. Sketch that symbol.

STEP NINE
Draw an outline of a human body. Place the two pictures you created on it.

What does this body tell you about your thinking potential?

STEP TEN
Read Step Two again. Choose the situation you most want to be different. Determine *how* your head and heart are out of sync by asking yourself these questions:

Is this a no brainer and I am overthinking the situation to the point of pressuring myself

or

do I need to be more sensible and think things through more completely?

Do I need to "put my heart" into what I am doing or stop "carrying my heart on my sleeve"?

After Juan* experienced this Taraka Yoga he decided to accept a job half a world away. He had been torn between his head telling him it was a chance of a lifetime opportunity and his heart strings being pulled by friends and loved ones who would miss him. Through entraining his minds he eliminated indecision by asking his girlfriend to marry him and come with him (a movement of head to heart) and by calculating how many trips home he could afford by taking the position (a movement of heart to head). By entraining his head and heart he knew the right course of action to take for him at this time in his life. The strength of this integration served him well in making the adjustments and aiding others to do the same.

For self-study, teaching aids can help. **The Dreamer's Dictionary** is an excellent resource for interpreting images in the Universal Language of Mind. For instance, Geoffrey's* picture of his head ruling showed flames encircling a large head on a small body. Fire symbolizes expansion therefore indicating that ideas expand Geoffrey's world. Whether this is productive or unproductive is a function of Geoffrey's concentration ability. When Self directed, Geoffrey is a creative thinker who mentally moves quickly. He can also "burn out" quickly, leaving many projects unfinished, many ideas untested. By adding heart, Geoffrey could focus upon purpose for his ideas. This would neutralize his tendency to be a "hothead" as his drawing suggested and give him the internal motivation needed for completing what he begins.

Deidre's* heart drawing shows her on an island with a very big heart radiating pink rays. Doves fly in the air and dolphins come up out of the waters to greet her. The sun shines in her picture and the sky is clear. In the language of mind, dream symbols, Deidre's picture reveals her need for Self possession midst internal and external stimuli. When she is removes her attention from distractions, symbolized by the island, her thoughts are clear (the sky), pure (doves), and spiritual (dolphins). She is centered and has connection with Superconsciousness (the sun).

This made sense to Diedre since her favorite pasttime is walking on the beach each evening. Before she moved to the Midwest, this was her custom. Since relocating she has felt the absence of this activity in her life, becoming more stressed. She thought it was the lack of water until this drawing. Now she could see what was missing in her life was time alone, the island time, which her head told her she could create anytime, anywhere.

Permanent Healing by Dr. Daniel Condron is an excellent resource to interpret energies expressing themselves through the body. In Step Nine, Faye's heart symbol was an opened heart with pink rays pouring out like a fountain. To her conscious mind this symbolized opening her heart and giving love. When her eight year old saw the drawing on the kitchen table she said, "Wow, Mom, who drew this?"

"I did. What do you think?"

"Looks like your heart is breaking," she answered.

Faye saw her drawing differently when she saw it through her child's eyes. The open heart was now a broken heart and the rays were blood pouring from the wound. Faye was surprised by what had been there all along that she had never seen. She realized that many of her "heart" moments were painful ones, ones of parting or hurt.

She consulted **Permanent Healing** for insight into heart. She found a description of the mental cause and remedy for heart problems. The one that made the most sense to her was: "pretending to be content in an area but actually discontent due to not being where one aspires to be or where one thinks one should be." Faye began taking stock of her life. She didn't like thinking that she is a pretender. She wanted to be authentic, real but she didn't know how.

Insight came in one of the suggestions given in **Permanent Healing**. She read: "decide what you want even if that is different from what everyone else wants. Live your life, not someone else's life." What stood out to Faye were the words *even if that is different*. In that moment, she realized why she had not followed her heart for many years. From the time she had become pregnant with her first child through later marrying her child's father through divorce, most of her choices had been swayed by others. She had not followed her heart. She had made the "logical" choice often based on fears. She had made emotional choices out of guilt. This was the root of her unhappiness and discontent.

Faye had always thought of herself as open-hearted, making

others happy. She could now see this was to the sacrifice of her own happiness, the bleeding heart her daughter saw. This newfound awareness birthed a desire for honesty in Faye. Her relationships began to change. Even when she was uncomfortable, she committed herself to making her thoughts and desires known. What she discovered was those who love her, not only stayed with her, they encouraged her changes and supported her in fulfilling her desires. Relationships with those who did not have her welfare in mind, where the other person was primarily self-serving, faded. Faye's life took on new meaning because she made a mental change bringing her closer to her ideal Self.

Those of us studying and teaching in the School of Metaphysics describe our common goal as "aiding any individual to become a whole, functioning self." Entrainment is the practice of becoming that Self. It can happen in a moment. It can occur spontaneously. For most, it comes and goes. When your mind is disciplined, entrainment can become a daily experience. The first way we teach this is through daily meditation.

Over time, each Essential Life Skill is taught and practiced. Each one providing the foundation for the one to come. Through calling into action the nine Essential Life Skills preceeding it, entrainment becomes your way of life and illumination the state of your consciousness. •

Jesus, the Borg, & the Healing Power of Music

In my mind this is the picture of my ideal for becoming a whole functioning Self - all parts being aligned and acting as one unit, one being like the Creator. It occurs when all parts have a role, and are moving toward one common goal.

I have experienced entrainment in many different ways. When we are singing for Cantatas or Christmas presentations, or performances, there comes a moment when everyone is focused on the image of the song, giving it to the people. There is no thought of Self, only the meaning, the picture of what is being sung. All the voices blend as one. It is a very powerful moment and I see people come to tears or feel a tingling up their spine or a stimulation of their crown chakra as they describe their experience.

I have experienced at times in each emperience that we have presented in ***"The Invitation"*** *as the Nobel Peace Laureates are embraced and their spirit comes to life. It was especially powerful in the Satyagraha emperience. I think this occurred because there was one point of focus, the life of Ghandi and Dr. Paul Blosser embraced that life, that philosophy, the spirit so well. Everyone's attention was focused on that one life and it came to be a whole and complete experience.*

The dictionary says that entrain means to drag along with or incorporate into the whole. This sounds like the Borg in "Star Trek" where they incorporate everything into the Borg. Another way to look at it is to get on the train, all aboard.

This is basically what Jesus does with all of his disciples and all the aspects of himself that he heals. He teaches to go out and teach the truth so that all aspects of the Self align with knowing that we are like the Creator, that we can know creation, that we can become enlightenment. The entrainment is to draw all parts of my Self toward enlightenment.∞ –Tad Messenger

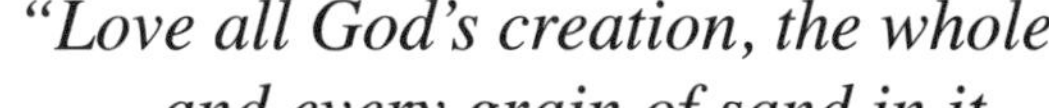

"Love all God's creation, the whole
and every grain of sand in it.
Love every leaf, every ray of
God's light. Love the animals,
love the plants, love everything.
If you love everything,
you will perceive the
divine mystery in things.
Once you perceive it,
you will begin to
comprehend it better
every day.
And you will come
at last to love the
whole world with
an all-embracing
love."

– Fyodor Dostoyevsky
1880, Russia

THE Whole Self

Rebuilding the Temple

There was once a teacher who lived with a large number of students in a run-down temple. The students supported themselves by begging for food in the streets of the nearby town. Some students grumbled about their humble living conditions.

Seeing the unrest, the old master said, "We must repair the walls of this temple yet since we spend our days in study and meditation, there is no time to earn the money we need. A solution entered my meditation this morning."

All the students gathered closer to hear the master's illumined thought.

"Each of you must go into town and steal goods that can be sold for money!" The monks' faces were expressionless. "In this way you will be able to do the good work of repairing our temple."

The students were shocked by this thought, but believing in the eternal guidance in meditation and divine order, they listened carefully to their master's instructions. "In order not to defile our excellent reputation by committing illegal and immoral acts, please be certain to steal when no one is looking. I do not want anyone to be caught."

When the teacher left, the students began talking amongst themselves. "It is wrong to steal," said one.

"Why has our master asked us to do this?" wondered another.

"It will rebuild the temple," another retorted. "It is a means to a good end."

They all agreed that whether they could understand it or not, the end justified the means. Leaving for town, they promised each other that they would not disgrace their temple by getting caught. "Take care," they called to one another.

As these students left, one lingered behind. The wise master approached him asking, "Why do you stay?"

The boy responded, "I cannot follow your instructions to steal where no one will see me."

Recognizing the boy's brilliance, the master asked, "What makes you say this?"

"Wherever I go, I am always there. Watching." The boys eyes filled with tears, as he felt torn though resolute. "My own eyes will see me steal, Master."

"Yes," the wise master embraced the boy. "This is a test of integrity, young brother, and you are the only one who is demonstrating this."

The boy went on to become a teacher himself.

As we move beyond extremes we gain the sight that brings mastery. Reasoning gives us the ability to see possibilities, intuition opens the mental eye to infinity, and entrainment, the marriage of the two, brings what the Tibetans call the Wisdom Eye.

It is our own experience of Truth that is universal which gives us the inner strength to see the good in all situations. Where were you polarized in reading this story? Was it from the beginning with the run-down temple filled with beggers? Was it when the leader asked others to steal? Or was it in a concept like "the means justifying the ends"? Neutralizing the polarity in our experience is the work of Self realization.

We possess the ability to move beyond labeling ourselves and others as right or wrong, good or bad, strong or weak, rich or poor, and the host of what the ancient teachings call the *pairs of opposites*. With these ten Essential Life Skills we have the tools to exercise it.

Each time we consciously choose use concentration or imagination or breath we are strengthening the integrity of our thought and our action. We are the change and to the degree we are awake to that Truth, we are One.•

Excerpted from an Intuitive Health Analysis (10132001BGC3)

Much of the hamonization of this one is pressed into service for physical desires and needs. We see this one tends to be very focused in the physical world. Upon what this one wants and what this one believes he should accomplish and therefore the mind is called upon to fulfill that which this one creates physically. We see that there is a great ability when this one employs reasoning and particularly his will to fashion and to create what this one desires, and the subconscious mind readily responds to this in bringing it to this one. We see that it is not always percieved by the conscious mind that what this one has wanted has been produced; however, it is a perfect mechanism in that it only reproduces what this one imagines.

We see that this then causes the working together of the two minds; however, there is not necessarily a harmony.

This difficulty arises because the conscious mind is not invested equally in returning something back to the inner mind; therefore, there is a slow depletion that is beginning to occur in the mind energies its self and its substance. We see that there is a need for this one in order to continue to experience the kind hamonization that this one has become accustomed to, to begin to expand this one's thinking to realizing a greater obligation within the mind. That the obligation goes beyond merely caring for or receiving what this one wants out in the physical material world, but that the obligation extends beyond the physicality of the self. There is some awareness of this however there is not the integration of it in the consciousness therefore it does not move itself within the life.

We see that although this one is able to pull upon the mind's energy and substance to produce what is desired there is the slow depletion of both because of it. In that regard it would be helpful for this one to begin to develop a stronger sense of purposes. This is not to say reasons for what this one wants but more where what this one wants will lead this one, the kind of person that it will aid this one to become, how it will build qualities and virtues and characteristics in the self that extend beyond merely the physical life and the materiality of the self. ***It is through the cultivation of this kind of thinking into the consciousness so that it becomes a part of the self that will aid this one in expanding and elevating the sense of harmony and will aid this one then to begin to return*** *the used energy back into the mind for the elevation of consciousness.* This is all.

This one says "Why do my thoughts often reflect on past relationships and events?"

This is relative to what has been given concerning purpose. When this one lacks purpose within the present time period of what this one is creating and building then the mind naturally goes to compulsive patterns and these compulsive patterns have been made in the past and are attached to the events and people in the past.

How can this one help to heal insecurities about this one's identity and awareness of the self as a creator.

By developing the reasoning ability. This will cause there to be a greater power within the conscious mind that this one will become aware of and it will then stimulate a more thoughtful and intelligent movement in the life which will naturally lend itself to the experiences and through the expereinces then will come the security of what this one knows.

How can this one eliminate thoughts of self doubt and increase this one's self revelation?

This one must reach a point of realizing that he can not do this alone. In order for this to be accomplished this one must be willing to make choices that enable this one to associate with others who either exhibit or are creating in a like manner. This one has not been willing to make these kinds of choices therefore the doubts still remain.

How can this one learn to discern a thought that comes from the highest or inner self or high self verses or one that comes from the conscious mind?

Illumined thoughts, thoughts that are comprehensive and multidimensional will also be universal thoughts. They will apply to anyone, any time, anywhere, any place within the known universe.

What suggestions will be given for atuning the conscious and subconscious minds to the superconscious mind for greater enlightenment and self awareness?

This one must be willing to turn the attention inward to be invested in the whole self and the willingness to give back to the self. It is very easy for this one to be tempted to give to the physical only and that is its own reward. In order for there to be attunement to superconsciousness the attention must be redirected inward there is no alternative this is the means by which superconsciousness becomes known. (10132001BGC3)

ELS#1-10

A Short Class on

Being Whole

JD: Healing class is a good example of a group of people working toward a common goal.

Dr. B: What is that common goal?

JD: To send healing to those requesting it.

LJ: To create wholeness in mind and body.

JM: To heal with the goodness of all concerned.

Dr. B: You each have an element of the success equation. The common goal is what Laurie said, to create wholeness. The purpose is goodness for all concerned. The activity is the projection of healing energies. When these three elements are present, the healing is effective, anytime, with any group.

Healing is where we teach the students that the ideal and purpose for creativity is wholeness. It's not about parts. It's about wholeness. All the time that we're teaching them the mechanics of how to separate thoughts, identify and admit them so they can wield them better we're also feeding them the idea that the ideal is wholeness. Realize everything is whole. Sometimes we only see a part, we look through a glass darkly, as Paul writes in the New Testament. Part of that whole is in shadows, darkness. This is why our inner light is used in mental projections. When we shine the light of our attention we can see the parts that make up the whole.

SF: That's where visualization comes in, in imagining something different. When you see something you don't like, you don't see as productive, you imagine how to make it better. How to improve the situation. That takes imagination otherwise you only have what you've done before.

Dr. B: Always be willing to ask yourself, "What is the whole truth?" •

Alpha and Omega email
It begins and ends with Self Respect

Dear Dr. Barbara,

During Taraka Yoga class there are many things that I put together. What got me to thinking was in a brief statement of how the Universal Laws are associated with the essential life skills. This in many ways is a no brainer but what it did was stimulate me to think about how certain Universal Laws are linked with a specific essential life skill. This is what came to me as I drove. Please let me know what you think.

I started with Self-respect and why that is the first essential life skill and which Universal Law describes that the best. Then as I thought more deeply I saw how each essential life skill aids in developing understandings in the Universal Law itself. That is the really exciting part because I believe in the power of aligning consciousness with the Universal Laws and what it produces in oneís life. I think as I become more proficiency in the life skills I will become more aligned with the universe and the laws that govern it. Okay on with how I paired them from what I understand thus far.

Self-Respect my first thought that held with even further thought was the Law of Divine Birthright or the Law of Will and the Law of Identity(I am doing this by memory so please bare with me) I thought of this because Self-Respect is the skill of using your will over and over again to look, to see your self again and again. Through doing this you activate the Law of Free Will and Identity. This made it clearer to me why Self-Respect is the first essential life skill and why it is constantly developed with each following skill.

Undivided Attention the next life skill I had to think a little more on so I went to the others for a while. When I came back to it I thought about the Law of Proper Perspective. how I saw this was that with the Law of Proper Perspective you are putting thoughts in order. This made more sense to me when I thought about how we teach the 10 most wanted list at the same time we initiate the Candle exercise. Undivided Attention gives us the skill to know what is most important, which is the ONE GOAL of knowing Self.

Concentration at first I linked to the Law of Proper Perspective thinking about follow through and completion. Then what dawned on me further was how concentration aids in the development of Prosperity. Prosperity is the ability to create long time productions. As I understand it, it is the epitome of adulthood. Prosperity is recognizing the unlimited resources we have around us, always having enough. Concentration is the skill in which we distill the essence of whatever we place our attention on. How I see that concentration is related to Prosperity is using concentration, the ability to hold your attention, to see the wealth and using it to the fullest. I am still developing this skill and I can see how when one knows how to concentrate they are abundant and prosperous. I thought about growing a garden. First you plant the seed, then water, fertilize, care for it. This must happen on a consistent basis. If the plants are left unattended they will wither and die, but with consistent practice of giving them attention they will produce and soon they will produce other plants that continually give thus leading to prosperity. (I hope I am clear enough, I did say this is my weakest essential life skill in class. I see how this may be connected with the karma of learning how to teach teachers.)

Memory, this took me a while, one attempting to remember what I have learned about the Universal Laws and comparing them to the life skills I saw my weakness and my strengths. However this does keep me energized for the car ride. What I came to was the Law of Evolution. I haven't quite figured out why yet. What I think so far is that the skill of memory let us know where we come from and therefore leads to knowing how things are built upon one another. I can see my weakness coming through in understanding what the Law of Evolution is. My theory is the more I utilize the essential life skill of memory the more I will understand the Universal Law of Evolution.

Listening, essential life skill number five. This came in a flash as I remembered more of the universal laws. (Remember I am driving at the time and I had a little difficulty in recalling the names of the Universal laws. This one came to me as I was asking the question so what would listening be related to? Get it related, ha ha it cracked me up:)) The Law of Relativity is the one that I gave to listening. I thought of this in terms of music. It is seen clearly on staff paper. Vibrational patterns. I describe listening as the ability to "be with". That is what i think this skill is. The Law of Relativity how I have come to understand it is seeing the connectedness to everyone and everything around us in our universe. The skill of listening gives us the skill of becoming one with and harmonizing self with creation itself.

Imagination I connected with the Law of Believing and Knowing. I thought about this in association with Kundalini and creation. You taught me that there is only one good use for imagination and that is how it is relative to the present to know I AM.

Breath was a given for me. Maybe too easy. I thought it connected with the Law of Giving and Receiving because of how energy is moved from one source to another. As one understands breath, the power of it, one can understand and utilize the Law of Giving and Receiving.

Reasoning this one stumped me for a while then I thought about cause and effect, oh yea, another Universal law, duh. This became clear to me as reasoning is the ability to use will, memory and imagination together which is essential in knowing how thinking is caused and what will be produced from it.

Intuition, maybe I should of chosen this as my weakest skill. For the life of me I couldn't think of a Universal Law that really strikes me as fitting or that I can a least have a line of thinking that would relate to it. The Law of Infinity kind of took this category by default. I am thinking more on this. Maybe it is that I have a underdeveloped concept of what the Law of Infinity is really about. One line of thinking I did come to is a line from the lessons, Spirit is and was one. By the Law of duality it becomes two. By the Law of Infinity multiplied by the law of relativity it becomes many. Now the many is endeavoring to make one. Maybe this has something to dowith it. I think this is in the friendship lesson, either seven or eight. I will do more research and let you know what I come up with.

Entrainment. This I thought was connected to the Law of Duality. Why? I think of it because entrainment is the conscious and subconscious minds aligned and connected with one another. When this is developed into a skill then the understanding of Duality will occur. I image it as a yin yang. This is where the conscious mind is now one with subconscious mind, thus they have the same mission, to know I AM.

I enjoyed this greatly. Let me know if you think I am just chasing butterflies or if the direction I am headed can really lead me somewhere. I want to know what you think, because I think with a little more development this could go somewhere, it probably already has and I am just dawning on it. That I think is the really fun part in this is that I do not have any attachments to what goes where. In the end I believe that each of the laws could go with any of the essential life skills. I really love seeing how things fit together. I guess i always have. Maybe it was this love that manifested in the desire to take things a part and put them back together again to see how it works. I welcome any feedback you may have for me and how this could be used more completely.

I send you my Circle of Love,
Laurie Jeanne Biswell

Laurie Jeanne!

You are becoming quite the thinker. As you write more often you will find your thoughts taking shape more easily and quickly. I know, I practiced it for years as well. I continue to hone communication skills. This is in response to state of consciousness.

Now content.....I smile at the ambiguity in your words. Of course meaning is relative! What is important is, is it relevant and to whom? Seeking Truth that is Universal is a duty, a full time job. Glad you are invested! There's a great line written by Ralph Waldo Emerson, a 19th century transcendental poet, king of a forerunner of thoday's metaphysician, that says something like "know in your own heart that what is true for you is true to all men, that is genius!" I believe in that idea. I live my life in the pursuit of manifesting its Univeral Truth. I belive you desire to do so also. That is what imspires me in what you wrote.

I know that this kind of thinking is what postiive thinking is built from and upon. There have been many times students and I have discused such maters til early in the morning. It is insightful, stimulating, and magnetic. It is the same energy as that of the Oracle. Such discussion makes consciousness tangible. This is beyond right or wrong, does this law go wih this skill? It is the pursuit of reaosning, being able to use the essential life skills to create, describe, and manifest your thought. Self Realization.

This thought project is worth exploring. (Sounds like a great thesis topic in fact!)

I send my circle, Dr. Barbara

Powers of Ten

As I was gathering all the pieces for this book and beginning the layout and design phase, I was also entertaining the concepts that are becoming a seminar on "Powers of Ten - Your Hidden Potential for Wholeness". I continually marvel at how the Universe reveals itself to me.

I intended the seminar to teach the deeper, universal truths found in the spiritual documentary THE SILVER CORD. Once I got into the subject matter and research in science and math, the Powers of Ten took on more meanings. The 10 Essential Life Skills taught in this book and in the School of Metaphysics course are the backbone of the seminar. The first Power of Ten is Self's potential. The Essential Life Skills enable you to explore and develop your whole Self.

From Self Respect through Entrainment, the skills build one upon the next. They illustrate the Universal Laws of Relativity and Infinity. Concentration becomes the baseline for listening. Listening evolves with practice into intuition. Undivided Attention makes it simple to remember. Memory is one of the elements that make reasoning possible. By the time you work up through Entrainment you have an entirely different vantage point for Self Respect and you have all the skills you need to continue growth and creating your life in your own image.

When I first began studying metaphysics at age 22, I was presented with the idea that each individual is a Self. The Self is multifaceted and, ultimately, multidimensional. Developing that whole Self, manifesting its potential, is the purpose of life.

Some people receive the study of metaphysics as a science, others view it as an art, still others as a spiritual quest. The School of Metaphysics teaches metaphysics as the study of the mind and the Universal Laws that govern creation. The Essential Life Skills enable anyone to use more of their mind's power.

Studying metaphysics is like breathing. It is simple, universal, and necessary in the scope of anyone's quest to know Self. Like breathing, each individual applies their own individual desires and characteristics to their study. Some draw upon Kundalini, the creative power in humans, to produce miraculous healings while others use it to project for a desired position or love relationship.

These life skills are so essential that they will someday be taught in educational systems. The day will come when teachers expect their students to excel in concentration, memory, listening, reasoning ***because they are teaching these skills***, not just preaching them. Imagine how that will change our world!

Each of us chooses the quality and the quantity of our thoughts. For those who believe and know from experience there is more to life than what meets the physical eyes and senses, the study of metaphysics is a natural evolutionary step. Now. For me this awareness came in the form of dreams when I was as young as six years old. It came in intuitive hunches that in time proved true. It came in visionary reason that aided friends in school. It expressed itself through acts of creation – art, music, writing. It made itself undeniable in the many "why" questions surfacing in my thinking.

I didn't tolerate well the college/university brand of metaphysics. Logic and existential courses left me baffled and cold. They seemed to move in circles, often talking in double-speak. I wasn't looking for intellectual development, I received plenty of that in public school, I was looking for ways to understand my experiences and to reproduce those I found beneficial. Exercising the Essential Life Skills gave me both. Through these I have learned how to align my head and my heart, a simple task that sometimes I've made challenging and difficult.

What is certain is this, after 30 years I use these basic principles and practices in my life now more than ever. I liken this to learning how to play an instrument. Repeated and enhanced experiences, over time, produce the music of a master. Life is like that too.

I trust what you read here is as valuable for you as it has been for those of us who made these experiences. I hope you will see your own in a new light and be inspired toward greater Self awareness and deeper understanding of the meaning in your life.

May peace be with you all ways.

Acknowledgements

My thanks and apppreciation go to all the many people - past, present and future - I have enjoyed as traveling companions in this life. Our desire to learn brought us together. Our fulfillment through experience gave birth to these life stories. May we inspire others to think and live more fully, more completely. To live in such a way that others benefit from the life you make, is to experience divine love and friendship. To Daniel, my husband, thank you for your still mind. To Hezekiah, thank you for your active one. To Dr. Terry Martin, Paul Madar, Tad Messenger, Ivy Norris, Dr. Laurel Clark, Dr. Pam Blosser, Stacy Ferguson, and others, your experiences can now increase the stature of others. To emailers including Amy Pawlus, Matthew Marian, Laurie Biswell, Jessica Hudson, and any who wished to remain anonymous, your thoughts can now stimulate others' minds toward fulfilling potential. To those in the College of Metaphysics Class of 2002 your participation in the morning Socratic explorations are now timeless and thereby able to aid others to arrive at a greater Truth. Thank you all for encouraging this book and for the part you provided in its fruition. - Barbara Condron

Information on the coursework, Spiritual Focus Weekends, Intuitive Reports, and the services described in this book can be gained in these ways.....

through writing

School of Metaphysics World Headquarters
163 Moon Valley Road
Windyville, Missouri 65783 USA

through calling

417-345-8411

through websites

www.som.org
www.dreamschool.org
www.societyforintuitiveresearch.org
www.peacedome.org

email: som@som.org

Additional titles available from SOM Publishing include:

The Purpose of Life by Dr. Daniel R. Cnodron
ISBN: 0944386-35-0 $15.00

Dharma: Finding Your Soul's Purpose by Dr. Laurel Clark
ISBN: 0944386-34-2 $10.00

The Wisdom of Solomon by Dr. Barbara Condron
ISBN: 094438633-4 $15.00

Every Dream is about the Dreamer by Dr. Barbara Condron
ISBN: 0944386-27-X $13.00

Peacemaking:
9 Lessons for Changing Yourself, Relationships, & World
Dr. Barbara Condron ISBN: 0944386-31-8 $12.00

The Tao Te Ching Interpreted & Explained
Dr. Daniel R. Condron ISBN: 0944385-30-x $15.00

How to Raise an Indigo Child
Dr. Barbara Condron ISBN: 0944386-29-6 $14.00

Atlantis: The History of the World Vol. 1
Drs. Daniel & Barbara Condron ISBN: 0944386-28-8 $15.00

Karmic Healing by Dr. Laurel Clark
ISBN: 0944386-26-1 $15.00

The Bible Interpreted in Dream Symbols - Drs. Condron, Condron, Matthes, Rothermel ISBN: 0944386-23-7 $18.00

Spiritual Renaissance
Elevating Your Conciousness for the Common Good
Dr. Barbara Condron ISBN: 0944386-22-9 $15.00

Superconscious Meditation
Kundalini & Understanding the Whole Mind
Dr. Daniel R. Condron ISBN 0944386-21-0 $13.00

First Opinion: Wholistic Health Care in the 21st Century
Dr. Barbara Condron ISBN 0944386-18-0 $15.00

The Dreamer's Dictionary by Dr. Barbara Condron
ISBN 0944386-16-4 $15.00

The Work of the Soul
Dr. Barbara Condron, ed. ISBN 0944386-17-2 $13.00

Uncommon Knowledge: Past Life & Health Readings
Dr. Barbara Condron, ed. ISBN 0944386-19-9 $13.00

The Universal Language of Mind
The Book of Matthew Interpreted by Dr. Daniel R. Condron
ISBN 0944386-15-6 $13.00

Dreams of the Soul - The Yogi Sutras of Patanjali
Dr. Daniel R. Condron ISBN 0944386-11-3 $9.95

Kundalini Rising: Mastering Your Creative Energies
Dr. Barbara Condron ISBN 0944386-13-X $13.00

To order write:

School of Metaphysics
World Headquarters
163 Moon Valley Road
Windyville, Missouri 65783 U.S.A.

Enclose a check or money order payable in U.S. funds to SOM with any order. Please include $5.00 for postage and handling of books, $10 for international orders.

A complete catalogue of all book titles, audio lectures and courses, and videos is available upon request.

Visit us on the Internet at *http://www.som.org*
e-mail: som@som.org

About the School of Metaphysics

We invite you to become a special part of our efforts to aid in enhancing and quickening the process of spiritual growth and mental evolution of the people of the world. The School of Metaphysics, a not-for-profit educational and service organization, has been in existence for three decades. During that time, we have taught tens of thousands directly through our course of study in applied metaphysics. We have elevated the awareness of millions through the many services we offer. If you would like to pursue the study of mind and the transformation of Self to a higher level of being and consciousness, you are invited to write to us at the School of Metaphysics World Headquarters in Windyville, Missouri 65783.

*The heart of the School of Metaphysic*s is a four-tiered course of study in understanding the mind in order to know the Self. Lessons introduce you to the Universal Laws and Truths which guide spiritual and physical evolution. Consciousness is explored and developed through mental and spiritual disciplines which enhance your physical life and enrich your soul progression. For every concept there is a means to employ it through developing your own potential. Level One includes concentration, visualization (focused imagery), meditation, and control of life force and creative energies, all foundations for exploring the multidimensional Self.

*As experts in the Universal Language of Min*d, we teach how to remember and understand the inner communication received through dreams. We are the sponsors of the National Dream Hotline®, an annual educational service offered the last weekend in April. Study centers are located throughout the Midwestern United States. If there is not a center near you, you can receive the first series of lessons through correspondence with a teacher at our headquarters.

For those desiring spiritual renewal, weekends at our Moon Valley Ranch on the College of Metaphysics campus in the Midwest U.S. offer calmness and clarity. Each weekend focuses on intuitive research done specifically for you in your presence. More than a traditional class or seminar, these gatherings are experiences in multidimensional awareness of who you are, why you are here, where you came from, and where you are going.

The Universal Hour of Peace was initiated by the School of Metaphysics on October 24, 1995 in conjunction with the 50th anniversary of the United Nations. We believe that peace on earth is an idea whose time has come. To realize this dream, we invite you to join with others throughout the world in the reading a document written by over two dozen spiritual teachers – the *Universal Peace Covenant* (see 350) – as you welcome the new year. During this time, students and faculty at the College of Metaphysics hold a 24 hour peace vigil in the world's Peace Dome. For more information visit www.peacedome.org .

There is the opportunity to aid in the growth and fulfillment of our work. Donations supporting the expansion of the School of Metaphysics' efforts are a valuable way for you to aid humanity. As a not-for-profit publishing house, SOM Publishing is dedicated to the continuing publication of research findings that promote peace, understanding and good will for all of Mankind. It is dependent upon the kindness and generosity of sponsors to do so. Authors donate their work and receive no royalties. We have many excellent manuscripts awaiting a benefactor.

One hundred percent of the donations made to the School of Metaphysics are used to expand our services. The world's first Peace Dome located on our college campus was funded entirely by individual contributions. Presently, donations are being received for the Octagon an international center for multidimensional living. Donations to the School of Metaphysics are tax-exempt under 501(c)(3) of the Internal Revenue Code. We appreciate your generosity. With the help of people like you, our dream of a place where anyone desiring Self awareness can receive education in mastering the mind, consciousness, and the Self will become a reality. *We send you our Circle of Love.*